THE SUPREME COURT AND CIVIL LIBERTIES POLICY

By
RICHARD C. CORTNER
University of Arizona

Mayfield Publishing Company

Copyright © 1975 by Richard C. Cortner
First edition 1975

All rights reserved. No portion of this book may be
reproduced in any form or by any means without
written permission of the publisher.

Library of Congress Catalog Card Number: 75-21071
International Standard Book Number: 0-87484-336-7

Manufactured in the United States of America
Mayfield Publishing Company
285 Hamilton Avenue, Palo Alto, California 94301

This book was set in Baskerville Medium and Baskerville
Bold by Libra Cold Type, and was printed and bound by
the George Banta Company. Sponsoring editor was C.
Lansing Hays, Carole Norton supervised editing, and
Zipporah Collins was manuscript editor. Michelle Hogan
supervised production, the book was designed by Nancy
Sears, and cover art was prepared by Howard Brodie.

CONTENTS

iii

PREFACE

This book is intended for use as a supplementary text in undergraduate university courses in American government, civil liberties, and the judicial process. It consists of relatively brief commentaries on the more salient issues of civil liberties policy that have been the subject of contemporary Supreme Court decisions, with accompanying case studies of specific decisions of the Court in those areas that have loomed large in recent years.

The text differs from the typical casebook in constitutional law, which commonly contains many excerpts from Supreme Court opinions plus brief explanatory notes. The bulk of this work is devoted to in-depth case studies of the litigation in six recent Supreme Court decisions in the civil liberties field. Its purpose is not only to acquaint students with some substantive areas of civil liberties policy, but also to emphasize the process of constitutional litigation as a policy-making process. The cases selected, therefore, concern the most salient areas of policy with which the Supreme Court has recently dealt, and the studies analyze the litigation in federal and state courts, trial and appellate, in the hope of conveying to students a sense of the judicial process and of the fact that cases do not arrive at the Supreme Court's doorstep like abandoned orphans in the night.

In writing such a text, many hard decisions must be made about what issues should be covered and particularly what cases should be the subjects of in-depth studies. Because a supplementary text of this length cannot conceivably embrace an analysis of all aspects of modern civil liberties policy as enunciated in the decisions of the Supreme Court, I believe I should indicate at the outset both to colleagues who may use this text in the classroom and to the students who with varying degrees of reluctance will be constrained to read it the reasons for my choices.

The backbone of modern civil liberties policy, as I see it, is the evolution of the meaning of the due process clause of the Fourteenth Amendment. In regard to civil liberties, this evolution has had two phases: the nationalization of the Bill of Rights, and (still in its early stages) the Court's interpretation of the due process clause to embrace rights not listed in the Bill of Rights or, indeed, elsewhere in the Constitution. Chapter I deals, therefore, with the nationalization process and the extension of the meaning of the due process clause. The remaining chapters deal with what, in my opinion, are the most important fields in which the Court's civil liberties decisions have concentrated in recent years: criminal procedure, free expression, church-state relations, and equal protection.

In the selection of the case studies I have followed essentially three criteria: (1) the inherent importance of the Court decision in providing a good summary of civil liberties policy; (2) the potential interest of the case to students; and (3) the likelihood that the decision will continue to represent civil liberties policy for some reasonable time in the future. I should add that these factors are listed roughly in order of their importance in my selection.

With these considerations in mind, I selected *Duncan v. Louisiana* to illustrate the nationalization of the Bill of Rights because of its inherently interesting background and because it contains the last major statements of the total incorporation, selective incorporation, and fundamental rights–fair trial approaches to interpretation of the due process clause of the

Fourteenth Amendment. As the case study on extension of the due process clause beyond the Bill of Rights, the obvious choice, I thought, had to be the *Abortion Cases (Roe v. Wade* and *Doe v. Bolton).*

The field of criminal procedure posed special selection problems, since this field above all other areas of civil liberties policy is likely to see great changes. I chose *Chimel v. California* as the subject of the case study because it illustrates the profound effects of the "revolution in criminal procedure" that was wrought in the 1960s, and because it involves one of the most important interpretations of the prohibition against unreasonable searches and seizures in recent years, however that interpretation may change under the Burger Court.

In the field of freedom of expression, I chose *Cohen v. California* for the case study because Justice Harlan's opinion in that case used most of the tests of the scope of free expression developed by the Court in determining whether Cohen's message was protected by the First and Fourteenth Amendments. The language with which *Cohen* deals will perhaps be offensive to some, but because of its offensiveness, perhaps, the Court dealt with some of the central problems in the field of free expression in that case.

In the field of church-state relations, I sought a case that raised both establishment clause and free exercise clause issues. *Wisconsin v. Yoder,* I think, fulfills that requirement and illustrates some of the more important and troubling problems that our somewhat conflicting constitutional guarantees of religious freedom involve.

Finally, I wanted a case study that would illustrate the different tests that the Court is currently applying in the field of equal protection policy, and I hoped to illustrate a frontier area in the equal protection field. I think the subject of sexual discrimination as raised in *Frontiero v. Richardson* reasonably fills both requirements.

The field of constitutional policy as enunciated in Supreme Court decisions is one of both continuity and change, especially as we have moved in recent years from the Warren Court to the Burger Court. These case studies should be viewed as snapshots of the judicial policy-making process in action, some illustrative of the continuity of constitutional policy, others perspectives from which changes in that policy may be viewed, as fate and the values represented on the Court determine. In both situations, I hope the material will add to the understanding of how constitutional policy is made.

In preparing this text, I have received generous assistance from several of the attorneys who were engaged in the litigation I have explored. I especially thank Richard Sobol for his help in regard to *Duncan v. Louisiana*; Keith Monroe for his generous responses to my questions on *Chimel v. California*; Professor Melville Nimmer of the UCLA Law School for his comments on *Cohen v. California*; and Joseph Levin, Jr., of the Southern Poverty Law Center for his assistance in regard to the litigation in *Frontiero v. Richardson*.

I express my appreciation also to C. Lansing Hays of the Mayfield Publishing Company for initially encouraging me to author a text of this kind and for his continuing words of support. Zipporah Collins has been tolerant in the extreme in editing a manuscript typed on an old, beat-up Remington, and Carole Norton has bolstered my courage in meeting the electronic age in the form of an Olivetti electric.

None of the above individuals is of course responsible for any sins of commission or omission in the text; on that point, the plea must be the traditional one: *mea culpa.*

R.C.C.

Tucson
Spring 1975

Chapter One

THE NATIONALIZATION OF THE BILL OF RIGHTS – AND BEYOND

Introduction The most important modern development in civil liberties policy as enunciated by the United States Supreme Court has been the nationalization of the Bill of Rights— that is, the process by which the Court has applied most of the rights in the Bill of Rights as restrictions on state power. The Bill of Rights was, of course, not a part of the original Constitution submitted to state ratifying conventions in 1787, but rather was proposed by Congress as amendments to the original Constitution and ratified by the states in 1791.[1] During the ratification, citizens expressed fear of the powers conferred on the new national government, and the Bill of Rights was directed at restricting the powers of that government, not the powers of the states. Having reviewed the historical reasons for adoption of the Bill of Rights, Chief Justice John Marshall ruled in 1833 in *Barron v. Baltimore* that the rights in the Bill of Rights were not limitations on the powers of the states, but rather were limitations exclusively on the powers of the national government.

1. The Bill of Rights usually is defined to include the first eight amendments to the Constitution; the Ninth and Tenth Amendments were of course adopted at the same time.

1

One of the most significant constitutional consequences of the Civil War, however, was adoption of the Fourteenth Amendment in 1868. It provides in part, "No State shall make or enforce any law which shall abridge the privileges or immunities of citizens of the United States; nor shall any State deprive any person of life, liberty, or property, without due process of law." These clauses, called the privileges and immunities clause and the due process clause respectively, were thus restrictions on the powers of the states. Litigants before the Supreme Court soon sought to convert the clauses into guarantees of a broad spectrum of rights against state power, including the rights in the Bill of Rights.

The Supreme Court proved highly resistant to arguments that the Fourteenth Amendment altered the federal system in such a fundamental way. In the *Slaughter House Cases,* decided in 1873, the Court held that most of the significant civil and political rights of individuals against exercises of state power still derived from state law and state constitutions. The Court refused to read the privileges and immunities clause as guaranteeing any significant rights against state power, thus essentially reducing that clause to a dead letter. Similarly, in *Hurtado v. California,* in 1884, the Court adopted reasoning that denied that any of the rights in the Bill of Rights could be guaranteed by the due process clause against state action. The Fourteenth Amendment, at this point, did not show much potential as a guarantee of civil and political liberties against the states.

Despite the reasoning adopted in *Hurtado,* however, the Court held in 1897, in *Chicago, Burlington & Quincy Ry. v. Chicago,* that the due process clause of the Fourteenth Amendment required the states to provide just compensation for private property that was taken for a public use. (This right was guaranteed to people against the national government by the just compensation clause of the Fifth Amendment.) And in *Twining v. New Jersey* in 1908 the Court conceded that the due process clause of the Fourteenth Amendment might guarantee against state action some rights that were similar to those in the Bill of Rights. Seventeen years later, in *Gitlow v. New York,* the Court assumed that the freedoms of speech and of the press were guaranteed against state action by the word "liberty" in the due process clause, an assumption that became a reality as the Court squarely held in a series of cases that both freedom of speech (*Fiske v. Kansas, Stromberg v. California*) and freedom of the press (*Near v. Minnesota*) were secured against invasion by the states by the due process clause.

Soon after this initial breakthrough, the Court held that freedom of assembly and petition (*DeJonge v. Oregon*) and freedom of religion (*Cantwell v. Connecticut*) were also guaranteed by the due process clause against infringement by the states. In *Everson v. Board of Education,* the Court held that the states were prohibited from establishing religions by the due process clause. By 1947, the Court had made every right guaranteed by the First Amendment applicable to the states via the due process clause of the Fourteenth Amendment.

Following the nationalization of First Amendment rights, the nationalization process virtually halted until 1961. In 1948, however, the Court did hold that the due process clause guaranteed the right to a public trial in state proceedings (in *In re Oliver*), a right also protected by the Sixth Amendment; and in 1949, in *Wolf v. Colorado,* the "core" of the Fourth Amendment prohibition against unreasonable searches and seizures was held to apply to the states. The Court declined, however, to apply the full Fourth Amendment to the states, and it refused to enforce the prohibition in state proceedings by holding that illegally seized evidence would be inadmissible in state criminal trials (the "exclusionary rule").

In the 1960s, "selective incorporationist" justices came to be a majority on the Court. They believed that most of the rights in the Bill of Rights applied to the states via the due process clause, and that these rights applied with the same scope and meaning as they applied to the federal government. While the Court was dominated by these views, between 1961 and 1969, most of the criminal procedure safeguards of the Bill of Rights were applied to the states.

The Court thus applied the full Fourth Amendment and the exclusionary rule in 1961 (*Mapp v. Ohio*); the Eighth Amendment prohibition against cruel and unusual punishments in 1962 (*Robinson v. California*); the full Sixth Amendment right to counsel in criminal proceedings in 1963 (*Gideon v. Wainwright*); the Fifth Amendment right against self-incrimination in 1964 (*Malloy v. Hogan*); the Sixth Amendment rights to confront and cross-examine witnesses in 1965 (*Pointer v. Texas*), to a speedy trial and to compulsory process in 1967 (*Klopfer v. North Carolina; Washington v. Texas*), and to a jury trial in serious criminal cases in 1968 (*Duncan v. Louisiana*); and, finally, the Fifth Amendment prohibition against double jeopardy in 1969 (*Benton v. Maryland*). By 1969, therefore, only the Second, Third, and Seventh Amendments, the grand jury clause of the Fifth Amendment, and the excessive fines and bail clause of the Eighth Amendment had not been made applicable to the states via the due process clause of the Fourteenth Amendment. (See table 1 for a summary of nationalization.)

From 1897 to 1969, when the nationalization of the Bill of Rights occurred, there were significant conflicts on the Court about what the process in fact involved. During the later stages of the nationalization process, a majority of the Court accepted a "selective incorporation" approach. The selective incorporationists believed that most but not all of the Bill of Rights applied to the states, and, if a right did apply, it applied with the same scope and meaning as it applied to the national government.

Justice Hugo Black, on the other hand, believed that it had been the intention of the framers of the Fourteenth Amendment to reverse the 1833 decision in *Barron v. Baltimore* and to make all of the Bill of Rights applicable to the states, a position he first announced in a dissenting opinion in *Adamson v. California* in 1947. Although three other justices supported Black's "total incorporation" position in the *Adamson* case, only Justice Douglas continued to support this theory in the later stages of the nationalization process, and the total incorporation approach never commanded a majority of the Court. Black's analysis of the intentions of the framers of the Fourteenth Amendment also was subjected to scholarly attack, especially from Professor Charles Fairman ("Does the Fourteenth Amendment Incorporate the Bill of Rights: The Original Understanding," *Stanford Law Review* 2 [1949]: 5), who concluded that "the record of history is overwhelmingly against" Black's total incorporation beliefs.

Table 1

APPLICABILITY OF BILL OF RIGHTS
TO STATES VIA DUE PROCESS CLAUSE OF
FOURTEENTH AMENDMENT

Right	Whether Applicable	Case and Date
FIRST AMENDMENT		
Freedom of speech*	yes	*Gitlow v. New York* (1925)
		Fiske v. Kansas (1927)
		Stromberg v. California (1931)
Freedom of the press*	yes	*Near v. Minnesota* (1931)
Freedom of assembly	yes	*DeJonge v. Oregon* (1937)
Freedom of religion	yes	*Cantwell v. Connecticut* (1940)
Establishment clause	yes	*Everson v. Board of Education* (1947)
SECOND AMENDMENT	no	
THIRD AMENDMENT	no	
FOURTH AMENDMENT	yes	*Wolf v. Colorado* (1949)
		Mapp v. Ohio (1961)
FIFTH AMENDMENT		
Grand jury clause	no	
Just compensation clause	yes	*Chicago, Burlington & Quincy Ry. v. Chicago* (1897)
Self-incrimination clause	yes	*Malloy v. Hogan* (1964)
Double jeopardy clause	yes	*Benton v. Maryland* (1969)
SIXTH AMENDMENT		
Notice	yes	In re *Oliver* (1948)†
Assistance of counsel clause	yes	*Gideon v. Wainwright* (1963)
Public trial clause	yes	In re *Oliver* (1948)
Confrontation clause	yes	*Pointer v. Texas* (1965)
Compulsory process clause	yes	*Washington v. Texas* (1967)
Speedy trial clause	yes	*Klopfer v. North Carolina* (1967)
Jury trial clause	yes	*Duncan v. Louisiana* (1968)
SEVENTH AMENDMENT	no	
EIGHTH AMENDMENT		
Cruel and unusual punishment clause	yes	*Robinson v. California* (1962)
Excessive fines and bail clause	no	

* There is disagreement on when freedom of speech and freedom of the press were nationalized; it is probably most accurate to say this occurred in a series of cases beginning with *Gitlow* in 1925 and ending with *Near* in 1931.

† Adequate notice of the charges is a traditional requirement of due process in a criminal case; in *Oliver*, the Court indicated that the due process clause requires notice in state criminal proceedings, without formally nationalizing the Sixth Amendment notice requirement.

The leading opponent of both selective incorporation and total incorporation during the later stages of the nationalization process was Justice John Marshall Harlan, whose grandfather, the first Justice Harlan, had been an adherent of the total incorporation position. The second Justice Harlan argued that the Fourteenth Amendment had not reversed *Barron v. Baltimore,* which held that the Bill of Rights applied only to the national government. On the other hand, he believed that the due process clause of the Fourteenth Amendment did guarantee against state action certain "fundamental" rights and the right to a "fair" hearing as far as criminal procedure was concerned. He thus conceded that the due process clause guaranteed certain rights that were similar to or parallel to rights in the Bill of Rights; but, for Harlan, the critical point of logic was that the due process clause did not apply any of the rights in the Bill of Rights to the states. The rights guaranteed by the due process clause were thus, in Harlan's view, not identical in scope and meaning to their Bill of Rights counterparts, as both the total and the selective incorporationists on the Court contended. The rights guaranteed against the states by the due process clause were merely similar to those in the Bill of Rights, in Harlan's opinion, allowing a broader scope for state regulation of such rights than the national government possessed under the Bill of Rights.

The last major theoretical clash on the Court between the selective incorporation and Black's total incorporation views on one hand and Harlan's fundamental rights/fair hearing views on the other occurred in 1968 in *Duncan v. Louisiana,* which resulted in application of the jury trial clause of the Sixth Amendment to the states. We shall now examine *Duncan* in detail.

Case Study
**JURY TRIALS AND THE LAW
IN PLAQUEMINES PARISH:
GARY DUNCAN'S CASE**

The right to trial by jury was considered to be a fundamental right of the individual by the generation of Americans who successfully rebelled against Great Britain and ultimately ratified the

Constitution. Among the many justifications for the Revolution, as stated in the Declaration of Independence, was the charge that King George III had deprived "us in many cases, of the benefits of Trial by Jury." Trial by jury was also one of the limited number of civil liberties contained in the original Constitution before addition of the Bill of Rights. Article III provides that the "Trial of all Crimes, except in Cases of Impeachment, shall be by Jury . . . ." With the addition of the Bill of Rights to the Constitution in 1791, two other jury trial provisions became constitutional guarantees under the Sixth and Seventh Amendments. The Sixth Amendment provides in part that in "all criminal prosecutions, the accused shall enjoy the right to a speedy and public trial, by an impartial jury of the State and district wherein the crime shall have been committed," and the Seventh Amendment provides that in civil suits at common law, "where the value in controversy shall exceed twenty dollars, the right of trial by jury shall be preserved . . . ."

Under the Supreme Court ruling in *Barron v. Baltimore* in 1833, of course, the Sixth and Seventh Amendments were applicable only in the federal courts, not state judicial proceedings. After adoption of the Fourteenth Amendment, however, attempts were made to persuade the Supreme Court that the jury trial requirements of the Sixth and Seventh Amendments were guaranteed also by the Fourteenth Amendment and were thus applicable in state trials. In 1876, the Court rejected the proposition that the Seventh Amendment applied to the states (*Walker v. Sauvinet*), and it has never reversed its position on that point. The states are therefore free to abolish jury trials in civil cases as far as the federal Constitution is concerned.

The Court also rejected the idea that the Sixth Amendment requirement of jury trials in criminal cases was applicable to the states, most notably in *Maxwell v. Dow,* a 1900 case involving Charles L. "Gunplay" Maxwell. There the Court refused to apply the jury trial clause of the Sixth Amendment to the states, and it upheld Utah's use of eight-person juries in criminal cases. "Trial by jury," the Court said, "has never been affirmed to be a necessary requisite of due process of law."

Although the Court subsequently repeated its belief that jury trials were not required in state criminal cases by the due process clause of the Fourteenth Amendment, in the 1960s it began to speak more respectfully of jury trials as a fundamental individual right. Thus, in 1961, the Court declared in *Irvin v. Dowd* that "England, from whom the Western World has largely taken its concepts of individual liberty and of the dignity and worth of every man, has bequeathed to us safeguards for their preservation, the most priceless of which is that of trial by jury." The Court's decisions nationalizing the Sixth Amendment assistance of counsel clause (*Gideon v. Wainwright* in 1963), confrontation clause (*Pointer v. Texas* in 1965), speedy and public trial clauses (*Klopfer v. North Carolina* in 1967 and *In re Oliver,* in 1948), and compulsory process clause (*Washington v. Texas* in 1967) also indicated that it might be ready to reconsider its 1900 ruling in *Maxwell.* This reconsideration was produced by Gary Duncan's difficulties with the law in Plaquemines Parish, Louisiana.

During the 1960s, the political boss of oil-rich Plaquemines Parish was Leander H. Perez, Sr., a skillful politician of the old school and a rabid segregationist. Perez considered the civil rights movement a "Zionist-Communist" conspiracy, and he adamantly fought any attempt to enforce desegregation or equal rights in Plaquemines Parish. When the federal government began to challenge voting discrimination in the parish in 1961, 6,714 of the 8,633 whites were registered voters, but only 45 of the 2,897 black residents had succeeded in registering. Anticipating civil rights demonstrations in the parish during the mid–1960s, Perez prepared Fort St. Phillip as a prison for demonstrators. The fort had been built by the Spanish in 1746; its powder magazines, some with water standing in them and all harboring swarms of mosquitoes, were converted into cells to hold what Perez called "anarchists, those who come here to overthrow the legally constituted government."

When the Catholic parochial schools in southeastern Louisiana were ordered to desegregate by church officials in 1962, Perez urged the people of Plaquemines Parish to resist and to cease contributing money to the church. Because of his leadership in resisting parochial school desegregation, Perez was excommunicated from the church, but he continued his defiance. "Our people realize that deep unswerving responsibility to protect their children against the immoral course of forced racial integration," he declared. "I am a life-long Catholic and will continue to be so, regardless of communistic infiltration and the influence of the National Council of Christians and Jews upon our church leadership."

Twelve years after the Supreme Court had declared public school segregation to be unconstitutional in the 1954 decision in *Brown v. Board of Education*, the rigidly segregated Plaquemines Parish public school system was challenged by the Justice Department in a suit filed in the United States District Court in New Orleans. Leander Perez again fought back with tenacity, addressing meetings throughout the parish urging the establishment of private segregated schools. He was so successful, the federal court had to enjoin parish officials from transferring public school property to the new private schools, and Perez himself was threatened with a contempt citation by United States District Judge Herbert W. Christenberry.

Perez responded to the Justice Department suit with an argument that the Fourteenth Amendment had been illegally adopted and was therefore inapplicable to Plaquemines Parish, but Judge Christenberry dismissed the argument as "old hat" and told Perez that it "might be all right for a meeting of laymen but not for lawyers." The judge issued what was, under the circumstances, a rather moderate desegregation decree requiring the immediate desegregation of the Plaquemines Parish public schools in grades one, seven, ten, twelve, and two others to be selected by school authorities. It is "difficult to understand at this date," the judge said, "how anyone can believe that he can operate a segregated school system." Leander Perez denounced the court's decision, however, declaring that when he saw what the Justice Department was demanding in regard to desegregation, "my reaction was, 'My God, we will have to give up our rights of citizenship as Americans.'" The future of Plaquemines Parish, he said, was "not in the lap of the gods, but in the hands of the sadistic mixers."[2]

2. The description of Leander Perez's role in the politics of Plaquemines Parish contained in this case study is drawn substantially from James Conaway, *Judge: The Life and Times of Leander Perez* (New York: Knopf, 1973).

The integration of the public schools in Plaquemines Parish in the fall of 1966 was, not unexpectedly, punctuated by racial incidents. For example, black students Bert Grant and his cousin Bernard St. Ann encountered harassment by white students, when they attended the parish's formerly all-white Boothville-Venice high school.

On October 18, 1966, their nineteen-year-old cousin Gary Duncan was driving south on highway 23 in the vicinity of the school, when he saw his two cousins, Grant and St. Ann, confronted by four white boys beside the highway. Duncan, a tow boat worker, stopped his car and inquired what the trouble was. His cousins responded that the white boys apparently wanted to fight. Duncan told his cousins to get into the car. What happened next was later a matter of dispute. After an exchange of words with the white boys, Duncan claimed that he told one of them, Herman M. Landry, Jr., to go home and touched him on the elbow. Landry claimed Duncan slapped him hard on his arm.

P. E. Lathum, the head of a private school established in response to desegregation of the parish public schools, observed the encounter between the boys and called a deputy sheriff. Duncan's car was intercepted by the deputy, and Duncan was returned to the scene of the encounter. After questioning the boys, however, the deputy said he did not believe that Duncan had assaulted young Landry, and Duncan was released. Nevertheless, three days later, on October 21, Duncan was arrested by Plaquemines Parish authorities and charged with cruelty to juveniles. Bail was set at $1,000.

Duncan's parents, Mr. and Mrs. Lambert R. Duncan, apparently felt that their son's arrest was part of the pattern of resistance to civil rights in the parish, and they traveled to New Orleans to contact a representative of the Lawyers Constitutional Defense Committee. The LCDC had been organized in 1964 by such groups as the American Civil Liberties Union, the American Jewish Congress, and the Congress of Racial Equality to provide attorneys in civil rights litigation in areas of the South where attorneys willing to take such cases were few and far between. The LCDC's national office in New York City deployed volunteer lawyers to Mississippi, Louisiana, and Alabama, and eventually the committee established regional offices in Jackson and New Orleans.

The services of LCDC attorneys were sorely needed in Plaquemines Parish, since few if any attorneys there were willing to engage in civil rights litigation. Yet willing outside attorneys were intimidated when they ventured into the parish. In 1961, for example, sheriff's deputies and members of the district attorney's office had raided a black bar in the parish called the Chicken Shack. The telephone was ripped off the wall, two deputies machine gunned the bottles and glasses on the bar and the shelves behind it, and over one hundred blacks were arrested on charges of disturbing the peace. Two NAACP lawyers, Earl Amedee and A. M. Trudeau, Jr., came from New Orleans to represent those arrested. When they arrived at the courthouse, however, they were confronted by Leander Perez and a group of whites. Perez demanded to know "what are you two niggers doing down here?" When the lawyers refused to respond, Perez threatened they "sure as hell will tell me or you're going to be in for some trouble." Amedee then said, "You know me, Judge. I'm Earl Amedee."

"You're a liar," Perez answered. "I don't know any goddamn niggers." He then announced, "I'll tell you one thing, those niggers have all pleaded guilty and paid their fines and gone back to their jobs where they should have been that night they were in the Chicken Shack." Fearing for their lives, Amedee and Trudeau quickly left Plaquemines Parish and, as Amedee said later, he had never returned.

Gary Duncan's parents contacted Richard Sobol, who was the chief staff counsel for the LCDC in New Orleans. Born in New York City, Sobol was a graduate of Union College and Columbia Law School, where he had been an editor of the *Columbia Law Review* in his senior year. He had served as a clerk for Judge Paul R. Hays on the United States Court of Appeals for the Second Circuit and had been on the staff of the Federal Trade Commission before joining the Washington, D.C., firm of Arnold, Fortas and Porter. He had given up this $24,000-a-year position to become a volunteer LCDC lawyer at $2,000 a year. As chief staff counsel, however, his salary had advanced to $15,000 a year.

Sobol and the other LCDC lawyers were at first reluctant to enter the *Duncan* case, since it seemed to be a relatively minor suit out of the mainstream of their concerns—primarily litigation implementing the Civil Rights Act of 1964. Sobol soon became convinced, however, that this incident was part of the pattern of anti-civil rights intimidation and harassment in Plaquemines Parish, and he finally agreed, with some "trepidation," to represent Duncan.

On November 21, 1966, a hearing was held before Judge Eugene E. Leon, Jr., in the Twenty-fifth Judicial District Court in Plaquemines Parish, on the charge of cruelty to juveniles. Representing Duncan at the hearing, Richard Sobol filed a motion to quash the charge on the ground that, under Louisiana law, "cruelty to juveniles" could only be charged against a person having some parental control or supervision over the juvenile abused. Since Duncan occupied no such position in relation to young Landry, Sobol argued that the charge was invalid.

After the hearing on this motion, Assistant District Attorney Darryl Bubrig advised Landry's parents that the charge was not going to stick. Mrs. Landry promptly signed an affidavit charging Duncan with simple battery. On November 25, Duncan was rearrested on the battery charge, and bond was set at $1,500. On January 4, 1967, Bubrig dropped the cruelty to juveniles charge, but Duncan was brought to trial on the battery charge on January 25.

Again representing Duncan, Sobol filed a demand for a jury trial. Noting that the offense was punishable by a maximum sentence of two years in prison, Sobol argued that the Sixth Amendment jury trial clause applied to the states via the due process clause of the Fourteenth Amendment; a jury trial was therefore required if a defendant could be sentenced on conviction to more than six months' imprisonment. Sobol based his argument on Supreme Court decisions holding that jury trials were required in federal criminal cases under the Sixth Amendment when the potential sentence was over six months.

Judge Leon rejected the demand for a jury, noting that he was "very familiar with [the Louisiana] statute fixing the juries." He explained, "Misdemeanors are not tried by jury with or without hard labor. It's a five-man jury with hard labor or a twelve-man jury and nine men concurring; capital must be a twelve-man jury, twelve men concurring. These are the requirements under the Louisiana law. The court is going to deny your request."

Sobol thus converted the *Duncan* case into a test of whether the jury trial clause of the Sixth Amendment applied to the states. Under Louisiana law, all offenses that were punishable by imprisonment but not at hard labor were tried without juries. If imprisonment at hard labor was the possible sentence, the defendant was entitled to a jury of five and a unanimous verdict. If imprisonment at hard labor was the mandatory sentence, a jury of twelve and conviction by nine were necessary. Only in capital cases did Louisiana law require a jury of twelve and a unanimous verdict. The offense of simple battery was classified as a high misdemeanor, punishable by a maximum of two years in prison but not at hard labor.

Gary Duncan was prosecuted by District Attorney Leander Perez, Jr., and Assistant District Attorney Darryl Bubrig. Herman Landry, called as a prosecution witness, testified that Duncan had hit him hard on the arm. This testimony was confirmed by two of Landry's companions. Duncan and his cousins denied that Duncan had hit Landry. P. E. Lathum, the head of the private school who had witnessed the incident, testified that Duncan had "made a pass at the white teenager, hitting him on the arm, knocking his arm up around his shoulders."

Judge Leon found Duncan guilty of simple battery. "The Court," he said, "taking into consideration Mr. Lathum's testimony, a man who was not even in the discussion, or whatever we may call it between six boys on the side of the street, and the testimony of the victim himself, Mr. Landry, that this blow was sufficient to sting him, I think the State for those reasons has proved to me beyond a reasonable doubt that the defendant is guilty of simple battery." Duncan was sentenced to pay a $150 fine and costs and serve sixty days in the parish prison, or an additional twenty days if the fine and costs were not paid. Bond for Duncan, pending an appeal, was set by Judge Leon at $1,500, a favorite figure. Duncan was rearrested and kept in jail a few hours until the bond was raised.

Sobol renewed his jury trial argument in a bill of exceptions filed February 1, 1967, which Judge Leon again rejected. The case was then appealed to the Louisiana Supreme Court, which affirmed Duncan's conviction on February 20. There was, the court said, no "error of law in the ruling complained of."

The next day, Sobol telephoned Judge Leon and sought an appointment with him to arrange for Duncan's bond to remain in effect pending an appeal to the United States Supreme Court. The judge promptly informed Assistant District Attorney Bubrig that Sobol was returning to Plaquemines Parish, and District Attorney Perez signed a bill of information charging Sobol with the unauthorized practice of law in Louisiana. Judge Leon then issued a bench warrant for Sobol's arrest, and he was arrested leaving the courthouse in Pointe a la Hache after his appointment with the judge. Sobol was taken to the parish prison, was photographed and fingerprinted, and had his personal effects seized. He was incarcerated for four hours until his bail, set at $1,500 was raised. Meanwhile Judge Leon issued a bench warrant for the arrest of Gary Duncan on the grounds that the refusal of the Louisiana Supreme Court to reverse his case had had the effect of cancelling his bond. Duncan was arrested late at night on February 23 by Plaquemines Parish officers who generally abused him on the trip to the prison. His relatives pledged $1,500 worth of property to bail him out of jail, but they were informed by the sheriff's office that twice that amount of property would have to be pledged for bail, despite the fact that Louisiana law specified a pledge of property equal to the amount of bail. Duncan was jailed for twenty-four hours before his $1,500 bail was raised.

After Sobol's release from the Plaquemines Parish prison, he filed suit in federal district court for an injunction and a declaratory judgment against the Louisiana statutes under which he was charged. He contended that enforcement against him of the state law regulating the unauthorized practice of law violated the First Amendment and the equal protection clause of the Fourteenth Amendment. Prohibiting his service as a nonresident attorney, in association with a member of the state bar, in no-fee civil rights suits, Sobol argued, would effectively prevent needy civil rights litigants from obtaining legal assistance.

While this federal suit was pending, Sobol pursued the appeal of *Duncan v. Louisiana* to the United States Supreme Court. The Court noted probable jurisdiction in the case on October 9, 1967. Sobol acknowledged in his argument that the 1900 Court in *Maxwell v. Dow* had held the Sixth Amendment jury trial clause inapplicable to the states, but he argued that the nationalization decisions of the 1960s undermined *Maxwell* as a precedent. *Maxwell* had been based on the premise that none of the rights in the Bill of Rights were applicable to the states. This premise was completely undermined by the Court's subsequent decisions applying all of the Sixth Amendment rights to the states except the jury trial clause. "Under the conception of Fourteenth Amendment Due Process recently affirmed in *Gideon, Pointer* and *Washington v. Texas,*" Sobol told the Court, "appellant submits that application of the Sixth Amendment jury trial guarantee to state criminal proceedings is required: (1) by historical and contempory recognition of the fundamental nature of the jury trial right in our system of criminal law; and (2) by the essential role which the jury serves in assuring a defendant a fair trial in accordance with due process of law."

During oral argument before the Supreme Court, on January 17, 1968, Sobol was asked by Justice Fortas just "what rule do you want us to apply" on this point. "The rule we are contending for," Sobol responded, "is the application of the Sixth Amendment right to a trial by jury to the states via the Fourteenth Amendment to the Constitution of the United States." Did he mean that all of the states must have juries composed of twelve persons, Fortas asked, and Sobol replied that the Court had consistently held in the past that the jury trial clause required this.

A persistent opponent to the kind of incorporation that Sobol was proposing, Justice Harlan asked if his argument would not also support application to the states of the Seventh Amendment requirement of jury trials in all civil cases involving over twenty dollars. "No, sir, that is not the logic of our position," Sobol said. Harlan persisted, asking how Sobol would pick and choose among the provisions of the Bill of Rights those that were to apply to the states. Sobol responded that juries were necessary in criminal trials in order to ensure fairness, but again Harlan interrupted. "How do you get this out of the Constitution? The theory of incorporation is not due process."

Despite Harlan's hostility, Sobol insisted that the Court should hold the jury trial clause applicable to the states in all serious criminal cases and should hold that a serious criminal case was one in which the potential sentence was more than six months' imprisonment. Since Duncan had faced a potential sentence of two years' imprisonment for the offense of simple battery under Louisiana law, Sobol argued that the Louisiana courts had violated the Constitution in their refusal to grant a jury trial in this case. The role of dispensing justice in a democracy, he concluded, "is a particularly sensitive task and the right of the people to participate directly in this important function of government has been preserved in the form of the criminal jury. The increasing complexity and influence of modern government, where in most matters popular control is several times removed from the decision making process, underscores the urgency of preserving inviolate the direct voice of the community in the administration of the criminal law."

In defending the validity of Duncan's conviction, the Louisiana attorney general's office argued that the due process clause of the Fourteenth Amendment merely required state criminal trials to be conducted fairly. Ever since *Maxwell* in 1900, the Court had rejected the proposition that a jury was essential for a fair trial in a criminal case. Even if the Court were to conclude that the due process clause required jury trials in state proceedings, the respondents argued, juries should be required only in "serious" criminal cases, and simple battery had historically been considered a "petty" not a "serious" offense. Moreover, if the Court defined a serious offense as one for which a person was imprisoned more than six months, Duncan's case did not meet this test, since he had been sentenced to only sixty days in jail. If jury trials were required in all cases involving imprisonment for more than six months, it was argued, the Court should look not at the maximum potential sentence for a given offense but rather the actual sentence imposed.

In pursuing the argument orally before the Court, Assistant Attorney General Dorothy D. Wolbrette was interrupted by Justice Black, who asked if the determination of whether a defendant was entitled to a jury trial had to be made after the trial had taken place and the length of sentence was determined. "Are you saying that a wait and see approach must be taken?" he asked. "Yes," she replied. "Do you say that this young man could have been sentenced to two years imprisonment without being afforded his right to trial by jury?" Black continued. "Why, of course," Wolbrette responded.

Simple battery was regarded as a petty offense in Louisiana, Wolbrette said, and was punishable by a sentence in the parish jail rather than in the state prison. "What is the difference between a parish jail and a penitentiary?" Justice Thurgood Marshall asked. Wolbrette replied that those sentenced to the state prison were compelled to perform hard labor and that such a sentence entailed more disgrace for the prisoner. "What is the maximum punishment that can be imposed in Louisiana for an offense that is not classified as a felony?" Justice Fortas wanted to know. Mrs. Wolbrette responded that a judge sitting without a jury could sentence a defendant to three years in jail for wearing a hood on the public streets except at Mardi Gras. "What if a person wears a hood during Mardi Gras?" Fortas asked. "Why, it would be a crime not to wear a hood during Mardi Gras," Wolbrette replied.

A fair trial, as required by the due process clause, was obtainable without a jury, Mrs. Wolbrette concluded. "I don't think it's essential in any case. A judge can try a defendant fairly." The state was not denying the value of jury trials in criminal cases, she said, but was arguing that there was "just not a constitutional mandate" requiring jury trials in state criminal proceedings.

The Court, however, did not agree, and in a decision announced on May 20, 1968, it held that the jury trial clause of the Sixth Amendment applied to the states via the due process clause of the Fourteenth Amendment. It therefore reversed Gary Duncan's conviction. Justice White wrote the majority opinion, joined by Chief Justice Warren and Justices Brennan and Marshall; Justice Black, joined by Justice Douglas, concurred in a separate opinion, as did Justice Fortas. Justice Harlan, joined by Justice Stewart, dissented.

DUNCAN V. LOUISIANA
391 U.S. 145, decided May 20, 1968

Mr. Justice White delivered the opinion of the Court. [White first summarized the facts in the case and then turned to the merits.]

The Fourteenth Amendment denies the States the power to "deprive any person of life, liberty, or property, without due process of law." In resolving conflicting claims concerning the meaning of this spacious language, the Court has looked increasingly to the Bill of Rights for guidance; many of the rights guaranteed by the first eight Amendments to the Constitution have been held to be protected against state action by the Due Process Clause of the Fourteenth Amendment. That clause now protects the right to compensation for property taken by the State; the rights of speech, press and religion covered by the First Amendment; the Fourth Amendment rights to be free from unreasonable searches and seizures and to have excluded from criminal trials any evidence illegally seized; the right guaranteed by the Fifth Amendment to be free of compelled self-incrimination; and the Sixth Amendment rights to counsel, to a speedy and public trial, to confrontation of opposing witnesses, and to compulsory process for obtaining witnesses.

The test for determining whether a right extended by the Fifth and Sixth Amendments with respect to federal criminal proceedings is also protected against state action by the Fourteenth Amendment has been phrased in a variety of ways in the opinions of this Court. The question has been asked whether a right is among those " 'fundamental principles of liberty and justice which lie at the base of all our civil and political institutions,' " . . . ; whether it is "basic in our system jurisprudence," . . . ; and whether it is "a fundamental right, essential to a fair trial," . . . . The claim before us is that the right to trial by jury guaranteed by the Sixth Amendment meets these tests. The position of Louisiana, on the other hand, is that the Constitution imposes upon the States no duty to give a jury trial in any criminal case, regardless of the seriousness of the crime or the size of the punishment which may be imposed. Because we believe that trial by jury in criminal cases is fundamental to the American scheme of justice, we hold that the Fourteenth Amendment guarantees a right of jury trial in all criminal cases which—were they to be tried in a federal court—would come within the Sixth Amendment's guarantee. Since we consider the appeal before us to be such a case, we hold that the Constitution was violated when appellant's demand for jury trial was refused.

The history of trial by jury in criminal cases has been frequently told. It is sufficient for present purposes to say that by the time our Constitution was written, jury trial in criminal cases had been in existence in England for several centuries and carried impressive credentials traced by many to Magna Carta. . . .

Objections to the Constitution because of the absence of a bill of rights were met by the immediate submission and adoption of the Bill of Rights. Included was the Sixth Amendment which, among other things, provided:

> "In all criminal prosecutions, the accused shall enjoy the right to a speedy and public trial, by an impartial jury of the State and district wherein the crime shall have been committed."

The constitutions adopted by the original States guaranteed jury trial. Also, the constitution of every State entering the Union thereafter in one form or another protected the right to jury trial in criminal cases.

Even such skeletal history is impressive support for considering the right to jury trial in criminal cases to be fundamental to our system of justice, an importance frequently recognized in the opinions of this Court. . . .

Jury trial continues to receive strong support. The laws of every State guarantee a right to jury trial in serious criminal cases; no State has dispensed with it; nor are there significant movements underway to do so. Indeed, the three most recent state constitutional revisions, in Maryland, Michigan, and New York, carefully preserved the right of the accused to have the judgment of a jury when tried for a serious crime.

We are aware of prior cases in this Court in which the prevailing opinion contains statements contrary to our holding today that the right to jury trial in serious criminal cases is a fundamental right and hence must be recognized by the States as part of their obligation to extend due process of law to all persons within their jurisdiction. Louisiana relies especially on Maxwell v. Dow, . . . Palko v. Connecticut, . . . and Snyder v. Massachusetts . . . . None of these cases, however, dealt with a State which had purported to dispense entirely with a jury trial in serious criminal cases. Maxwell held that no provision of the Bill of Rights applied to the States—a position long since repudiated—and that the Due Process Clause of the Fourteenth Amendment did not prevent a State from trying a defendant for a noncapital offense with fewer than 12 men on the jury. It did not deal with a case in which no jury at all had been provided. In neither Palko nor Snyder was jury trial actually at issue, although both cases contain important dicta asserting that the right to jury trial is not essential to ordered liberty and may be dispensed with by the States regardless of the Sixth and Fourteenth Amendments. These observations, though weighty and respectable, are nevertheless dicta, unsupported by holdings in this Court that a State may refuse a defendant's demand for a jury trial when he is charged with a serious crime. . . .

The guarantees of jury trial in the Federal and State Constitutions reflect a profound judgment about the way in which law should be enforced and justice administered. A right to jury trial is granted to criminal defendants in order to prevent oppression by the Government. Those who wrote our constitutions knew from history and experience that it was necessary to protect against unfounded criminal charges brought to eliminate enemies and against judges too responsive to the voice of higher authority. The framers of the constitutions strove to create an independent judiciary but insisted upon further protection against arbitrary action. Providing an accused with the right to be tried by a jury of his peers gave him an inestimable safeguard against the corrupt or overzealous prosecutor and against the compliant, biased, or eccentric judge. If the defendant preferred the common-sense judgment of a jury to the more tutored but perhaps less sympathetic reaction of the single judge, he was to have it. Beyond this, the jury trial provisions in the Federal and State Constitutions reflect a fundamental decision about the exercise of official power—a reluctance to entrust plenary powers over the life and liberty of the citizen to one judge or to a group of judges. Fear of unchecked power, so typical of our State and Federal Governments in other respects, found expression in the criminal law in this insistence upon community participation in the determination of guilt or innocence. The deep commitment of the Nation to the right to jury trial in serious criminal cases as a defense against arbitrary law enforcement qualifies for protection under the Due Process Clause of the Fourteenth Amendment, and must therefore be respected by the States. . . .

The State of Louisiana urges that holding that the Fourteenth Amendment assures a right to jury trial will cast doubt on the integrity of every trial conducted without a jury. Plainly, this is not the import of our holding. Our conclusion is that in the American States, as in the federal judicial system, a general grant of jury trial for serious offenses is a fundamental right, essential for preventing miscarriages of justice and for assuring that fair trials are provided for all defendants. We would not assert, however, that every criminal trial—or any particular trial—held before a judge alone is unfair or that a defendant may never be as fairly treated by a judge as he would be by a jury. Thus we hold no constitutional doubts about the practices, common in both federal and state courts, of accepting waivers of jury trial and prosecuting petty crimes without extending a right to jury trial. . . .

Louisiana's final contention is that even if it must grant jury trials in serious criminal cases, the conviction before us is valid and constitutional because here the petitioner was tried for simple battery and was sentenced to only 60 days in the parish prison. We are not persuaded. It is doubtless true that there is a category of petty crimes or offenses which is not subject to the Sixth Amendment jury trial provision and should not be subject to the

Fourteenth Amendment jury trial requirement here applied to the States. Crimes carrying possible penalties up to six months do not require a jury trial if they otherwise qualify as petty offenses. . . . But the penalty authorized for a particular crime is of major relevance in determining whether it is serious or not and may in itself, if severe enough, subject the trial to the mandates of the Sixth Amendment. . . . We need not, however, settle in this case the exact location of the line between petty offenses and serious crimes. It is sufficient for our purposes to hold that a crime punishable by two years in prison is, based on past and contemporary standards in this country, a serious crime and not a petty offense. Consequently, appellant was entitled to a jury trial and it was error to deny it.

The judgment below is reversed and the case is remanded for proceedings not inconsistent with this opinion.

Mr. Justice Fortas, concurring.[3]

I join the judgments and opinions of the Court in these cases because I agree that the Due Process Clause of the Fourteenth Amendment requires that the States accord the right to jury trial in prosecutions for offenses that are not petty. . . .

But although I agree with the decision of the Court, I cannot agree with the implication . . . that the tail must go with the hide: that when we hold, influenced by the Sixth Amendment, that "due process" requires that the States accord the right of jury trial for all but petty offenses, we automatically import all of the ancillary rules which have been or may hereafter be developed incidental to the right to jury trial in the federal courts. I see no reason whatever, for example, to assume that our decision today should require us to impose federal requirements such as unanimous verdicts or a jury of 12 upon the States. We may well conclude that these and other features of federal jury practice are by no means fundamental—that they are not essential to due process of law—and that they are not obligatory on the States. . . .

The Due Process Clause commands us to apply its great standard to state court proceedings to assure basic fairness. It does not command us rigidly and arbitrarily to impose the exact pattern of federal proceedings upon the 50 States. On the contrary, the Constitution's command, in my view, is that in our insistence upon state observance of due process, we should, so far as possible, allow the greatest latitude for state differences. It requires, within the limits of the lofty basic standards that it prescribes for the States as well as the Federal Government, maximum opportunity for

3. Justice Fortas's concurring opinion was recorded in a companion case to *Duncan, Bloom v. Illinois*, 391 U.S. 194, 211-15 (1968).

diversity and minimal imposition of uniformity of method and detail upon the States. Our Constitution sets up a federal union, not a monolith.

This Court has heretofore held that various provisions of the Bill of Rights . . . "are all to be enforced against the States under the Fourteenth Amendment according to the same standards that protect those personal rights against federal encroachment." . . . I need not quarrel with the specific conclusion in these specific instances. But unless one adheres slavishly to the incorporation theory, body and substance, the same conclusion need not be superimposed upon the jury trial right. I respectfully but urgently suggest that it should not be. Jury trial is more than a principle of justice applicable to individual cases. It is a system of administration of the business of the State. While we may believe (and I do believe) that the right of jury trial is fundamental, it does not follow that the particulars of according that right must be uniform. We should be ready to welcome state variations which do not impair—indeed, which may advance—the theory and purpose of trial by jury.

Mr. Justice Black, with whom Mr. Justice Douglas joins, concurring.

[Black endorsed the opinion and decision of the Court and noted that *Duncan* was but another step toward what he had urged over twenty years ago in 1947 in *Adamson v. California*—total incorporation of the Bill of Rights into the due process clause. He then sought to answer the concurring opinion by Justice Fortas and the dissenting opinion by Justice Harlan by again reiterating his total incorporation theory.]

I do not believe that it is necessary for me to repeat the historical and logical reasons for my challenge to the Twining holding contained in my Adamson dissent and Appendix to it. What I wrote there in 1947 was the product of years of study and research. My appraisal of the legislative history followed 10 years of legislative experience as a Senator of the United States, not a bad way, I suspect, to learn the value of what is said in legislative debates, committee discussions, committee reports, and various other steps taken in the course of passage of bills, resolutions, and proposed constitutional amendments. My Brother Harlan's objections to my Adamson dissent history, like that of most of the objectors, relies most heavily on a criticism written by Professor Charles Fairman and published in the Stanford Law Review . . . . I have read and studied this article extensively, including the historical references, but am compelled to add that in my view it has completely failed to refute the inferences and arguments that I suggested in my Adamson dissent. Professor Fairman's "history" relies very heavily on what was *not* said in the state legislatures that passed on the Fourteenth Amendment. Instead of relying on this kind of negative pregnant, my legislative experience has convinced me that it is far wiser to rely on what *was* said, and most importantly, said by the men who actually sponsored the Amendment in the Congress. . . . The historical appendix to my Adamson dissent leaves no doubt in my mind that both its sponsors and those who opposed it believed the Fourteenth Amendment made the first eight Amendments of the Constitution (the Bill of Rights) applicable to the States. . . .

While I do not wish at this time to discuss at length my disagreement with Brother Harlan's forthright and frank restatement of the now discredited Twining doctrine, I do want to point out what appears to me to be the basic difference between us. His view, as was indeed, the view of Twining, is that "due process is an evolving concept" and therefore that it entails a "gradual process of judicial inclusion and exclusion" to ascertain those "immutable principles . . . of free government which no member of the Union may disregard." Thus the Due Process Clause is treated as prescribing no specific and clearly ascertainable constitutional command that judges must obey in interpreting the Constitution, but rather as leaving judges free to decide at any particular time whether a particular rule or judicial formulation embodies an "immutable principle of free government" or is "implicit in the concept of ordered liberty," or whether certain conduct "shocks the judge's conscience" or runs counter to some other similar, undefined and undefinable standard. Thus due process, according to my Brother Harlan, is to be a phrase with no permanent meaning, but one which is found to shift from time to time in accordance with judges' predilections and understandings of what is best for the country. If due process means this, the Fourteenth Amendment, in my opinion, might as well have been written that "no person shall be deprived of life, liberty or property except by laws that the judges of the United States Supreme Court shall find to be consistent with the immutable principles of free government." It is impossible for me to believe that such unconfined power is given to judges in our Constitution that is a written one in order to limit governmental power. . . .

Finally I want to add that I am not bothered by the argument that applying the Bill of Rights to the States, "according to the same standards that protect those personal rights against federal encroachment," interferes with our concept of federalism in that it may prevent States from trying novel social and economic experiments. I have never believed that under the guise of federalism the States should be able to experiment with the protections afforded our citizens through the Bill of Rights. . . .

It seems to me totally inconsistent to advocate, on the one hand, the power of this Court to strike down any state law or practice which it finds "unreasonable" or "unfair" and, on the other hand, urge that the States be given maximum power to develop their own laws and procedures. Yet the due process approach of my Brothers Harlan and Fortas . . . does just that since in effect it restricts the States to practices which a majority of this Court is willing to approve on a case-by-case basis. No one is more concerned than I that the States be allowed to use the full scope of their powers as their citizens see fit. And that is why I have continually fought against the expansion of this Court's authority over the States through the use of a broad, general interpretation of due process that permits judges to strike down state laws they do not like.

In closing I want to emphasize that I believe as strongly as ever that the Fourteenth Amendment was intended to make the Bill of Rights applicable to the States. I have been willing to support the selective incorporation doctrine, however, as an alternative, although [it is] perhaps less historically supportable than complete incorporation. The selective incorporation process, if used properly, does limit the Supreme Court in the Fourteenth Amendment field to specific Bill of Rights' protections only and keeps judges from roaming at will in their own notions of what policies outside the Bill of Rights are desirable and what are not. And, most importantly for me, the selective incorporation process has the virtue of having already worked to make most of the Bill of Rights' protections applicable to the States.

Mr. Justice Harlan, whom Mr. Justice Stewart joins, dissenting.
. . . The Court's approach to this case is an uneasy and illogical compromise among the views of various Justices on how the Due Process Clause should be interpreted. The Court does not say that those who framed the Fourteenth Amendment intended to make the Sixth Amendment applicable to the States. And the Court concedes that it finds nothing unfair about the procedure by which the present appellant was tried. Nevertheless, the Court reverses his conviction: it holds, for some reason not apparent to me, that the Due Process Clause incorporates the particular clause of the Sixth Amendment that requires trial by jury in federal criminal cases—including, as I read its opinion, the sometimes trivial accompanying baggage of judicial interpretation in federal contexts. I have raised my voice many times before against the insistence upon fastening on the States federal notions of criminal justice, and I must do so again in this instance. With all respect, the Court's approach and its reading of history are altogether topsy-turvy.

I believe I am correct in saying that every member of the Court for at least the last 135 years has agreed that our Founders did not consider the requirements of the Bill of Rights so fundamental that they should operate directly against the States. They were wont to believe rather that the security of liberty in America rested primarily upon the dispersion of governmental power across a federal system. The Bill of Rights was considered unnecessary by some but insisted upon by others in order to curb the possibility of abuse of power by the strong central government they were creating.

The Civil War Amendments dramatically altered the relation of the Federal Government to the States. . . . The question has been: Where does the Court properly look to find the specific rules that define and give content to such terms as "life, liberty, or property" and "due process of law?"

A few members of the Court have taken the position that the intention of those who drafted the first section of the Fourteenth Amendment was simply, and exclusively, to make the provisions of the first eight Amendments applicable to state action. This view has never been accepted by this Court. In my view, often expressed elsewhere, the first section of the Fourteenth Amendment was meant neither to incorporate, nor to be limited to, the specific guarantees of the first eight Amendments. The overwhelming historical evidence marshalled by Professor Fairman demonstrates, to me conclusively, that the Congressmen and state legislators who wrote, debated, and ratified the Fourteenth Amendment did not think they were "incorporating" the Bill of Rights. . . . In short, neither history, nor sense, supports using the Fourteenth Amendment to put the States in a constitutional strait-jacket with respect to their own development in the administration of criminal or civil law.

Although I therefore fundamentally disagree with the total incorporation view of the Fourteenth Amendment, it seems to me that such a position does at least have the virtue, lacking in the Court's selective incorporation approach, of internal consistency: we look to the Bill of Rights, word for word, clause for clause, precedent for precedent because, it is said, the men who wrote the Amendment wanted it that way. . . .

Apart from the approach taken by the absolute incorporationists, I can see only one method of analysis that has any internal logic. That is to start with the words "liberty" and "due process of law" and attempt to define them in a way that accords with American traditions and our system of government. This approach, involving a much more discriminating process of adjudication than does "incorporation," is, albeit difficult, the one that was followed throughout the 19th and most of the present century. It entails a "gradual process of judicial inclusion and exclusion," seeking, with due recognition of constitutional tolerance for state experimentation and disparity, to ascertain those "immutable principles . . . of free government which no member of the Union may disregard." . . .

The relationship of the Bill of Rights to this "gradual process" seems to me to be twofold. In the first place it has long been clear that the Due Process Clause imposes some restrictions on state action that parallel Bill of Rights restrictions on federal action. Second, and more important than this accidental overlap, is the fact that the Bill of Rights is evidence, at various points, of the content Americans find in the term "liberty" and of American standards of fundamental fairness. . . .

The logically critical thing, however, was not that the rights had been found in the Bill of Rights, but that they were deemed, in the context of American legal history, to be fundamental. . . .

Today's Court still remains unwilling to accept the total incorporationists' view of the history of the Fourteenth Amendment. This, if accepted, would afford a cogent reason for applying the Sixth Amendment to the States. The Court is also, apparently, unwilling to face the task of determining whether denial of trial by jury in the situation before us, or in other situations, is fundamentally unfair. Consequently, the Court has compromised on the ease of the incorporationist position, without its internal logic. It has simply assumed that the question before us is whether the Jury Trial Clause of the Sixth Amendment should be incorporated into the Fourteenth, jot-for-jot and case-for-case, or ignored. Then the Court merely declares that the clause in question is "in" rather than "out."

The Court has justified neither its starting place nor its conclusion. . . . The argument that jury trial is not a requisite of due process is quite simple. . . . "[D]ue process of law" requires only that criminal trials be fundamentally fair. As stated above, apart from the theory that it was historically intended as a mere shorthand for the Bill of Rights, I do not see what else "due process of law" can intelligibly be thought to mean. If due process of law requires only fundamental fairness, then the inquiry in each case must be whether a state trial process was a fair one. The Court has held, properly I think, that in an adversary process it is a requisite of fairness, for which there is no adequate substitute, that a criminal defendant be afforded a right to counsel and to cross-examine opposing witnesses. But it simply has not been demonstrated, nor, I think, can it be demonstrated, that trial by jury is the only fair means of resolving issues of fact. . . .

This Court, other courts, and the political process are available to correct any experiments in criminal procedure that prove fundamentally unfair to defendants. That is not what is being done today: instead, and quite without reason, the Court has chosen to impose upon every State one means of trying criminal cases; it is a good means, but it is not the only fair means, and it is not demonstrably better than the alternatives States might devise.

I would affirm the judgment of the Supreme Court of Louisiana.

Despite Justice Harlan's renewed protest against the incorporation theory, the majority of the Court had applied the jury trial clause of the Sixth Amendment to state criminal proceedings via the due process clause of the Fourteenth Amendment. The *Duncan* decision left several important questions unanswered, however. The Court had failed to say whether the requirement would be applied retroactively, where exactly the line between petty and serious offenses lay, and whether the clause required unanimous verdicts by juries of twelve.

The Court held later that year in *DeStafano v. Woods* that the jury trial clause would not be retroactively applicable to cases tried in state courts. And during the next four years the Court cleared up the other questions left unanswered in *Duncan*. In *Baldwin v. New York,* decided in 1970, it ruled that "serious" criminal offenses requiring jury trials were those in which the potential sentence exceeded six months' imprisonment, and it held that states could continue to try "petty" offenses (those with potential sentences of up to six months' imprisonment) without juries. Also in 1970, in *Williams v. Florida,* the Court held that the Sixth and Fourteenth Amendments did not require juries of twelve, although the traditional common law jury had been composed of twelve persons and the Court had consistently held in the past that juries of twelve were required under the Sixth Amendment. The purpose of a jury trial, it held, was to "safeguard against arbitrary law enforcement," and the traditional requirement of a twelve-person jury was a "historical accident, unrelated to the great purposes which gave rise to the jury in the first place." Under the Sixth and Fourteenth Amendments, the Court concluded, juries could be composed of fewer than twelve persons as long as they were "large enough to promote group deliberation, free from outside attempts at intimidation, and to provide a fair possibility for obtaining a representative cross-section of the community."

Finally, in *Apodaca v. Oregon* and *Johnson v. Louisiana,* decided in 1972, the Court held that the jury trial requirement imposed on the states did not require unanimous verdicts. It therefore sustained jury verdicts by a vote of nine to three in Louisiana and ten to two in Oregon. Such nonunanimous jury verdicts, the Court held, did not undermine the due process requirement that the state prove its case beyond a reasonable doubt.

The deciding vote in the *Johnson* and *Apodaca* cases was cast by Justice Powell, who agreed with the contention of Justice Fortas in the *Duncan* case that the due process clause did not impose on the states the requirement of unanimous verdicts by juries of twelve. On the other hand, Powell contended that the Sixth Amendment did require unanimous verdicts in federal criminal cases. Justices Douglas, Brennan, Stewart, and Marshall dissented in these cases. The rather anomalous result of *Apodaca* and *Johnson* was to allow nonunanimous verdicts in state criminal cases but not in federal cases.

Richard Sobol had also participated in *Apodaca,* arguing that the Sixth and Fourteenth Amendments required unanimous jury verdicts, but fate and the Nixon appointees to the Court since *Duncan* were against him. Still, Sobol had established jury trials as a constitutional requirement in *Duncan,* and he had successfully challenged the Perez regime in Plaquemines Parish. His suit for a declaratory judgment and an injunction against the Louisiana unauthorized–practice–of–law statutes resulted in the first important federal court challenge to the attempts by southern states to bar out-of-state attorneys from representing civil rights litigants. Hearings were held before a three-judge federal court in New Orleans during January and February of 1968 and on July 22, 1968, the federal court delivered its opinion in *Sobol v. Perez,* tonguelashing the Plaquemines Parish authorities. The court reviewed Sobol's outstanding legal qualifications and the proceedings in *Duncan v. Louisiana,* noting that Gary Duncan had been arrested four times in Plaquemines Parish and compelled to post $5,500 in bail, while earning $65 a week and supporting a wife and baby. The court also noted the events surrounding the unauthorized-practice arrest of Sobol and the fact that District Attorney Leander Perez, Jr., had investigated Sobol and learned from the telephone and utilities companies in New Orleans when Sobol had established residence in Louisiana, in obvious anticipation of filing the unauthorized-practice charge against him. The court also noted Perez's public statement in 1965 that "if any known agitator were to appear in Plaquemines Parish, his mere presence would amount to a disturbance of the peace, since he was an outsider."

"We are impressed most strongly," the court said, "by the fact Sobol was charged and arrested without a word having been said to him by the court or the district attorney to indicate to him that he was practicing law improperly. Remanding him to the jail, removing his personal effects, photographing him and setting bail without having him appear before the judge are so out of keeping with what normally would be done to a person of Sobol's professional status that they can only be interpreted as harassment."

The prosecution instituted by the Plaquemines Parish authorities against Sobol, the court concluded, "was meant to show Sobol that civil rights lawyers were not welcome in the parish, and that their defense of Negroes involved in cases growing out of civil rights efforts would not be tolerated. It was meant also as a warning to other civil rights lawyers and to Negroes in the parish who might consider retaining civil rights lawyers to advance their rights to equal opportunity and equal treatment under the Equal Protection Clause of the Fourteenth Amendment."

The three-judge court concluded that while the Louisiana unauthorized-practice statutes were not unconstitutional on their face, they were inapplicable to the kind of civil rights practice in which Sobol had been engaged in association with members of the Louisiana bar. District Judge Fred Cassibry thus issued an injunction prohibiting Plaquemines Parish officials from proceeding against Sobol under the statutes.

Although Leander Perez, Sr., died on March 19, 1969, his sons continued to maintain the iron grip of the Perez family on Plaquemines Parish. Despite the Supreme Court's decision reversing Duncan's conviction, District Attorney Perez indicated he would reprosecute the battery case against Duncan. Attorneys of the Lawyers Constitutional Defense Committee, however, filed a suit in federal district court for an injunction against the reprosecution, and on October 20, 1970, the court granted the injunction in *Duncan v. Perez.*

The court noted that, between 1965 and 1970, there had been eighty-four prosecutions for battery in Plaquemines Parish and in only fifteen of those cases were mandatory jail terms imposed. In only five of the cases had the sentences exceeded the sixty-day term given to Duncan. The court also noted the cancellation of Duncan's bond pending appeal to the Supreme Court, his subsequent arrest late at night, his harassment by the arresting officers, and the rejection of sufficient property pledged as bail for his release. It concluded that the "plaintiff has maintained the heavy burden required for an injunction against a pending state criminal proceeding," since the "proceeding against Duncan in state court is maintained by the defendant in bad faith and for purposes of harassment." There was, the court held, "no legitimate state interest in the reprosecution of Duncan." The alleged violation of the law by Duncan, the court said, "was so slight and technical as to be generally reserved for law school hypotheticals rather than criminal prosecutions." If Duncan were required to face retrial on the battery charge, the court concluded, "it would constitute an unmistakable message to Negroes in Plaquemines Parish that it is unprofitable to step outside familiar patterns and to seek to rely on federal rights to oppose the policies of certain parish officials."

The district court thus enjoined Perez from further prosecution of Gary Duncan on the battery charge. Perez appealed to the Fifth Circuit Court of Appeals, but on June 14, 1971, that court affirmed the district court's injunction. The United States Supreme Court was asked to review the case but it refused on November 9, 1971. For the first time in five years, Gary Duncan was free from the threat of prosecution in Plaquemines Parish.

No cases nationalizing parts of the Bill of Rights have been decided by the Supreme Court since *Benton v. Maryland* in 1969 applied the Fifth Amendment double jeopardy clause to the states. Since most of the Bill of Rights now applies, little further extension of the nationalization process can be expected. A possible exception is application of the excessive fines and bail clause of the Eighth Amendment to the states in some future case.

The nationalization of the Bill of Rights has radically altered the nature of our federal system and of American constitutional litigation. Before the Civil War, the protection of political and civil liberties against state action was almost exclusively a matter of state law; as a result of the nationalization process, the federal Constitution now guarantees almost all the rights in the Bill of Rights against interference by the states as well as by the federal government. In addition, the majority of the cases in which the important rights in the Bill of Rights are interpreted by the Supreme Court are now cases involving challenges to state power. This is true not only in the fields of freedom of expression and religion but also in regard to the most important criminal procedure rights. (See table 2.) The nationalization process may thus be said to have transformed the due process clause of the Fourteenth Amendment into our second bill of rights—one that is in many ways more salient to the average citizen than the original Bill of Rights adopted in 1791.

With most of the Bill of Rights made applicable to the states, the nationalization process ceased to be the most significant line of policy development under the due process clause of the Fourteenth Amendment in the middle 1960s, and it was supplanted by the question of whether the Court would interpret the clause to embrace rights that were not listed in the Bill of Rights. Justice Black, who had fought for total incorporation during most of his career on the Court, vehemently rejected the proposition that the due process clause embraced any rights beyond those in the Bill of Rights. The Bill of Rights, he argued, supplied the total meaning of the due process clause. For the Court to read rights beyond those in the Bill of Rights into the due process clause, he contended, would be an abuse of judicial power, allowing the justices to impose their own personal predilections on the meaning of the due process clause.

Black's view was not accepted by the Court, however, and in *Griswold v. Connecticut,* decided in 1965, a majority of the Court invalidated a Connecticut prohibition against use of contraceptives to prevent conception, holding it to be an invasion of the "right to privacy in marriage" protected by the due process clause, although such a right was nowhere mentioned in the Bill of Rights or elsewhere in the Constitution. A majority of the Court in *Griswold* found that the right to privacy in marriage was guaranteed either as an "emanation" from the rights guaranteed in the First, Third, Fourth, Fifth, and Ninth Amendments in the Bill of Rights, or by

Table 2

THE IMPACT OF THE NATIONALIZATION PROCESS
UPON CONSTITUTIONAL INTERPRETATION

Field of Supreme Court Decisions*	Number of Decisions	Percentage (Rounded)
Freedom of expression cases decided		
from 1931 to 1970†	175	100%
State cases	122	70
Federal cases	53	30
Free exercise of religion cases decided		
from 1940 to 1970	34	100%
State cases	29	85
Federal cases	5	15
Search and seizure cases decided		
from 1961 to 1970	66	100%
State cases	35	53
Federal cases‡	31	47
Right to counsel cases decided		
from 1963 to 1970	20	100%
State cases	17	85
Federal cases	3	15
Self-incrimination cases decided		
from 1964 to 1970	40	100%
State cases	23	57.5
Federal cases	17	42.5

* Includes only cases decided with opinions.

† Freedom of expression here includes freedom of speech and freedom of the press but not freedom of assembly or freedom of association.

‡ The number of federal search and seizure cases is considerably inflated by the fifteen cases considered in *Giordano v. United States*.

inference from the theory of the Ninth Amendment, which provides that "enumeration in the Constitution, of certain rights, shall not be construed to deny or disparage others retained by the people." As Justice Goldberg emphasized in a concurring opinion in *Griswold*, the Ninth Amendment thus appeared to contemplate the preservation of unenumerated individual rights, such as the right to privacy in marriage, that had gone unmentioned in the Constitution.

Griswold was heavily relied on by the Court in *Eisenstadt v. Baird,* a 1972 decision that invalidated a Massachusetts statute banning the distribution of contraceptives to unmarried persons. Although *Eisenstadt* was decided under the equal protection clause of the Fourteenth Amendment, the Court did expand its holding in *Griswold* by saying that if "the right of privacy means anything, it is the right of the *individual,* married or single, to be free from unwarranted governmental intrusion into matters so fundamentally affecting a person as the decision whether to bear or beget a child."

In *Griswold v. Connecticut,* therefore, the Court had indicated that the meaning of the due process clause of the Fourteenth Amendment was not to be confined to rights in the Bill of Rights, but rather was elastic, potentially embracing fundamental individual rights beyond those mentioned in the Bill of Rights. And in *Eisenstadt* the Court held that the right of privacy it had recognized in *Griswold* embraced a right to be free from "unwarranted governmental intrusion" into the "decision whether to bear or beget a child." This interpretation of the due process clause was to serve as the basis for challenges to the most prevalent governmental interference with that decision—anti-abortion statutes. In the next case study we examine in detail how the right of privacy that was developed in the *Griswold* and *Eisenstadt* cases was applied in litigation of the *Abortion Cases* of 1973.

Case Study
THE CASES OF THE PSEUDONYMOUS WOMEN: THE ABORTION CASES

The current emotions aroused by the abortion issue have not, apparently, always characterized its treatment under Anglo-American law. It appears that under British common law, abortions induced during the early stages of pregnancy at least were not regarded as criminal offenses, and there is some doubt whether abortion was regarded as an offense whenever it was performed. At the very least, the common law did not make abortion an offense until after a pregnancy had reached the stage of "quickening," estimated to be between sixteen and eighteen weeks after conception, during which movements of the fetus are detectable. This common law treatment of abortion was inherited by the American states, and thus abortion was not a significant subject of American criminal law during most of the first half of the nineteenth century.

Although Connecticut adopted a statute prohibiting abortions after quickening in 1821, most state legislation modifying the common law on the subject occurred after the Civil War. Two important modifications in the common law approach to abortion then become discernible. First, the state statutes modifying the common law treatment of abortion tended to treat abortion as a rather serious criminal offense, although it was not treated as homicide. Secondly, the common law distinction between abortions performed in early pregnancy and those performed after quickening, was abandoned in most state legislation dealing with the subject. In nineteenth-century statutes, therefore, abortion became a criminal offense at whatever stage during pregnancy it occurred, although an exception was generally recognized for abortions performed to preserve the lives of mothers. Some jurisdictions, although not a majority, also allowed abortions for pregnancies initiated by rape or incest. What had been a largely unregulated matter in 1800, therefore, had become a statutory crime by 1900.

Although the reasons for adoption of the anti-abortion statutes during the latter part of the nineteenth century remain obscure, it has been speculated that Victorian sexual mores were responsible. From the standpoint of the development of medical science, however, there were obvious compelling reasons for prohibiting abortions until relatively recent times. Not until the 1840s did American doctors become generally aware that clean hands were advisable during gynecological examinations, and not until 1867 did Joseph Lister propose the novel idea that antiseptic techniques were required during surgery. Moreover, not until the turn of the century did antiseptic techniques become generally accepted as mandatory in American surgical practices.

As a consequence, before 1900 major surgery was generally

considered inadvisable unless death was imminent. The mortality rate for major operations during this period commonly ran from 50 to 100 percent. Abortions at the time usually required the internal use of surgical instruments and thus posed grave risks for the pregnant woman. Whatever other motives may have induced American legislatures to prohibit abortion during the post–Civil War period, preservation of the health, or indeed the very life of the woman could have been a compelling motive.

Several factors contributed to a changed attitude toward abortion during the 1960s and 1970s, not least among them the diminished hazards of abortion that medical advances had produced. In marked contrast to the risks in the nineteenth century, by the 1960s abortion, especially during the early stages of pregnancy, had become a relatively safe medical procedure. In the late 1960s, for example, the mortality rate for women giving birth was 28 per 100,000 live births. The mortality rate for appendectomies was 400 per 100,000; for gall bladder operations, 1,600 per 100,000; for tonsillectomy-adenoidectomy, 5.2 per 100,000. For legally performed abortions the rate was 10.3 per 100,000. An abortion, at least during the early stages of pregnancy, had thus become somewhat safer for a woman than giving birth, and it was medically safer than an appendectomy or a gall bladder operation. If the medical hazards of abortions had motivated the existing antiabortion legislation, this rationale was thus substantially undermined by advances in medicine during the twentieth century.

In addition, there developed, especially during the 1960s, a heightened awareness that laws permitting abortions only to preserve the lives of mothers too narrowly defined the legitimate justifications for the procedure. Such laws did not permit the abortion of pregnancies resulting from rape or incest, nor did they allow the probability of serious mental or physical defects in the child to be considered in the abortion decision. Finally, most state abortion laws did not allow the medical justification for an abortion to include psychological and other factors that were important to the preservation of the overall health of women.

Perhaps no event in the 1960s focused more attention on the restrictive nature of most state abortion legislation than the discovery that thalidomide, a tranquilizing drug, when used by women during pregnancy, produced a high percentage of grossly deformed children. The typical "thalidomide baby" was born without arms or legs or both; in Germany, where the drug had been widely used, more than five thousand deformed babies had been born by 1962. Yet, despite the prospect that many women who had used thalidomide would bear deformed children, under most state abortion laws at the time, such women could not legally obtain abortions. The problem of the thalidomide babies was further publicized in 1962, when Mrs. Sherri Finkbine of Phoenix, Arizona, a widely known television personality, the mother of four children and pregnant with a fifth child, discovered that she had used thalidomide during her current pregnancy. Mrs. Finkbine was unable to secure a legal abortion in Arizona, since the state law prohibited abortions except when the life of the mother was endangered by a pregnancy. Mrs. Finkbine instituted legal proceedings in the Arizona courts, but when these failed to clarify the legal situation, she traveled to Sweden and secured an abortion there. The doctor performing the operation later said that, if she had carried her child to term, it would have been deformed.

Also contributing significantly to the growing focus on abortion as a public policy issue was the rapid development of the women's rights movement during the 1960s. The movement was comprised of a broad coalition of groups, and its concerns ranged from primary emphasis on sexual discrimination in employment to a rethinking of the traditional status and role of women in American society. As part of this rising consciousness regarding women's rights, many women's groups attacked the prevailing abortion laws and demanded their reform or repeal. Some groups soon adopted the position that whether or not to bear a child should be the exclusive decision of the woman involved, in consultation with her physician. Women had a fundamental right to control what happened to their own bodies, it was argued, and the prevailing governmental regulation of abortion invaded that fundamental, personal right.

Within this changing climate of opinion, alterations in abortion policy began to occur within at least some jurisdictions. The

American Law Institute in 1959 proposed a revision of abortion policy in its Model Penal Code, to allow abortions by licensed physicians if there was "substantial risk that continuance of the pregnancy would gravely impair the physical or mental health of the mother or that the child would be born with grave physical or mental defect, or that the pregnancy resulted from rape, incest, or other felonious intercourse." By the early 1970s, approximately fourteen states had adopted some version of this ALI proposal. Four states, Alaska, Hawaii, New York, and Washington, repealed criminal penalties for abortions performed during the early stages of pregnancy, if performed by a licensed physician and under certain procedural safeguards.

The support for liberalizing abortion laws was finally countered in the early 1970s, however, by "right-to-life" groups, which were slower to organize and act on the issue of abortion than the groups favoring repeal or reform of restrictive policies. Public opinion polls in the early 1970s indicated that a majority of Americans disapproved of unregulated abortions even during the first stages of pregnancy, and the right-to-life forces were able to slow if not stop the trend toward less restrictive legislation. The liberal New York abortion law, for example, generated strong emotional responses, and during 1972 the legislature was constrained to consider its modification or repeal. Large public demonstrations for retention of the liberalized policy were countered by demonstrations by right-to-life forces in which abortion was denounced as murder.

Although the Commission on Population Growth appointed by President Nixon reported proposals favoring liberalization of abortion laws in the spring of 1972, Nixon announced his opposition to the proposals. A day later, on May 7, 1972, Nixon publicly intervened in the New York abortion dispute through a letter to Cardinal Cooke in which he stated that he "would personally like to associate myself with the convictions you deeply feel and eloquently express." The New York legislature subsequently repealed the state's liberalized abortion policy, but Governor Nelson Rockefeller vetoed the repeal, thus leaving the liberalized policy in effect.

Although Rockefeller blocked a major defeat of the pro-abortion forces, those forces soon received other setbacks. They had placed referenda on the question of changing state abortion policy on the ballots in North Dakota and Michigan. In the 1972 elections in both states the voters overwhelmingly rejected the proposed liberalizations of state policy.

With legislative changes in abortion policy slowed if not halted, the proponents of abortion reform turned increasingly to the courts. Between 1970 and 1973, state abortion laws were challenged in approximately thirty proceedings in the lower federal and state courts, with most of the decisions favoring the pro-abortion forces. Perhaps the most notable victory for these forces before 1972 was the 1969 California Supreme Court decision in *People v. Belous,* reversing the conviction of a doctor who had made abortion referrals and invalidating the California abortion law. The California court held that the right to privacy recognized in *Griswold v. Connecticut* was sufficiently broad to embrace the decision of a woman to secure an abortion. Although the United States Supreme Court denied review in *Belous,* it seemed inevitable that the validity of abortion laws would sooner or later be contested before the Court, given the increasing litigation by pro-abortion groups.

In the context of these events, a twenty-five-year-old unmarried waitress, Norma McCorvey, became pregnant in Dallas, Texas. As a consequence of her pregnancy she lost her job, and, when she consulted a physician regarding a possible abortion, she was advised that the 1856 Texas law did not permit abortions except "by medical advice for the purpose of saving the life of the mother." Since her pregnancy was not life-threatening, Ms. McCorvey was advised that she could not secure a legal abortion in Texas. Because of her financial situation, she was unable to travel elsewhere. As Ms. McCorvey said later, "I was a woman alone with no place to go and no job. No one wanted to hire a pregnant woman. I felt there was no one in the world who could help me."

Although it was estimated that three thousand illegal abortions, costing between $150 and $1,000 each, were performed in Dallas in 1969, Ms. McCorvey did not resort to that alternative, but rather contacted an attorney, Linda N. Coffee. Ms. Coffee was twenty-seven years old and had graduated from the University of

Texas Law School the previous year, but despite her inexperience as a practicing attorney she began proceedings that would result in one of the most bitterly contested United States Supreme Court decisions of recent times.

On March 3, 1970, Coffee filed a complaint on behalf of Norma McCorvey in the United States District Court for the Northern District of Texas, challenging the Texas abortion statute. The complaint requested a three-judge district court,[4] a declaratory judgment that the Texas abortion statute was unconstitutional, and an injunction prohibiting further enforcement of the statute. For purposes of the suit, Norma McCorvey adopted the pseudonym "Jane Roe," and the complaint was filed both for her and as a class action on behalf of "all other women who have sought, are seeking, or in the future will seek to obtain a legal medically safe abortion but whose lives are not critically threatened by the pregnancy."

The Texas abortion statute, the complaint alleged, deprived "women and their physicians of rights protected by the First, Fourth, Fifth, Ninth and Fourteenth Amendments, in that [the statute is] neither narrowly drawn nor supported by any overriding and compelling state interest." The statute thus denied women adequate medical advice, deprived them of "the fundamental right . . . to choose when and where to bear children," and invaded their right to privacy in the doctor-patient relationship and their right to personal privacy.

In a personal affidavit justifying her use of a pseudonym, Norma McCorvey stated that she was unmarried and pregnant and had had extreme difficulty in finding employment because of her pregnancy. "I feared the notoriety occasioned by the lawsuit would make it impossible for me to secure any employment in the near future and would severely limit my advancement in any employment which I might secure at some later date," she said. "I consider the decision of whether to bear a child a highly personal

---

4. A suit seeking an injunction against enforcement of a state statute on the ground of its federal constitutional invalidity requires a three-judge district court. Congress has required this procedure because of the feeling that a state policy should not be judged invalid and enjoined by a single federal judge. If a three-judge district court either issues or denies an injunction, that decision is appealable directly to the United States Supreme Court, bypassing the courts of appeals.

one and feel that the notoriety occasioned by the lawsuit would result in a gross invasion of my personal privacy." She wished to terminate her pregnancy, she continued, because of the economic hardship it entailed and "because of the social stigma attached to the bearing of illegitimate children in our society. I consider myself to be a law-abiding citizen and have never wanted to participate in an act deemed by the State of Texas to be a felony offense." She noted that because she had only a tenth grade education, she lacked formal training that would have prepared her for a well-paying job, and thus she could not afford to travel out-of-state for an abortion. "I believe that the enforcement of the Texas Abortion Laws against licensed physicians has forced me into the dilemma of electing whether to bear an unwanted child or to risk my life by submitting to an abortion at the hands of unqualified personnel outside of clinical settings."

In addition to the *Roe* complaint, attorney Coffee subsequently filed a complaint against the statute on behalf of "John and Mary Doe," a married couple who also adopted pseudonyms for the litigation. The Does' complaint alleged that Mary Doe suffered a neural-chemical disorder and that her physician had advised her against becoming pregnant, yet she had also been required to discontinue taking contraceptive pills, also on medical advice. The Does also alleged that for "highly personal reasons" they did not want to become parents in the near future. They thus feared that, because of contraceptive failure, "they may face the prospect of becoming parents before they are properly prepared to accept the responsibilities of parenthood and before Mary Doe is able to undergo pregnancy without suffering considerable harm to her health and well-being." If Mary Doe were to become pregnant, therefore, the Does would seek an abortion for her, but Texas law would deny her one. They therefore joined Jane Roe in seeking a court decision holding the Texas abortion law unconstitutional.

The *Roe* case attracted still another plaintiff. On March 20, the court granted a motion allowing Dr. James Hubert Hallford to intervene in *Roe* and file a complaint. Dr. Hallford was a graduate of the University of Texas Southwestern Medical School in Dallas and had been licensed to practice medicine in Texas since 1958. He had, however, been arrested several times for performing abortions in violation of the Texas law, and he was at the time under indictment for performing a criminal abortion. His trial in state court would soon commence, and Hallford thus sought a ruling by the federal court that the Texas law was invalid, and an injunction against his prosecution in the state court. The Texas law, he argued, violated the due process clause of the Fourteenth Amendment by preventing him from practicing medicine "according to the highest standards of medical practice because of the uncertainty and broad potential sweep and application" of its provisions.

Dr. Hallford was represented by his own counsel in his intervention in the *Roe* case. The litigation on behalf of Jane Roe and John and Mary Doe was, on the other hand, sponsored by the Population Law Center, an organization founded in 1969 by an attorney, Roy Lucas, and devoted to litigation involving birth control and population control matters. Having secured private foundation support for the PLC, Lucas and his organization sponsored the attack on the Texas abortion statute for the purpose, he said, of freeing women from the "tyranny of pregnancy." Linda Coffee continued to serve as counsel in the *Roe* case, but she was joined as counsel before the three-judge court by Sarah Weddington, a state legislator from Austin.

The right to privacy had been recognized as a guarantee of the due process clause of the Fourteenth Amendment in *Griswold v. Connecticut.* This suit faced the problem of translating it into a right broad enough to invalidate the Texas abortion law. In addition the *Roe* case faced other difficulties. For example, the complaints had named as defendant the district attorney of Dallas County, Henry Wade, and the case thus became *Roe v. Wade.* It would have been more appropriate, however, to name the state attorney general as defendant, since an injunction against Wade would affect enforcement of the abortion law only in Dallas County, while an injunction against the attorney general would have statewide application. Although representatives of the attorney general's office appeared at the hearing of *Roe* before the three-judge court, the attorney general did not become a defendant in the case. When one of the judges pointed out this omission to Coffee and Weddington and noted the limitations of an injunction against Wade alone, Weddington forthrightly admitted, "We goofed."

Much more serious threshold problems faced the *Roe* litigation, however. Assuming the case were pursued to the Supreme Court, it would be impossible to obtain a decision on the merits before Jane Roe's pregnancy came to term. It could thus be argued by Texas that the issues in the case were moot, since Roe would no longer be pregnant during most stages of the litigation. And if Roe were no longer pregnant at any stage of the proceedings, it could also be argued that she lacked standing to maintain the suit, since she would no longer have a concrete, personal interest in the outcome of the proceedings. The complaint of the Does could also be attacked on the ground of lack of ripeness, since their objections to the abortion law were based upon a series of contingencies that might never occur. Under the doctrine of ripeness, federal courts often refuse to entertain cases in which the issues appear to be unduly hypothetical in nature.[5] Finally, Dr. Hallford's complaint sought an injunction from the federal court against a pending state prosecution; however the Supreme Court had generally held in the past that a federal court could not hear an attack on a state statute that was the basis for a pending state prosecution, unless there was a showing that the prosecution was undertaken in bad faith and for the purpose of harassment. It was therefore also doubtful that Dr. Hallford's complaint could be successfully maintained in the federal court.[6]

Thus, even if the Texas abortion statute violated the right of privacy guaranteed by the due process clause, or invalidly inter-

5. The jurisdiction of the federal courts, including the Supreme Court, is limited by Article III of the Constitution to "cases or controversies" arising under the Constitution, federal laws, or treaties. The phrase *cases and controversies* has been interpreted by the Court to impose limitations on federal judicial power. In order to be entertained by the federal courts a case thus must be "justiciable," and among the elements of a justiciable case or controversy are standing to sue and ripeness. Standing to sue, or simply standing, generally requires that a party bringing suit in a federal court must demonstrate a concrete, personal stake in the outcome of the case. Ripeness requires that the issues in a suit be neither hypothetical nor theoretical in nature.

6. The leading cases on this point were decided in 1971, after the three-judge court's ruling on Hallford's standing to intervene in *Roe*. They are *Younger v. Harris* and *Samuels v. Mackell*. For an example of a case in which a federal court was justified in enjoining a pending state prosecution on the grounds of bad faith and harassment by prosecutorial authorities, see *Duncan v. Perez,* discussed earlier in this chapter.

fered with Dr. Hallford's right to pursue his profession, these substantive claims were under constant threat of dismissal because of the problems of mootness, standing, and ripeness, and the federal policy against enjoining enforcement of a statute while a state prosecution is pending. In answering the complaints in *Roe,* the Dallas district attorney and the Texas attorney general not only denied that the Texas abortion statute was invalid under the due process clause, but also argued that the case could not be entertained by the three-judge court because it did not present a "justiciable case or controversy."

The court, composed of District Judges Sarah T. Hughes and W. N. Taylor and Fifth Circuit Court of Appeals Judge Irving L. Goldberg, denied the defendants' motions to dismiss, however, and a hearing was held on May 22, 1970. Again the defendants argued that there was no justiciable case or controversy and suggested that Jane Roe had already had her child. Interrupting the argument of Assistant Attorney General Jay Floyd on this point, however, Judge Sarah Hughes wanted to know what would give anyone "standing in a case like this to test the constitutionality of this statute? Apparently you don't think anybody has standing."

Judge Hughes had, of course, reached the heart of the problem of standing and mootness in pregnancy litigation. If the courts were to hold that termination of a pregnancy mooted the issues in such cases, no pregnancy litigation could ever reach the Supreme Court, or indeed most trial courts, because of the time involved.

Going beyond the issue of justiciability, the defendants argued on the merits that the state had a justifiable interest in prohibiting abortions except to save the life of the mother. The fetus deserved the state's protection, they contended, since it represented at least the potential of human life. Assistant District Attorney John Tolle stated the defendants' position that "the life of every person starts somewhere. Every person in this room at one time was the most primitive form of embryo. We say the State has got the right to protect life that is in being at whatever stage it may be in being, and if there is no absolute fact as to when life occurs, then it becomes, I think, for the purpose of public order, a legislative problem as to when they're going to set up an arbitrary time." The case involved a conflict between the life of the unborn child and the woman's right to privacy, Tolle said, and the question was whether the state had "an interest in the life of the unborn child sufficient to regulate the woman's right to privacy." He concluded, "This is a very difficult question, and I think that it is properly a legislative question."

The plaintiffs argued, on the other hand, that there was no compelling state interest in protecting the potential human life represented by the fetus that was sufficient to justify the Texas statute's absolute prohibition of abortions except to save the mother's life. Arguing for the plaintiffs, Sarah Weddington told the court that the state had advanced only one justification for its abortion statute—that "of protecting what they term the life of the unborn child." Life was an ongoing process, she said, and was present even in the ova and the sperm. But under questioning by Judge Goldberg, Weddington did admit that allowing abortions at any stage of pregnancy did give her "some pause," and that perhaps abortions could be validly prohibited after the twenty-second or twenty-sixth week of pregnancy, "when the fetus is able to live outside the body of the mother." However, Texas had not demonstrated a compelling interest that would justify the abortion statute it had enacted, she contended.

The opinion of the three-judge court was announced on June 17, 1970. The court concluded that the Texas abortion statute was invalid under the due process clause of the Fourteenth Amendment. On the standing and mootness issues, it concluded that Jane Roe and Dr. Hallford had sufficiently concrete stakes in the outcome of the litigation to maintain their suits, but that the Does lacked standing to maintain theirs. On the merits, the court relied on *Griswold v. Connecticut* to justify a holding that the due process clause, inspired by the Ninth Amendment, protected a right of privacy of women to decide, at least during the early stages of pregnancy, to obtain an abortion. In regard to Dr. Hallford, the court also held that the Texas statute was unconstitutionally vague because it did not define sufficiently the conditions under which an abortion could be performed in order to preserve the life of the mother.

On the principal issue, the right of a woman to obtain an abortion, the court held that this right was a "fundamental" right under the due process clause and the Ninth Amendment, and the Texas law infringed on it. Therefore "the burden is on the defendant to demonstrate to the satisfaction of the Court that such infringement is necessary to support a compelling state interest. The defendant has failed to meet this burden." The court noted that the state could perhaps demonstrate a compelling interest in seeing to it that abortions were performed only by licensed physicians and in adequate clinical settings, and that a state could perhaps also justify prohibiting abortions during the later stages of pregnancy, especially after "quickening." The difficulty with the Texas abortion law, the court said, was that, even if it promoted these valid state interests, it far outstripped them "by prohibiting *all* abortions except those performed 'for the purpose of saving the life of the mother.'" While thus recognizing that the right to privacy protected by the due process clause was not "unqualified or unfettered," the court held that any state interference with the right had to be justified by a compelling state interest, and the Texas prohibition of abortions with one exception did not meet this test. The district court issued a declaratory judgment holding the Texas law invalid, but it declined to issue an injunction against the law's enforcement, since it concluded that the plaintiffs had not demonstrated sufficient reasons for such a federal judicial intrusion into state affairs.

The court's rulings proved unsatisfactory to both the plaintiffs and the state. Assistant District Attorney John Tolle informed Sarah Weddington on July 22 that the Dallas district attorney's office would continue its policy of enforcing the abortion law "in all abortion cases in which indictments are returned by the Dallas County Grand Jury." Dr. Paul C. MacDonald, the chairman of the Department of Obstetrics and Gynecology at the University of Texas Southwestern Medical School and Chief of the Obstetrics and Gynecology Service of Parkland Memorial Hospital, also requested advice from the Dallas district attorney's office regarding the impact of *Roe v. Wade* on the hospital's abortion policy. He was told that the hospital should "follow . . . the same policy which has prevailed in the past, as regards to any abortion." Other physicians in the Dallas area received similar advice from the district attorney's office.

The plaintiffs' victory in gaining a declaratory judgment on the merits therefore had little meaning. Without an injunction against continued enforcement of the abortion statute, the "invalid" policy continued in force. The state, on the other hand, was dissatisfied with the declaratory judgment. Both sides therefore decided to appeal the decision.

Congress has provided that a decision of a three-judge federal court either granting or denying an injunction against enforcement of a state statute is appealable directly to the Supreme Court, bypassing the courts of appeals. But an adverse declaratory judgment by a three-judge court is appealable to the appropriate court of appeals. The plaintiffs in *Roe v. Wade* could thus appeal directly to the Supreme Court, since they had been denied the injunction they had sought. But the defendants had lost on the merits in the declaratory judgment and had to take their appeal to the United States Court of Appeals for the Fifth Circuit, not to the Supreme Court. Appeals and cross-appeals were therefore filed in both courts. On the motion of the plaintiffs, the Fifth Circuit Court of Appeals issued an order holding the proceedings before it in abeyance, pending a decision by the Supreme Court, and the Supreme Court granted the plaintiffs' appeal on May 3, 1971, while postponing the issue of its jurisdiction until a hearing on the merits. Despite the complexities besetting *Roe v. Wade* in the appellate process, the case was therefore finally assured of a hearing in the Supreme Court.

Almost simultaneously with the litigation in *Roe,* an attack was launched on the validity of Georgia's abortion statutes. Unlike the Texas law, which had its origins in the nineteenth century, the Georgia statutes had been adopted in 1968 and were based on the American Law Institute's Model Penal Code. The 1968 statutes legalized abortions when, in the best clinical judgment of a physician, the continuation of a pregnancy would endanger the life of a woman, would permanently injure her health, or would very likely result in the birth of a child with a grave, permanent, and irremediable physical or mental defect, or when the pregnancy resulted from forcible or statutory rape. Abortions under other conditions were still criminal offenses.

The Georgia statutes, however, imposed formidable procedural requirements on the performance of legal abortions. The woman involved was required to swear that she was a legal resident of Georgia, and the physician involved was required to swear that he had no reason to believe otherwise. Two other physicians had to personally examine the woman and certify that an abortion was required. The operation also had to be approved by a majority of a committee of at least three of the medical staff of the hospital where it was to be performed. The abortion had to be performed in a hospital licensed by the State Board of Health and accredited by the Joint Commission on Accreditation of Hospitals. If the justification for the abortion was rape, the woman was required to make a written statement of the date, time, and place of the rape and the name of the rapist, if known. In addition, the law required a certified copy of any report of the rape to any law enforcement agency and a statement by the solicitor general of the judicial circuit where the rape allegedly occurred certifying that there was probable cause to believe that the rape had occurred. These written reports, opinions, and statements had to be filed permanently with the hospital, with the solicitor general of the judicial district, and with the director of the State Department of Public Health. Finally, the solicitor general of any judicial circuit in which an abortion was about to be performed, or any relative of the woman involved "within the second degree of consanguinity" could petition the circuit court to protect the legal or constitutional rights of the fetus. If the court decided that the rights of the fetus would be violated by an abortion, it could enjoin the operation. It is easy to understand why during the first year of the new law only seventy legal abortions were performed in Georgia.

Although the Georgia statutes were more liberal than the Texas law or the laws enforced in most states, they nonetheless raised a series of imposing hurdles before a legal abortion was obtainable, as well as restricting the conditions of pregnancy under which an abortion was legal. Because of these procedural and substantive restrictions, a coalition of individuals and groups attacked the constitutionality of the statutes in complaints filed in the United States District Court for the Northern District of Georgia in April 1970. The plaintiffs included the Planned Parenthood Association of Atlanta, the Georgia Citizens for Hospital Abortion, and groups of physicians, nurses, clergymen, and social workers who counseled women regarding birth control and abortion. The suit was also supported by the American Civil Liberties Union, and the National Legal Program on Health Problems of the Poor intervened in the case as *amicus curiae* (friend of the court).

The principal complaint was filed by attorneys Margie Pitts Hames, Tobiane Schwartz, Elizabeth Rindskopf, and Betty Kehrer on behalf of a twenty-two-year-old pregnant woman who adopted the pseudonym Mary Doe. She was the mother of three children, one of whom had been placed with adoptive parents, while the other two had recently been placed in foster homes because of Doe's poverty and inability to care for them properly. Doe had been married five years, but was separated from her husband and was living with her indigent parents, who themselves had eight children. In March 1970, she had applied to the Abortion Committee of Grady Memorial Hospital in Atlanta for an abortion, but her request was denied because her situation did not come within the legal abortion provisions of the Georgia statutes. In the complaint, Doe challenged the Georgia statutes because they did not permit a woman to secure an abortion when she did not have the financial means to care for the child she was carrying. Because the hospital's abortion committee "has denied plaintiff's application for a therapeutic abortion," the complaint alleged, "plaintiff Doe has been forced to either relinquish her right to decide when and how many children she will bear or to seek an abortion which must be termed illegal" in violation of her constitutional rights "guaranteed by the First, Ninth, and Fourteenth Amendments." As in the Texas case, Mary Doe's suit was filed as a class action on behalf of herself and all other women similarly situated.

Complaints were also filed on behalf of the physicians, nurses, social workers, clergymen, Planned Parenthood Association, and Georgia Citizens for Hospital Abortion. These alleged that the Georgia statutes prevented the physicians from practicing their professions by giving their patients the benefit of the best medical knowledge and treatment, and thus the statutes violated the due process clause of the Fourteenth Amendment. The nurses, social workers, clergymen, and others were, the complaints alleged, deterred "in the practice of their professions and the exercise of their constitutionally guaranteed right of free speech because of the unconstitutional Georgia law." The plaintiffs sought a declaratory judgment that the Georgia abortion statutes were unconstitutional and an injunction against the defendants to prevent enforcement of the statutes.

The defendants in *Doe* were Georgia Attorney General Arthur K. Bolton, Fulton County (Atlanta) District Attorney Lewis R. Slaton, and Atlanta Chief of Police Herbert T. Jenkins. They argued that there was no case or controversy before the federal court, since they could not be sure of the existence of Mary Doe. To settle the point, they moved that the court allow a physical examination of Doe and require the revelation of her true name, but the court denied these motions. The defendants argued further that the other plaintiffs lacked standing because the complaints they had filed were unduly hypothetical.

The three-judge court convened to hear *Doe v. Bolton* was composed of Fifth Circuit Court of Appeals Judge Lewis R. Morgan and United States District Court Judges Sidney O. Smith and Albert J. Henderson. On June 15, 1970, they heard arguments in the case.

Counsel for the plaintiffs of course denied the defendants' allegations and indicated that Mary Doe not only existed but indeed was twenty weeks pregnant at the time of the hearing. Mary Doe was actually present in the courtroom, but again the judges declined to order her to be identified further.

On the merits, counsel for the plaintiffs contended that, by unduly limiting the legal justifications for abortions, the Georgia statutes interfered with a woman's right to privacy as enunciated in *Griswold v. Connecticut* and its progeny. Moreover the statutes were unconstitutionally vague and indefinite. And the procedural obstacles they raised violated the constitutional right to travel by imposing a residence requirement; denied equal protection of the laws by denying equal access to abortions to the poor; and imposed vague conditions that violated the freedom of speech of physicians, nurses, social workers, and the other plaintiffs subject to the statutes.

Defense counsel renewed their objection that there was no case or controversy, particularly since they could not be certain that Mary Doe even existed or was pregnant. Arguing on behalf of District Attorney Slaton, Assistant District Attorney Tony H. Hight thus told the court that the defendants "don't even know who Mary Doe is and we ask the Court to inform us so we could properly investigate the case." The *Griswold* case, he said, had vindicated the right of marital privacy, but abortion was an entirely different matter. A woman seeking an abortion, Hight told the court, was "coming out and asking the court to say, I have a constitutional right at any time to go to a hospital, to go to a doctor and say that I am entitled to an abortion. Now, this is not the private marital state that is referred to in *Griswold*."

Assistant Attorney General Dorothy T. Beasley also argued on behalf of the defendants that women had means to avoid pregnancy, including contraceptive methods, sterilization, and "most traditionally, abstention." Mary Doe, she contended, "has voluntarily put herself in the position to have this child and once that life is kindled in her, the state takes the position that it has the right to be born because it is regarded as a life." Asked by the court about the Georgia policy of allowing abortions of pregnancies resulting from rape, Beasley responded that this policy was justified because "the state takes the position that that repayment can be done to a person who has been the victim of such a crime."

Despite the defendants' arguments the three-judge court on July 31, 1970, held several sections of the Georgia abortion statutes unconstitutional. The judges held that Mary Doe had alleged a sufficiently concrete stake in the outcome of the case to maintain her complaint. Although it held that the plaintiff physicians, nurses, social workers, and others had standing to attack the Georgia statutes, it found that they had failed to establish sufficiently that they were actually affected adversely by the statutes, and their complaints were accordingly dismissed.

On the merits, the court relied on *Griswold* and its progeny in holding that "the concept of personal liberty [guaranteed by the due process clause of the Fourteenth Amendment] embodies a right to privacy which apparently is also broad enough to include the decision to abort a pregnancy." This right to privacy, however, the court continued, was not absolute, since, "unlike the decision to use contraceptive devices, the decision to abort a pregnancy affects other interests than those of the woman alone, or even husband and wife alone." Thus, said the court, "Once conception takes place and an embryo forms, for better or worse the woman carries a life form with the *potential* of independent human existence. Without positing the existence of a new being with its own identity and federal constitutional rights, we hold its development cannot be considered a purely private one affecting only husband and wife, man and woman."

Since the court recognized that the decision to obtain an abortion was not an absolute right, but rather had to be balanced against the interests of the potential human life represented by the fetus, it ruled that only parts of the Georgia abortion statutes were unconstitutional. The court thus held (1) that Georgia could not validly limit abortions to those intended to save the life or preserve the health of women, or to pregnancies involving potentially defective children or resulting from rape; (2) that the requirement of written statements by the woman involved and the solicitor general certifying probable cause that a rape had occurred was invalid; (3) and that the provision for judicial review of the abortion decision at the instance of a solicitor general or a relative of the woman involved was invalid.

On the other hand, the court upheld those sections imposing a residence requirement, requiring a personal examination of the woman involved and certification that the abortion was appropriate by two physicians other than the woman's personal physician, requiring that abortions be performed in specifically licensed and accredited hospitals, and requiring that the abortion be approved by an abortion committee of the hospital. As a consequence, despite the court's decision, an abortion could be performed legally in Georgia only on a woman who was a legal resident of Georgia, with the approval of a minimum of five physicians, and in a hospital meeting the statutes' licensing and accreditation standards (only 54 of Georgia's 159 counties had such hospitals).

In addition, although the court declared parts of the statutes invalid, it refused to issue an injunction prohibiting enforcement of those portions.

It is not surprising, therefore, that neither side in *Doe v. Bolton* was satisfied with the decision. Attorney General Arthur Bolton protested what he regarded as the court's "rewriting of state law" in the case, and indicated that he would appeal. Although Margie Pitts Hames praised the decision as "a real victory for American civil liberties and for females," she also indicated that the decision was not totally satisfactory to the plaintiffs. One of the clergymen plaintiffs commented, "At least we won—whether the victory means anything or not. But I can't see how this is greatly going to affect what actually happens."

Since the three-judge court had refused to issue an injunction in the case, attorney Hames filed another complaint with the court, this time on behalf of a "Jane Roe," alleging that Roe was pregnant but had been denied an abortion by the Georgia Baptist Hospital despite the court's declaratory judgment. The complaint sought an injunction to compel the hospital's compliance. The hospital, however, subsequently reversed its position, and the court dismissed the complaint. The plaintiffs thus still had not secured an injunction against enforcement of the invalidated laws.

As in the Texas case, they decided on November 14, 1970, to appeal the denial of an injunction directly to the Supreme Court, and the Court indicated on May 3, 1971, that it would hear *Doe v. Bolton* as well as *Roe v. Wade.* The court thus appeared ready to consider the explosive issue of the constitutional validity of state abortion laws.

The issue was on the Court's docket in May 1971, but the Court's response to the issue was long delayed. The *Abortion Cases,* as *Roe* and *Doe* came to be called, were not decided on the merits until January 22, 1973. They were argued originally in December 1971, but were restored to the Court's docket for reargument on October 11, 1972. The delay tended to aid the pro-abortion forces, because of several legal developments that occurred during the interim.

The first development helpful to the pro-abortion forces was the 1972 decision of *Eisenstadt v. Baird*, in which the Supreme

Court amplified the right of privacy it had enunciated in *Griswold* to include "the right of the *individual,* married or single, to be free from unwarranted governmental intrusion into matters so fundamentally affecting a person as the decision whether to bear or beget a child." This obviously bolstered the core argument in the *Abortion Cases* that the prevailing abortion laws unduly infringed on a woman's right to privacy in the decision to obtain an abortion.

Further aiding the pro-abortion forces was the Court's opinion in *United States v. Vuitch,* decided in 1971 only a month before the *Abortion Cases* were docketed. In *Vuitch,* the Court considered a federal district court ruling on the District of Columbia abortion statute that permitted legal abortions only to preserve the mother's life or health. The district court concluded that the term "health" was so imprecise as to be unconstitutionally vague. The Supreme Court reversed and held that the statute should be interpreted to include consideration of mental as well as physical health; so construed, the statute was valid, it stated. Although the Court had thus demonstrated a reluctance to invalidate an abortion statute, it had implicitly rejected the idea that an unborn fetus was a "person" in the constitutional sense. If the Court had considered the fetus a "person," it would have invalidated the District of Columbia statute and held that the government could not authorize taking the life of a person in order to preserve the mental health of a woman. The implication of *Vuitch,* therefore, further encouraged the pro-abortion forces in the *Abortion Cases.*

The *Abortion Cases* drew an unusually large number of *amicus curiae* briefs—on both sides of the issue, although the pro-abortion groups again appeared to have organized more rapidly for the Supreme Court test. The individuals and groups participating as *amici* are listed in table 3.

Before arguments on the merits could be considered, however, the parties had to address the problem of whether a justiciable case or controversy was presented. The principal problem for the appellants on this score was, of course, the fact that both Jane Roe and Mary Doe could not possibly still be pregnant; counsel for both Georgia and Texas argued to the Court that the cases should be dismissed, because neither Doe nor Roe possessed stand-

Table 3

AMICUS CURIAE PARTICIPANTS
IN ABORTION CASES*

Pro–Abortion Participants

American Association of Planned
　Parenthood Physicians
American Association of University
　Women
American College of Obstetricians
　and Gynecologists
American Ethical Union
American Friends Service Committee
American Humanist Association
American Jewish Congress
American Medical Women's
　Association
American Public Health
　Association
American Psychiatric Association
Board of Christian Social Concerns
　of United Methodist Church
California Committee to Legalize
　Abortion
Community Action for Legal Services
Episcopal Diocese of New York
Group of 178 Physicians
National Abortion Action Coalition
National Board of the YWCA
National Legal Program on Health
　Problems of the Poor
National Organization for Women
National Welfare Rights Organization
National Women's Conference of the
　American Ethical Union
New Women Lawyers
New York Academy of Medicine
New York Council of Churches
Planned Parenthood Federation of
　America
Professional Women's Caucus
South Bay (California) Chapter of
　National Organization of Women
State Communities Aid Association

Twenty–six Individual Women
Union of American Hebrew Congre-
　gations
Unitarian–Universalist Association
Unitarian–Universalist Women's
　Federation
United Church of Christ
Women's Alliance of the First
　Unitarian Church of Dallas
Women's Health and Abortion
　Project, Inc.
Zero Population Growth

Anti–Abortion Participants

Americans United for Life
Attorneys General of Arizona,
　Connecticut, Kentucky,
　Nebraska, and Utah
Celebrate Life
Certain Individual Doctors and
　Nurses
Certain Physicians, Professors,
　and Fellows of the American
　College of Obstetrics and
　Gynecology
Ferdinand Buckley
League for Infants, Fetuses,
　and the Elderly (LIFE)
Minnesota Citizens Concerned
　for Life
New York State Council of
　Columbiettes
Women Concerned for the
　Unborn Child
Women for the Unborn

* Most *amicus curiae* briefs filed in the *Abortion Cases* were joint briefs, representing
several individuals and groups listed.

ing, and, since their pregnancies had ended, the issues in the cases were moot. Appellants answered by pointing out that, if the rules of standing and mootness were applied so rigidly, no pregnancy litigation could ever reach the Court as a justiciable controversy, with the result that allegedly invalid abortion statutes could never be successfully attacked before the Court. The Court was thus urged to hold that Doe and Roe possessed standing, despite the termination of their pregnancies during the pendency of the litigation.

In the Texas case, appellants also argued that John and Mary Doe had standing because of the current adverse effect of the state's abortion policy on their marriage. And Dr. Hallford also had standing, it was argued, since he was under the threat of criminal prosecution for performing illegal abortions. Counsel for Texas replied, however, that the Does had alleged only hypothetical and contingent issues in their attack on the state law, and that their complaint was therefore not justiciable. And Dr. Hallford, respondents argued, could not obtain an injunction against a pending state criminal prosecution under the Supreme Court's decisions forbidding such interference by federal courts in state affairs.

In the Georgia case, appellants further argued that the physicians, nurses, clergymen, social workers, and pro-abortion organizations that had joined Mary Doe in her attack on the state statutes also possessed standing, since they performed functions that were likely to cause the statutes to be enforced against them. Again, however, counsel for Georgia denied that Mary Doe or her coplaintiffs had standing to maintain their challenge.

On the merits, counsel for the appellants and their *amicus* allies in both cases argued that the constitutional right of privacy recognized by the Court in *Griswold* and *Eisenstadt* embraced the right of a woman to decide to terminate a pregnancy. This right was protected by the due process clause of the Fourteenth Amendment and by the Ninth Amendment, it was argued, and the Georgia and Texas laws invalidly infringed on that right by unduly restricting a woman's right to obtain an abortion. Counsel for Texas and Georgia did not deny that the due process clause protected a right of privacy, but they denied that the constitutional right of privacy protected a woman's right to obtain an abortion free of state regulation. As the Georgia attorney general said, appellants had indicated by their position that they "were patently unconcerned with 'the potential human life'" represented by the fetus "and instead display in bold relief the uncompromising assertion that the removal of an unwanted fetus is just as much a right as the removal of an unwanted mole."

The core of the arguments was whether there was a "compelling state interest" justifying governmental regulation or prohibition of abortions, given the invasion of a woman's right to privacy that such governmental policies entailed. Appellants argued that the nineteenth-century legislation restricting abortions had been prompted by unsafe medical practices and that, given modern medical advances, this was no longer a valid justification for anti-abortion laws; indeed, abortions were now safer for women statistically than giving birth. It was also pointed out to the Court that abortion had never been considered murder of the fetus. Women obtaining illegal abortions or inducing abortions themselves had almost never been prosecuted at all, much less for murder, and persons performing illegal abortions were never prosecuted for homicide. The states had not evidenced any great concern for protecting the lives of fetuses until they had been compelled to defend their abortion policies before the courts. Thus, appellants argued, the states could not belatedly assert a "compelling interest" in preserving the life of the unborn that was sufficient to override the woman's recognized right to privacy under the due process clause.

Counsel for Texas and Georgia, however, argued strenuously that there was a compelling state interest in preserving the life of the fetus and that this justified regulation of the abortion decision by a woman. At a minimum, the states argued, the fetus represented the potential of human life, and governments had a compelling interest in protecting that potential life from indiscriminate destruction on the whim of an individual woman. Counsel for Texas traced the stages of fetal development and argued that the "whole thrust of medicine is in support of the notion that the child in its mother is a distinct individual in need of the most diligent study and care, and that he is also a patient whom science and medicine treats just like it does any other person." In view of this, "Whatever personal right of privacy a pregnant woman may have with respect to the disposition and use of her body," counsel for Texas argued, "must be balanced against the personal right of the unborn child to life." The Texas statute thus protected the fetus's right to life.

Defending its much more moderate statute, Georgia counsel also denied that a woman had an absolute right to terminate a pregnancy and instead argued that the state's abortion statutes were a reasonable compromise between the interests of the fetus and the rights of the woman. Georgia had "sought to strike a balance between the competing interests of the woman and the unborn child. It has therefore afforded to the developing fetus not an absolute legal right but rather a right circumscribed by limitations which are reasonably related to other legitimate state goals."

In addition to these central arguments in the *Abortion Cases,* appellants attacked the Texas and Georgia statutes on the grounds that they unduly restricted the right of physicians to practice their professions and that they were invalidly vague in violation of the due process clause. The Georgia provisions imposing a residence requirement, requiring the approval of an abortion by several physicians, and requiring that abortions be performed in accredited hospitals were also attacked as interfering with a woman's right to privacy, invalidly restricting a physician's right to practice, interfering with the right to travel interstate,[7] and discriminating against the poor in violation of the equal protection clause of the Fourteenth Amendment. Counsel for the states argued, on the contrary, that a physician had no right to violate a valid criminal statute in his practice, and that the state statutes were not unduly vague but rather sufficiently precise in what they prohibited. Georgia counsel additionally argued that the state's procedural restrictions on the performance of abortions were justified by the state's interest in regulating a woman's decision to have an abortion and preventing indiscriminate destruction of the unborn fetus.

7. The right to travel interstate had been recognized by the Court as early as 1868 in *Crandall v. Nevada* and had recently been reaffirmed in *Shapiro v. Thompson* in 1969.

After oral argument in December 1971, the cases were restored to the docket for reargument in October 1972. Behind this postponement was a story of internal conflict on the Court that illustrates some of the difficulties of the transition from the Warren Court to the Burger Court.

Chief Justice Burger was President Nixon's first appointee to the Court in 1969. After the Nixon administration's nominations of Clement Haynsworth and Harrold Carswell to the Court were defeated,[8] Chief Justice Burger's longtime friend from Minnesota, Judge Harry Blackmun, was successfully named to the Court. Burger and Blackmun quickly became known as the "Minnesota Twins" because of their tendency to vote together on most issues. While the *Abortion Cases* were pending before the Court, Justices Hugo Black and John Harlan resigned and then died, creating two more vacancies on the bench in the fall of 1971. The first argument in the *Abortion Cases* was thus heard by only seven justices.

It was reported[9] that Chief Justice Burger had attempted to select the justices who would write the opinions of the Court even when he was in the minority. This was contrary to the tradition of the Court that the chief justice could assign an opinion only when he voted with the majority in a case, but that the power to assign an opinion fell to the senior associate justice in the majority when the chief justice voted with the minority. Justices Black and Harlan had reportedly blocked Burger's attempts to assign opinions when he was in the minority while they remained on the Court.

In the conference after the first argument in the *Abortion Cases,* the justices divided five to two, with the majority, appar-

8. Haynsworth and Carswell were nominated for the seat vacated by Justice Abe Fortas, who had resigned under fire because of his financial involvement with financier Louis Wolfson. For accounts of the Fortas tragedy as well as the disastrous Haynsworth and Carswell episodes, see Robert Shogan, *A Question of Judgment* (New York: Bobbs-Merrill, 1972); Richard Harris, *Decision* (New York: Ballantine Books, 1970); and James F. Simon, *In His Own Image: The Supreme Court in Richard Nixon's America* (New York: David McKay Co., 1973).

9. Washington *Post,* July 4, 1972, p. A-1. See also Joel B. Grossman and Richard S. Wells, *Supplemental Cases for Constitutional Law and Judicial Policy Making* (New York: John Wiley, 1973), p. 26. The *Post* article is inaccurate in reporting that Douglas did not dissent from the decision to restore the *Abortion Cases* to the Court's docket for reargument. See 408 U.S. 918 (1972).

ently composed of Justices Douglas, Brennan, Stewart, Marshall, and Blackmun, voting to invalidate the Georgia and Texas abortion laws, while Chief Justice Burger and Justice White were opposed to this. Over the objections of Justice Douglas, the senior associate justice in the majority, Burger assigned the opinion of the Court to Justice Blackmun.

In an attempt to temper the dispute between Burger and Douglas, Blackmun promised to write an opinion that would be acceptable to everyone, and he circulated an opinion in 1972 that was agreeable to the majority justices. In the meantime, however, Justices Lewis Powell and William Rehnquist had joined the Court, replacing Black and Harlan, and Blackmun withdrew his opinion, urging instead that the *Abortion Cases* be restored to the docket for reargument before a full Court. Again, Douglas strenuously objected, but a majority of five justices agreed to order reargument on June 26, 1972. After reargument was heard on October 11, 1972, Douglas, Brennan, Stewart, Marshall, and Blackmun again voted to invalidate the statutes, joined by the newly appointed Justice Powell. Chief Justice Burger reportedly again voted with Justices White and Rehnquist in the minority, but when Blackmun circulated his opinion, Burger decided to join the majority. The ultimate vote in the *Abortion Cases* was therefore seven to two, with Justices White and Rehnquist the only dissenters.

ROE V. WADE
410 U.S. 113, decided January 22, 1973

Mr. Justice Blackmun delivered the opinion of the Court.

This Texas federal appeal and its Georgia companion, Doe v. Bolton, . . . present constitutional challenges to state criminal abortion legislation. The Texas statutes under attack here are typical of those that have been in effect in many States for approximately a century. The Georgia statutes, in contrast, have a modern cast and are a legislative product that, to an extent at least, obviously reflects the influences of recent attitudinal change, of advancing medical knowledge and techniques, and of new thinking about an old issue.

We forthwith acknowledge our awareness of the sensitive and emotional nature of the abortion controversy, of the vigorous opposing views, even among physicians, and of the deep and seemingly absolute convictions that the subject inspires. One's philosophy, one's experiences, one's exposure to the raw edges of human existence, one's religious training, one's attitudes toward life and family and their values, and the moral standards one establishes and seeks to observe, are all likely to influence and to color one's thinking and conclusions about abortion.

In addition, population growth, pollution, poverty, and racial overtones tend to complicate and not to simplify the problem.

Our task, of course, is to resolve the issue by constitutional measurement, free of emotion and of predilection. We seek earnestly to do this, and, because we do, we have inquired into, and in this opinion place some emphasis upon, medical and medical-legal history and what that history reveals about man's attitudes toward the abortion procedure over the centuries. . . .

The Texas statutes that concern us here . . . make it a crime to "procure an abortion," as therein defined, or to attempt one, except with respect to "an abortion procured or attempted by medical advice for the purpose of saving the life of the mother." Similar statutes are in existence in a majority of the States . . . .

Jane Roe, a single woman who was residing in Dallas County, Texas, instituted this federal action in March 1970 against the District Attorney of the county. She sought a declaratory judgment that the Texas criminal abortion statutes were unconstitutional on their face, and an injunction restraining the defendant from enforcing the statutes. . . .

James Hubert Hallford, a licensed physician, sought and was granted leave to intervene in Roe's action. In his complaint he alleged that he had been arrested previously for violations of the Texas abortion statutes and that two such prosecutions were pending against him. . . .

John and Mary Doe, a married couple, filed a companion complaint to that of Roe. They also named the District Attorney as defendant, claimed like constitutional deprivations, and sought declaratory and injunctive relief. . . .

On the merits, the District Court held that the "fundamental right of single women and married persons to choose whether to have children is protected by the Ninth Amendment, through the Fourteenth Amendment," and that the Texas criminal abortion statutes were void on their face because they were both unconstitutionally vague and constituted an overbroad infringement of the plaintiffs' Ninth Amendment rights. The court then held that abstention was warranted with respect to the requests for an injunction.

It therefore . . . declared the abortion statutes void, and dismissed the application for injunctive relief. . . .

The plaintiffs Roe and Doe and the intervenor Hallford, . . . have appealed to this Court from that part of the District Court's judgment denying the injunction. The defendant District Attorney has purported to cross-appeal . . . from the court's grant of declaratory relief to Roe and Hallford. Both sides also have taken protective appeals to the United States Court of Appeals for the Fifth Circuit. That court ordered the appeals held in abeyance pending decision here. We postponed decision on jurisdiction to the hearing on the merits. . . .

We are next confronted with issues of justiciability, standing, and abstention. Have Roe and the Does established that "personal stake in the outcome of the controversy," . . . that insures that "the dispute sought to be adjudicated will be presented in an adversary context and in a form historically viewed as capable of judicial resolution" . . . ? And what effect did the pendency of criminal abortion charges against Dr. Hallford in state court have upon the propriety of the federal court's granting relief to him as a plaintiff-intervenor?

. . . *Jane Roe.* Despite the use of the pseudonym, no suggestion is made that Roe is a fictitious person. For purposes of her case, we accept as true, and as established, her existence; her pregnant state, as of the inception of her suit in March 1970 and as late as May 21 of that year when she filed an alias affidavit with the District Court; and her inability to obtain a legal abortion in Texas.

Viewing Roe's case as of the time of its filing and thereafter until as late as May, there can be little dispute that it then presented a case or controversy and that, wholly apart from the class aspects, she, as a pregnant single woman thwarted by the Texas criminal abortion laws, had standing to challenge those statutes. . . . Indeed we do not read the appellee's brief as really asserting anything to the contrary. The "logical nexus between the status asserted and the claim sought to be adjudicated," . . . and the necessary degree of contentiousness . . . are both present.

The appellee notes, however, that the record does not disclose that Roe was pregnant at the time of the District Court hearing on May 22, 1970, or on the following June 17 when the court's opinion and judgment were filed. And he suggests that Roe's case must now be moot because she and all other members of her class are no longer subject to any 1970 pregnancy.

The usual rule in federal cases is that an actual controversy must exist at stages of appellate or certiorari review, and not simply at the date the action is initiated. . . .

But when, as here, pregnancy is a significant fact in the litigation, the normal 266-day gestation period is so short that the pregnancy will come to term before the usual appellate process is complete. If that termination makes a case moot, pregnancy litigation seldom will survive much beyond the trial stage, and appellate review will be effectively denied. Our law should not be that rigid. Pregnancy often comes more than once to the same woman, and in the general population, if man is to survive, it will always be with us. Pregnancy provides a classic justification for a conclusion of nonmootness. It truly could be "capable of repetition, yet evading review" . . . .

We, therefore, agree with the District Court that Jane Roe had standing to undertake this litigation, that she presented a justiciable controversy, and that the termination of her 1970 pregnancy has not rendered her case moot.

Dr. Hallford. The doctor's position is different. He entered Roe's litigation as a plaintiff-intervenor. . . .

Dr. Hallford is . . . in the position of seeking, in a federal court, declaratory and injunctive relief with respect to the same statutes under which he stands charged in criminal prosecutions simultaneously pending in state court. Although he stated that he has been arrested in the past for violating the State's abortion laws, he makes no allegation of any substantial and immediate threat to any federally protected right that cannot be asserted in his defense against the state prosecutions. Neither is there any allegation of harassment or bad-faith prosecution. In order to escape the rule . . . that, absent harassment and bad faith, a defendant in a pending state criminal case cannot affirmatively challenge in federal court the statutes under which the State is prosecuting him, Dr. Hallford seeks to distinguish his status as a present state defendant from his status as a "potential future defendant" and to assert only the latter for standing purposes here.

We see no merit in that distinction. . . . Dr. Hallford's complaint in intervention, therefore, is to be dismissed. He is remitted to his defenses in the state criminal proceedings against him. We reverse the judgment of the District Court insofar as it granted Dr. Hallford relief and failed to dismiss his complaint in intervention.

The Does. . . . We . . . have as plaintiffs a married couple who have, as their asserted immediate and present injury, only an alleged "detrimental effect upon [their] marital happiness" because they are forced to "the choice of refraining from normal sexual relations or of endangering Mary Doe's health through a possible pregnancy." Their claim is that sometime in the future Mrs. Doe might become pregnant because of possible failure of contraceptive measures, and at that time in the future she might want an abortion that might then be illegal under the Texas statutes.

This very phrasing of the Does' position reveals its speculative character. Their alleged injury rests on possible future contraceptive failure, possible future pregnancy, possible future unpreparedness for parenthood, and possible future impairment of health. Any one or more of these several possibilities may not take place and all may not combine. In the Does' estimation, these possibilities might have some real or imagined impact on their marital happiness. But we are not prepared to say that the bare allegation of so indirect an injury is sufficient to present an actual case or controversy. . . .

The Does therefore are not appropriate plaintiffs in this litigation. Their complaint was properly dismissed by the District Court, and we affirm that dismissal.

The principal thrust of appellant's attack on the Texas statutes is that they improperly invade a right, said to be possessed by the pregnant woman, to choose to terminate her pregnancy. Appellant would discover this right in the concept of personal "liberty" embodied in the Fourteenth Amendment's Due Process Clause; or in personal, marital, familial, and sexual privacy said to be protected by the Bill of Rights or its penumbras, see Griswold v. Connecticut . . . ; Eisenstadt v. Baird . . . ; or among those rights reserved to the people by the Ninth Amendment . . . . Before addressing this claim, we feel it desirable briefly to survey, in several aspects, the history of abortion, for such insight as that history may afford us, and then to examine the state purposes and interests behind the criminal abortion laws. . . .

It perhaps is not generally appreciated that the restrictive criminal abortion laws in effect in a majority of States today are of relatively recent vintage. Those laws, generally proscribing abortion or its attempt at any time during pregnancy except when necessary to preserve the pregnant woman's life, are not of ancient or even of common law origin. Instead, they derive from statutory changes effected, for the most part, in the latter half of the 19th century. . . .

[Justice Blackmun then summarized the history of the law's treatment of abortion from ancient to modern times. He noted that, although abortions were severely punished in the Persian Empire, they appeared to be freely performed during the Greek and Roman eras, and Greek and Roman law afforded slight protection to the unborn. The Hippocratic Oath, bearing the name of the great Greek doctor, requires a pledge that "I will not give to a woman a pessary to produce abortion." Hippocrates' views, however, were subject to dispute during his own lifetime and were accepted by only a small segment of Greek opinion. At the common law in England, abortions performed before "quickening"—before the sixteenth to eighteenth week of pregnancy—were not indictable offenses. And the predominant view of common law scholars was that even the abortion of a quick fetus constituted an offense less than homicide and was at most a misdemeanor, if indeed it was a common law crime at all. Connecticut was the first American state to enact antiabortion legislation, modifying or supplanting the received common law, but it was not until after the Civil War that the states generally began to enact legislation prohibiting abortions. During the middle and late nineteenth century, the common law distinction between unquick and quick fetuses was abandoned, and state legislation prohibited abortions unless performed to preserve the life of the mother.]

It is thus apparent that at common law, at the time of the adoption of our Constitution, and throughout the major portion of the 19th century, abortion was viewed with less disfavor than under most American statutes currently in effect. Phrasing it another way, a woman enjoyed a substantially broader right to terminate a pregnancy than she does in most States today. At least with respect to the early stage of pregnancy, and very possibly without such a limitation, the opportunity to make this choice was present in this country well into the 19th century. Even later, the law continued for some time to treat less punitively an abortion procured in early pregnancy. . . .

[Justice Blackmun then summarized the positions of certain professional associations on the subject of abortions, including the American Medical Association, the American Public Health Association, and the American Bar Association.]

Three reasons have been advanced to explain historically the enactment of criminal abortion laws in the 19th century and to justify their continued existence.

It has been argued occasionally that these laws were the product of a Victorian social concern to discourage illicit sexual conduct. Texas, however, does not advance this justification in the present case, and it appears that no court or commentator has taken the argument seriously. The appellants and amici contend, moreover, that this is not a proper state purpose at all and suggest that, if it were, the Texas statutes are overbroad in protecting it since the law fails to distinguish between married and unwed mothers.

A second reason is concerned with abortion as a medical procedure. When most criminal abortion laws were first enacted, the procedure was a hazardous one for the woman. This was particularly true prior to the development of antisepsis. Antiseptic techniques, of course, were based on discoveries by Lister, Pasteur, and others first announced in 1867, but were not generally accepted and employed until about the turn of the century. Abortion mortality was high. Even after 1900, and perhaps until as late as the development of antibiotics in the 1940's, standard modern techniques such as dilation and curettage were not nearly so safe as they are today. Thus, it has been argued that a State's real concern in enacting a criminal abortion law was to protect the pregnant woman, that is, to restrain her from submitting to a procedure that placed her life in serious jeopardy.

Modern medical techniques have altered this situation. Appellants and various amici refer to medical data indicating that abortion in early pregnancy, that is, prior to the end of the first trimester, although not without its risk, is now relatively safe. Mortality rates for women undergoing early abortions, where the procedure is legal, appear to be as low as or lower than the rates for normal childbirth. Consequently, any interest of the State in protecting the woman from an inherently hazardous procedure, except when it would be equally dangerous for her to forgo it, has largely disappeared. Of course, important state interests in the area of health and medical standards do remain.

The State has a legitimate interest in seeing to it that abortion, like any other medical procedure, is performed under circumstances that insure maximum safety for the patient. This interest obviously extends at least to the performing physician and his staff, to the facilities involved, to the availability of aftercare, and to adequate provision for any complication or emergency that might arise. The prevalence of high mortality rates at illegal "abortion mills" strengthens, rather than weakens, the State's interest in regulating the conditions under which abortions are performed. Moreover, the risk to the woman increases as her pregnancy continues. Thus, the State retains a definite interest in protecting the woman's own health and safety when an abortion is proposed at a late stage of pregnancy.

The third reason is the State's interest—some phrase it in terms of duty—in protecting prenatal life. Some of the argument for this justification rests on the theory that a new human life is present from the moment of conception. The State's interest and general obligation to protect life then extends, it is argued, to prenatal life. Only when the life of the pregnant mother herself is at stake, balanced against the life she carries within her, should the interest of the embryo or fetus not prevail. Logically, of course, a legitimate state interest in this area need not stand or fall on acceptance of the belief that life begins at conception or at some other point prior to live birth. In assessing the State's interest, recognition may be given to the less rigid claim that as long as at least *potential* life is involved, the State may assert interests beyond the protection of the pregnant woman alone.

Parties challenging state abortion laws have sharply disputed in some courts the contention that a purpose of these laws, when enacted, was to protect prenatal life. Pointing to the absence of legislative history to support the contention, they claim that most state laws were designed solely to protect the woman. Because medical advances have lessened this concern, at least with respect to abortion in early pregnancy, they argue that with respect to such abortions the laws can no longer be justified by any state interest. There is some scholarly support for this view of original purpose. The few state courts called upon to interpret their laws in the late 19th and 20th centuries did focus on the State's interest in protecting the woman's health rather than in preserving the embryo and fetus. Proponents of this view point out that in many States, including Texas, by statute or judicial interpretation, the pregnant woman herself could not be prosecuted for self-abortion or for cooperating in an abortion performed upon her by another. They claim that adoption of the "quickening" distinction through received common law and state statutes tacitly recognized the greater health hazards inherent in late abortion and impliedly repudiates the theory that life begins at conception.

It is with these interests, and the weight to be attached to them, that this case is concerned.

The Constitution does not explicitly mention any right of privacy. In a line of decisions, however, ... the Court has recognized that a right of personal privacy, or a guarantee of certain areas or zones of privacy, does exist under the Constitution. In varying contexts, the Court or individual Justices have, indeed, found at least the roots of that right in the First Amendment ... ; in the Fourth and Fifth Amendments ... ; in the penumbras of the Bill of Rights ... ; or in the concept of liberty guaranteed by the first section of the Fourteenth Amendment .... These decisions make it clear that only personal rights that can be deemed "fundamental" or "implicit in the concept of ordered liberty" ... are included in this guarantee of personal privacy. They also make it clear that the right has some extension to activities relating to marriage ... ; procreation ... ; contraception ... ; family relationships ... ; and child rearing and education : ...

This right of privacy, whether it be founded in the Fourteenth Amendment's concept of personal liberty and restrictions upon state action, as we feel it is, or, as the District Court determined, in the Ninth Amendment's reservation of rights to the people, is broad enough to encompass a woman's decision whether or not to terminate her pregnancy. The detriment that the State would impose upon the pregnant woman by denying this choice altogether is apparent. Specific and direct harm medically diagnosable even in early pregnancy may be involved. Maternity, or additional offspring, may force upon the woman a distressful life and future. Psychological harm may be imminent. Mental and physical health may be taxed by child care. There is also the distress, for all concerned, associated with the unwanted child, and there is the problem of bringing a child into a family already unable, psychologically and otherwise, to care for it. In other cases, as in this one, the additional difficulties and continuing stigma of unwed motherhood may be involved. All these are factors the woman and her responsible physician necessarily will consider in consultation.

On the basis of elements such as these, appellant and some amici argue that the woman's right is absolute and that she is entitled to terminate her pregnancy at whatever time, in whatever way, and for whatever reason she alone chooses. With this we do not agree. Appellant's arguments that Texas either has no valid interest at all in regulating the abortion decision, or no interest strong enough to support any limitation upon the woman's sole determination, is unpersuasive. The Court's decisions recognizing a right of privacy also acknowledge that some state regulation in areas protected by that right is appropriate. As noted above, a State may properly assert important interests in safeguarding health, in maintaining medical standards, and in protecting potential life. At some point in pregnancy, these respective interests become sufficiently compelling to sustain regulation of the factors that govern the abortion decision. The privacy right involved, therefore, cannot be said to be absolute. In fact, it is not clear to us that the claim asserted by some amici that one has an unlimited right to do with one's body as one pleases bears a close relationship to the right of privacy previously articulated in the Court's decisions. The Court has refused to recognize an unlimited right of this kind in the past. . . .

We, therefore, conclude that the right of personal privacy includes the abortion decision, but that this right is not unqualified and must be considered against important state interests in regulation.

We note that those federal and state courts that have recently considered abortion law challenges have reached the same conclusion. . . .

Although the results are divided, most of these courts have agreed that the right of privacy, however based, is broad enough to cover the abortion decision; that the right, nonetheless, is not absolute and is subject to some limitations; and that at some point the state interests as to protection of health, medical standards, and prenatal life, become dominant. We agree with this approach.

Where certain "fundamental rights" are involved, the Court has held that regulation limiting these rights may be justified only by a "compelling state interest," . . . and that legislative enactments must be narrowly drawn to express only the legitimate state interests at stake. . . .

The District Court held that the appellee failed to meet his burden of demonstrating that the Texas statute's infringement upon Roe's rights was necessary to support a compelling state interest, and that, although the appellee presented "several compelling justifications for state presence in the area of abortions," the statutes outstripped these justifications and swept "far beyond any areas of compelling state interest." . . . Appellant and appellee both contest that holding. Appellant, as has been indicated, claims an absolute right that bars any state imposition of criminal penalties in the area. Appellee argues that the State's determination to recognize and protect prenatal life from and after conception constitutes a compelling state interest. As noted above, we do not agree fully with either formulation.

The appellee and certain amici argue that the fetus is a "person" within the language and meaning of the Fourteenth Amendment. In support of this, they outline at length and in detail the well-known facts of fetal development. If this suggestion of personhood is established, the appellant's case, of course, collapses, for the fetus' right to life is then guaranteed specifically by the Amendment. The appellant conceded as much on reargument. On the other hand, the appellee conceded on reargument that no case could be cited that holds that a fetus is a person within the meaning of the Fourteenth Amendment.

The Constitution does not define "person" in so many words. . . . But [in nearly all instances in which the word is used or alluded to in the Constitution] the use of the word is such that it has application only postnatally. None indicates, with any assurance, that it has any possible prenatal application.

All this, together with our observation . . . that throughout the major portion of the 19th century prevailing legal abortion practices were far freer than they are today, persuades us that the word "person," as used in the Fourteenth Amendment, does not include the unborn. This is in accord with the results reached in those few cases where the issue has been squarely presented. . . .

This conclusion, however, does not of itself fully answer the contentions raised by Texas, and we pass on to other considerations.

The pregnant woman cannot be isolated in her privacy. She carries an embryo and, later, a fetus, if one accepts the medical definitions of the developing young in the human uterus. . . . The situation therefore is inherently different from marital intimacy, or bedroom possession of obscene material, or marriage, or procreation, or education, with which Eisenstadt, Griswold, Stanley, Loving, Skinner, Pierce, and Meyer were respectively concerned. As we have intimated above, it is reasonable and appropriate for a State to decide that at some point in time another interest, that of health of the mother or that of potential human life, becomes significantly involved. The woman's privacy is no longer sole and any right of privacy she possesses must be measured accordingly.

Texas urges that, apart from the Fourteenth Amendment, life begins at conception and is present throughout pregnancy, and that, therefore, the State has a compelling interest in protecting that life from and after conception. We need not resolve the difficult question of when life begins. When those trained in the respective disciplines of medicine, philosophy, and theology are unable to arrive at any consensus, the judiciary, at this point in the development of man's knowledge, is not in a position to speculate as to the answer.

It should be sufficient to note briefly the wide divergence of thinking on this most sensitive and difficult question. There has always been strong support for the view that life does not begin until live birth. This was the belief of the Stoics. It appears to be the predominant, though not the unanimous, attitude of the Jewish faith. It may be taken to represent also the position of a large segment of the Protestant community, insofar as that can be ascertained; organized groups that have taken a formal position on the abortion issue have generally regarded abortion as a matter for the conscience of the individual and her family. As we have noted, the common law found greater significance in quickening. Physicians and their scientific colleagues have regarded that event with less interest and have tended to focus either upon conception, upon live birth, or upon the interim point at which the fetus becomes "viable," that is, potentially able to live outside the mother's womb, albeit with artificial aid. Viability is usually placed at about seven months (28 weeks) but may occur earlier, even at 24 weeks. The Aristotelian theory of "mediate animation," that held sway throughout the Middle Ages and the Renaissance in Europe, continued to be official Roman Catholic dogma until the 19th century, despite opposition to this "ensoulment" theory from those in the Church who would recognize the existence of life from the moment of conception. The latter is now, of course, the official belief of the Catholic Church. As one of the briefs amicus discloses, this is a view strongly held by many non-Catholics as well, and by many physicians. Substantial problems for precise definition of this view are posed, however, by new embryological data that purport to indicate that conception is a "process" over time, rather than an event, and by new medical techniques such as menstrual extraction, the "morning-after" pill, implantation of embryos, artificial insemination, and even artificial wombs.

In areas other than criminal abortion, the law has been reluctant to endorse any theory that life, as we recognize it, begins before live birth or to accord legal rights to the unborn except in narrowly defined situations and except when the rights are contingent upon live birth. For example, the traditional rule of tort law denied recovery for prenatal injuries even though the child was born alive. That rule has been changed in almost every jurisdiction. In most States, recovery is said to be permitted only if the fetus was viable, or at least quick, when the injuries were sustained, though few courts have squarely so held. In a recent development, generally opposed by the commentators, some States permit the parents of a still-born child to maintain an action for wrongful death because of prenatal injuries. Such an action, however, would appear to be one to vindicate the parents' interest and is thus consistent with the view that the fetus, at most, represents only the potentiality of life. Similarly, unborn children have been recognized as acquiring rights or interests by way of inheritance or other devolution of property, and have been represented by guardians ad litem. Perfection of the interests involved, again, has generally been contingent upon live birth. In short, the unborn have never been recognized in the law as persons in the whole sense.

In view of all this, we do not agree that, by adopting one theory of life, Texas may override the rights of the pregnant woman that are at stake. We repeat, however, that the State does have an important and legitimate interest in preserving and protecting the health of the pregnant woman, whether she be a resident of the State or a nonresident who seeks medical consultation and treatment there, and that it has still *another* important and legitimate interest in protecting the potentiality of human life. These interests are separate and distinct. Each grows in substantiality as the woman approaches term and, at a point during pregnancy, each becomes "compelling."

With respect to the State's important and legitimate interest in the health of the mother, the "compelling" point, in the light of present medical knowledge, is at approximately the end of the first trimester. This is so because of the now-established medical fact . . . that until the end of the first trimester mortality in abortion may be less than mortality in normal child-birth. It follows that, from and after this point, a State may regulate the abortion procedure to the extent that the regulation reasonably relates to the preservation and protection of maternal health. Examples of permissible state regulation in this area are requirements as to the qualifications of the person who is to perform the abortion; as to the licensure of that person; as to the facility in which the procedure is to be performed, that is, whether it must be a hospital or may be a clinic or some other place of less-than-hospital status; as to the licensing of the facility; and the like.

This means, on the other hand, that, for the period of pregnancy prior to this "compelling" point, the attending physician, in consultation with his patient, is free to determine, without regulation by the State, that, in his medical judgment, the patient's pregnancy should be terminated. If that decision is reached, the judgment may be effectuated by an abortion free of interference by the State.

With respect to the State's important and legitimate interest in potential life, the "compelling" point is at viability. This is so because the fetus then presumably has the capability of meaningful life outside the mother's womb. State regulation protective of fetal life after viability thus has both logical and biological justifications. If the State is interested in protecting fetal life after viability, it may go so far as to proscribe abortion during that period, except when it is necessary to preserve the life or health of the mother.

Measured against these standards, Art. 1196 of the Texas Penal Code, in restricting legal abortions to those "procured or attempted by medical advice for the purpose of saving the life of the mother," sweeps too broadly. The statute makes no distinction between abortions performed early in pregnancy and those performed later, and it limits to a single reason, "saving" the mother's life, the legal justification for the procedure. The statute, therefore, cannot survive the constitutional attack made upon it here.

This conclusion makes it unnecessary for us to consider the additional challenge to the Texas statute asserted on grounds of vagueness. . . .

To summarize and to repeat:

1. A state criminal abortion statute of the current Texas type, that excepts from criminality only a *life-saving* procedure on behalf of the mother, without regard to pregnancy stage and without recognition of the other interests involved, is violative of the Due Process Clause of the Fourteenth Amendment.

(a) For the stage prior to approximately the end of the first trimester, the abortion decision and its effectuation must be left to the medical judgment of the pregnant woman's attending physician.

(b) For the stage subsequent to approximately the end of the first trimester, the State, in promoting its interest in the health of the mother, may, if it chooses, regulate the abortion procedure in ways that are reasonably related to maternal health.

(c) For the stage subsequent to viability, the State in promoting its interest in the potentiality of human life may, if it chooses, regulate, and even proscribe, abortion except where it is necessary, in appropriate medical judgment, for the preservation of the life or health of the mother.

2. The State may define the term "physician" . . . to mean only a physician currently licensed by the State, and may proscribe any abortion by a person who is not a physician as so defined.

In Doe v. Bolton, 410 U.S. 179 . . . , procedural requirements contained in one of the modern abortion statutes are considered. That opinion and this one, of course, are to be read together.

This holding, we feel, is consistent with the relative weights of the respective interests involved, with the lessons and examples of medical and legal history, with the lenity of the common law, and with the demands of the profound problems of the present day. The decision leaves the State free to place increasing restrictions on abortion as the period of pregnancy lengthens, so long as those restrictions are tailored to the recognized state interests. The decision vindicates the right of the physician to administer medical treatment according to his professional judgment up to the points where important state interests provide compelling justifications for intervention. Up to those points, the abortion decision in all its aspects is inherently, and primarily, a medical decision, and basic responsibility for it must rest with the physician. If an individual practitioner abuses the privilege of exercising proper medical judgment, the usual remedies, judicial and intra-professional, are available.

Our conclusion that Art. 1196 is unconstitutional means, of course, that the Texas abortion statutes, as a unit, must fall. . . .

Although the District Court granted plaintiff Roe declaratory relief, it stopped short of issuing an injunction against enforcement of the Texas statutes. The Court has recognized that different considerations enter into a federal court's decision as to declaratory relief, on the one hand, and injunctive relief, on the other. . . .

We find it unnecessary to decide whether the District Court erred in withholding injunctive relief, for we assume the Texas prosecutorial authorities will give full credence to this decision that the present criminal abortion statutes of that State are unconstitutional.

The judgment of the District Court as to intervenor Hallford is reversed, and Dr. Hallford's complaint in intervention is dismissed. In all other respects, the judgment of the District Court is affirmed. Costs are allowed to the appellee.

It is so ordered.

In the Georgia case, *Doe v. Bolton,* decided the same day as *Roe v. Wade,* the Court upheld the district court decision invalidating the provisions that prohibited abortions unless performed to preserve the life or health of the mother, unless the fetus would likely be born with a grave mental or physical defect, or unless the pregnancy resulted from forcible or statutory rape. Under the principles enunciated in the Texas case, the Court held, the abortion decision could not be subjected to such restrictions by state law. In addition, however, the Court invalidated many of the procedural requirements of the Georgia law as exceeding the state's interest in regulating the abortion decision and as violating the woman's right to privacy. The provisions struck down were those (1) that required abortions to be performed in hospitals accredited by the Joint Commission on Accreditation of Hospitals; (2) that required an abortion to be approved by a hospital abortion committee; (3) that required two other physicians to concur with the woman's personal physician that an abortion was appropriate; and (4) that limited abortions to Georgia residents. The first three requirements were held not to be justified by a compelling state interest in regulating the abortion decision, particularly during the early stages of pregnancy, under the standards spelled out in *Roe,* and the fourth restriction was held to violate the right to travel interstate, a right long recognized by the Court as protected by the Constitution.

Chief Justice Burger concurred in both of the Court's decisions in a brief opinion, but indicated he would have upheld a state's power to require the certification of two physicians before an abortion could be performed. Justice Douglas also wrote a concurring opinion in which he emphasized the right of privacy as a "fundamental" right subject to regulation by government only upon a showing of a "compelling interest."

Although he had dissented from the Court's decision in *Griswold v. Connecticut,* the case upholding the right of privacy in marriage that had become the doctrinal basis of the *Abortion Cases,* Justice Stewart also concurred in *Roe* and *Doe.* Noting that the Court in *Griswold* had invalidated a statute that violated neither a right in the Bill of Rights nor any other provision of the Constitution, Stewart said that it

> was clear to me then, and it is equally clear to me now, that the Griswold decision can be rationally understood only as a holding that the Connecticut statute substantively invaded the "liberty" that is protected by the Due Process Clause of the Fourteenth Amendment. As so understood, Griswold stands as one in a long line of . . . cases decided under the doctrine of substantive due process, and I now accept it as such.

The Court's decisions in the *Abortion Cases* could not be

accepted with such equanimity by Justices White and Rehnquist, and they filed the following dissenting opinions:

Mr. Justice White, with whom Mr. Justice Rehnquist joins, dissenting.

. . . With all due respect, I dissent. I find nothing in the language or history of the Constitution to support the Court's judgment. The Court simply fashions and announces a new constitutional right for pregnant mothers and, with scarcely any reason or authority for its action, invests that right with sufficient substance to override most existing state abortion statutes. The upshot is that the people and the legislatures of the 50 States are constitutionally disentitled to weigh the relative importance of the continued fetus, on the one hand, against a spectrum of possible impacts on the mother, on the other hand. As an exercise of raw judicial power, the Court perhaps has authority to do what it does today; but in my view its judgment is an improvident and extravagant exercise of the power of judicial review that the Constitution extends to this Court.

The Court apparently values the convenience of the pregnant mother more than the continued existence and development of the life or potential life that she carries. Whether or not I might agree with that marshaling of values, I can in no event join the Court's judgment because I find no constitutional warrant for imposing such an order of priorities on the people and legislatures of the States. In a sensitive area such as this, involving as it does issues over which reasonable men may easily and heatedly differ, I cannot accept the Court's exercise of its clear power of choice by interposing a constitutional barrier to state efforts to protect human life and by investing mothers and doctors with the constitutionally protected right to exterminate it. This issue, for the most part, should be left with the people and to the political processes the people have devised to govern their affairs. . . .

Mr. Justice Rehnquist, dissenting.

The Court's opinion brings to the decision of this troubling question both extensive historical fact and a wealth of legal scholarship. While the opinion thus commands my respect, I find myself nonetheless in fundamental disagreement with those parts of it that invalidate the Texas statute in question, and therefore dissent. . . .

The Court's opinion decides that a State may impose virtually no restriction on the performance of abortions during the first trimester of pregnancy. Our previous decisions indicate that a necessary predicate for such an opinion is a plaintiff who was in her first trimester of pregnancy at some time during the pendency of her law-suit. While a party may vindicate his own constitutional rights, he may not seek vindication for the rights of others. . . . The Court's statement of facts in this case makes clear, however, that the record in no way indicates the presence of such a plaintiff. We know only that plaintiff Roe at the time of filing her complaint was a pregnant woman; for aught that appears in this record, she may have been in her *last* trimester of pregnancy as of the date the complaint was filed. . . .

Even if there were a plaintiff in this case capable of litigating the issue which the Court decides, I would reach a conclusion opposite to that reached by the Court. I have difficulty in concluding, as the Court does, that the right of "privacy" is involved in this case. Texas, by the statute here challenged, bars the performance of a medical abortion by a licensed physician on a plaintiff such as Roe. A transaction resulting in an operation such as this is not "private" in the ordinary usage of that word. . . .

I agree with the statement of Mr. Justice Stewart in his concurring opinion that the "liberty," against deprivation of which without due process the Fourteenth Amendment protects, embraces more than the rights found in the Bill of Rights. But that liberty is not guaranteed absolutely against deprivation, only against deprivation without due process of law. The test traditionally applied in the area of social and economic legislation is whether or not a law such as that challenged has a rational relation to a valid state objective. . . . But the Court's sweeping invalidation of any restrictions on abortion during the first trimester is impossible to justify under that standard, and the conscious weighing of competing factors that the Court's opinion apparently substitutes for the established test is far more appropriate to a legislative judgment than to a judicial one. . . .

As in Lochner and similar cases applying substantive due process standards to economic and social welfare legislation, the adoption of the compelling state interest standard will inevitably require this Court to examine the legislative policies and pass on the wisdom of these policies in the very process of deciding whether a particular state interest put forward may or may not be "compelling." The decision here to break pregnancy into three distinct terms and to outline the permissible restrictions the State may impose in each one, for example, partakes more of judicial legislation than it does of a determination of the intent of the drafters of the Fourteenth Amendment. . . .

By the time of the adoption of the Fourteenth Amendment in 1868, there were at least 36 laws enacted by state or territorial legislatures limiting abortion. . . . There apparently was no question concerning the validity of this [Texas statute] or of any of the other state statutes when the Fourteenth Amendment was adopted. The only conclusion possible from this history is

that the drafters did not intend to have the Fourteenth Amendment with-
draw from the States the power to legislate with respect to this matter. . . .
    For all of the foregoing reasons, I respectfully dissent.

The Court had thus extended the right of privacy protected
by the due process clause to protect the right of a woman to
obtain an abortion. At the same time, however, it had recognized
that at some point during pregnancy the potential for human life
was sufficient to justify governmental regulation of the woman's
abortion decision. It had held, therefore, that (1) there was no
compelling interest to justify governmental interference with the
right of a woman to obtain an abortion under a physician's care up
to approximately the first trimester of a pregnancy; (2) because of
public health considerations, after a pregnancy proceeded beyond
the first trimester, governments might regulate the procedures
attendant to abortions, if reasonably justified by concern for
maternal well-being; and (3) after the fetus achieved viability,
governmental policy could justifiably even prohibit abortions
except those to preserve the life or health of the mother. The
abortion laws in force in most states were, under these criteria,
unconstitutional.

Reactions to the Court's decisions in the *Abortion Cases* may
have been muted by the death of ex-President Lyndon Johnson on
the same day the decisions were announced, but they were nonetheless as emotional as the issue had been for some years. In what
was perhaps the sharpest denunciation of a Supreme Court
decision by the Catholic hierarchy in modern times, Cardinal
Cooke of New York characterized the decisions as "shocking" and
"horrifying." Whatever the Court's rationale was, Cardinal Cooke
declared, "seven men have made a tragic utilitarian judgment
regarding who shall live and who shall die. They have made
themselves a 'super legislature.' They have gone against the will of
those American people who spoke their minds in favor of life as
recently as last November in referendums in Michigan and North
Dakota. They have usurped the powers and responsibilities of the
legislatures of the 50 states to protect human life."

Speaking for the National Council of Catholic Bishops, Cardinal Krol of Philadelphia denounced the decisions as an "unspeakable tragedy for this nation." He found it "hard to think of any decision in the 200 years of our history which has had more disastrous implications for our stability as a civilized society." The Court had used "bad logic and bad law," and as a consequence had done a "monstrous injustice" to thousands of unborn children. "Abortion at any stage of pregnancy is evil," he asserted. The National Council of Catholic Bishops later pledged to explore "every legal possibility" to overturn the Court's decisions, and again denounced abortion as "still morally wrong." In its view, "no court opinion can change the law of God prohibiting the taking of innocent life." A conservative Catholic lay group, the Society for a Christian Commonwealth, even called for the excommunication of Justice William Brennan, the only Catholic on the Court, for his "collaboration" in the *Abortion Cases.*

The pro-abortion forces were elated by the Court's decisions. A spokesman for the Planned Parenthood Federation praised them as "a wise and courageous stroke for the right to privacy, and for the protection of the woman's physical and emotional health." Because of the Court's action, the spokesman said, "hundreds of thousands of American women every year will be spared the medical risks and emotional horrors of back-street and self-induced abortions. And as a nation, we shall be a step further toward assuring the birthright of every child to be welcomed by its parents at the time of its birth."

Reverend Howard A. Spragg, director of the Board of Homeland Ministries of the United Church of Christ, also praised the Court's decisions as "historic not only in terms of women's individual rights but also in terms of the relationships of church and state." And women lawyers of the Center for Constitutional Rights hailed the decisions as a "tribute to the coordinated efforts of women's organizations, women lawyers and all women throughout this country."

As they had pledged when the decisions were announced, anti-abortion forces, with the Catholic Church and the National Right to Life Committee in the forefront, supported constitutional amendments to reverse the Court's action. Approximately eighteen such amendments have been introduced in Congress, ranging from proposals that would allow the states to regulate abortion free of federal constitutional restraints, to proposals that would prohibit the deprivation of life "from the moment of conception" or defining the word "person" in the due process clauses to include "all human beings, including their unborn off-spring at every stage of their biological development." Although the right-to-life forces organized a large rally in Washington, D.C., during 1974 to support a constitutional amendment banning abortion, the proposals have not been decisively acted on by Congress, and their prospects appear dim. Congress has, on the other hand, passed or considered several laws discouraging or limiting the opportunities for abortions in government-funded facilities, and these actions will undoubtedly furnish the bases for future litigation on the abortion issue.

Anti-abortion moves either in Congress or elsewhere, how-ever, will perhaps be discouraged by recent public opinion polls. Although polls before the Court's decisions in the *Abortion Cases* had indicated a majority of Americans opposed abortions, even during the early stages of pregnancy, after the decisions a majority of the public switched to a position sympathetic to abortions during the early stages of pregnancy. Heavy majorities among younger people (under thirty) favor abortion, irrespective of reli-gious affiliation, while older people have been more reluctant to accept abortion as a public policy.

Considered from the standpoint of constitutional develop-ment, the *Abortion Cases* are remarkable. As the Nixon appointees came to the Court, most observers believed that the rapid pace of constitutional change that had characterized the Warren Court era had ended, and that bold innovations in constitutional policy were unlikely. This observation has generally proved true, but the *Abortion Cases* are a glaring exception. Not only did a Court that was widely expected to eschew bold innovation make the decisions, but three out of the four Nixon appointees, Burger, Powell, and Blackmun, joined the majority.

The *Abortion Cases* are also remarkable from the standpoint of due process policy, since the doctrinal basis for the Court's decisions in those cases did not emerge until *Griswold v. Connecti-*

cut in 1965. From *Griswold* it appeared that a majority of the justices was prepared to interpret the due process clause to embrace rights beyond those in the Bill of Rights. If there were any doubts about the permanance of the Court's acceptance of that approach, the *Abortion Cases* certainly dispelled them. Since nationalization of the Bill of Rights via the due process clause has been largely completed, the most important line of development under the due process clause now is the one proceeding under the *Griswold-Abortion* line of cases, a development that involves judicial recognition and protection of rights beyond those listed in the Bill of Rights or elsewhere in the Constitution.

As often happens in constitutional developments with such controversial and national impact as that of the *Abortion Cases,* the individuals whose legal problems served as vehicles for the enunciation of policy by the Court were overlooked or forgotten. One of the ironies of the *Abortion Cases* is that the Court's decisions came too late for the women who were the principal litigants. Even when the district court in Atlanta announced its decision in *Doe v. Bolton,* Margie Pitts Hames said that Jane Doe was "too far along to get aborted now," since "it would not be medically safe." Hames indicated that Doe would have her child, and that it would be put up for adoption, since the mother was on welfare and financially unable to care for another child.

Norma McCorvey, ("Jane Roe") also had her baby. Following the announcement of the decisions in the *Abortion Cases,* Ms. McCorvey admitted that many times during her pregnancy she had felt desperate, wondering why she should go on. "No one," she said, "showed me any compassion except my doctor and lawyers." She had given birth to her child while *Roe v. Wade* was being litigated and had put the child up for adoption because she was financially unable to care for it. "It's great to know that other women will not have to go through what I did," she said of the *Abortion Cases.* "I'm glad the court decided that women, in consultation with a doctor, can control their own bodies."

Chapter Two

THE REVOLUTION IN CRIMINAL PROCEDURE AND ITS AFTERMATH: THE CASE OF SEARCHES AND SEIZURES

Introduction No other field of American constitutional policy has been as profoundly affected by the nationalization of the Bill of Rights as the field of criminal procedure. Throughout most of United States history, the states were largely free from federal constitutional restraints in the administration of their criminal laws. It was not until the 1930s that the Supreme Court used the due process clause of the Fourteenth Amendment to impose significant restrictions on state criminal procedures, and it was not until the height of nationalization during the 1960s that most of the criminal procedure provisions of the Bill of Rights were applied with full force to the states. Nationalization of these provisions during the 1960s was effected by decisions of the Supreme Court that, taken together, were characterized with little exaggeration as "the revolution in criminal procedure."

Many criminal procedure rights in the Bill of Rights were applied to the states without causing profound repercussions and great controversy. This was true of the Sixth Amendment requirements of a speedy (*Klopfer v. North Carolina* in 1967), public (*In re Oliver* in 1948) trial by jury (*Duncan v. Louisiana* in 1968), the right to confront witnesses (*Pointer v. Texas* in 1965), the right to compulsory process (*Washington v. Texas* in 1967), and even the full right to counsel (*Gideon v. Wainwright* in 1963). The Eighth Amendment prohibition of cruel and unusual punishment (*Robinson v. California* in 1962) and the Fifth Amendment double jeopardy clause (*Benton v. Maryland,* in 1969) were applied to the states with relatively little controversy.

Application to the states of the Fifth Amendment self-incrimination clause (*Malloy v. Hogan* in 1964) and the Fourth Amendment prohibition of unreasonable searches and seizures (*Mapp v. Ohio* in 1961), on the other hand, engendered considerable dispute. The Court's application of the self-incrimination clause led, in conjunction with the full guarantee of a right to counsel in state criminal proceedings, to the decision in *Miranda v. Arizona* in 1966. In *Miranda,* the Court required both state and federal law enforcement officials who had taken a suspect into custody and had begun to question him for the purpose of eliciting a confession, to warn the suspect of his right to remain silent under the self-incrimination clause, his right to have an attorney present during questioning, and his right to appointed counsel if he was unable to afford an attorney. The *Miranda* decision became a symbol to critics of the Warren Court who charged that the Court was "soft on criminals" and was enforcing policies that "handcuffed the police."

The Warren Court's full application to the states of the Fourth Amendment prohibition against unreasonable searches and seizures also proved one of its most controversial policy initiatives. The Fourth Amendment provides that the "right of the people to be secure in their persons, houses, papers, and effects, against unreasonable searches and seizures, shall not be violated, and no Warrants shall issue, but upon probable cause, supported by Oath or affirmation, and particularly describing the place to be searched, and the persons or things to be seized."

Historically, the Fourth Amendment was included in the Bill of Rights to a great extent in reaction to the use of "writs of assistance" by British authorities during the period leading up to the Revolution. Writs of assistance were general search warrants that authorized customs officials to search for contraband goods smuggled into the colonies in violation of Acts of Parliament imposing duties upon such goods. In February 1761, James Otis denounced the writs as "the worst instrument of arbitrary power, the most destructive of English liberty and the fundamental principles of law, that ever was found in an English law book," since the writs placed "the liberty of every man in the hands of every officer." Otis argued that "no acts of Parliament can establish such a writ; though it should be made in the very words of the petition, it would be void. An act against the [British] Constitution is void." Commenting on Otis's denunciation of these writs, John Adams later remarked, "Then and there was the first scene of the first act of opposition to the arbitrary claims of Great Britain. Then and there the child Independence was born."

In response to the general searches undertaken by the British, the Fourth Amendment outlawed the arbitrary use of general warrants and required that search and arrest warrants[10] be issued by a neutral judge or magistrate, who had to determine that there was information constituting probable cause to believe either that a particular individual had committed a crime (in order for an arrest warrant to issue) or that seizable items were at a particular place. In addition, warrants were to specify the person or things to be seized and the place to be searched. The Fourth Amendment thus theoretically placed between law enforcement officers and the individual a neutral magistrate who had to find probable cause to arrest or search on the basis of information supplied by law enforcement officers, before a search or arrest would be authorized. General searches, such as those authorized by the writs of assistance, were prohibited by the requirement that the place to be searched and the person or things to be seized were to be specified in the warrant.

Like the rest of the Bill of Rights, the Fourth Amendment was originally applicable only to the federal government. In *Weeks v. United States,* decided in 1914, the Supreme Court held that the amendment would be enforced in the federal courts by an exclusionary rule prohibiting the admission of evidence seized by

10. The arrest of an individual is a "seizure" of his person within the meaning of the Fourth Amendment.

federal officers in violation of Fourth Amendment requirements. Then in 1949 the Court held, in *Wolf v. Colorado,* that at least the "core" of the Fourth Amendment's prohibition of unreasonable searches and seizures applied to the states via the due process clause of the Fourteenth Amendment. The Court refused, however, to require state courts to exclude evidence seized in violation of the prohibition against unreasonable searches and seizures, even though the federal courts were required to do so under the *Weeks* rule.

Finally, in 1961, the Court held in *Mapp v. Ohio* that state courts must exclude illegally seized evidence, and it confirmed in 1963, in *Ker v. California,* that the full Fourth Amendment, not merely its "core," was applicable to the states. As a result of *Mapp,* the full force of the Fourth Amendment was applicable to the states for the first time. States that had previously admitted illegally seized evidence in criminal trials could no longer do so, and the often more stringent federal standards governing searches and seizures were, after 1961, applicable to the states.

The Fourth Amendment, of course, prohibits only "unreasonable" searches and seizures, and the courts have long held that arrests executed without warrants may be "reasonable" in certain circumstances. If, for example, a police officer sees a crime committed or has sufficient information to lead to a finding of probable cause that a particular person has committed a crime, the officer may arrest the individual without a warrant. The courts have also recognized that searches without warrants are reasonable in certain situations. Among these are:

(1) The search of a moving vehicle without a warrant is valid when officers have probable cause to believe the vehicle is carrying contraband or other seizable items (under *Carroll v. United States* and *Brinegar v. United States*). The rationale is that, if officers had to secure a warrant before searching such a vehicle, the vehicle could escape before a warrant could be issued in conformity with the provisions of the Fourth Amendment.

(2) There may be a warrantless search of a dwelling by officers who are in "hot pursuit" of a criminal suspect when the suspect has taken refuge in the dwelling. Under *Warden v. Hayden,* decided in 1967, the officers may search the dwelling for the

suspect, for evidence of the crime, and for the fruits and instruments of the crime.

(3) An officer may make a limited search for weapons without a warrant when an individual is behaving suspiciously and the officer has "reasonable cause" to suspect that he is about to commit a crime and may be armed, if the suspect fails to explain his behavior when challenged by the officer. The search must be limited to a "frisk" or "patdown" for weapons, absent probable cause for a more extensive search, according to *Terry v. Ohio* and *Sibron v. New York,* both decided in 1968.

(4) An individual may waive his right against an unreasonable search and seizure, and, he need not be advised of his Fourth Amendment rights by officers who conduct a search (*Schneckloth v. Bustamonte*).

(5) Finally, when officers make a valid arrest, a search of the person arrested and the immediately surrounding environment is justified without a warrant. The justification is to prevent the suspect from seizing weapons by which he may escape and to prevent him from destroying evidence within his reach at the time of arrest. These searches "incident to lawful arrests" are probably the most common searches that occur without warrants.

The standards governing searches incident to valid arrests have also fluctuated considerably over the years in the decisions of the Supreme Court. The Court first indicated that a search of an arrested suspect himself was valid in *Weeks v. United States* in 1914. By 1925, however, the doctrine of searches incident to valid arrests had been fully recognized by the Court in *Agnello v. United States.* There the Court held that the "right without a search warrant contemporaneously to search persons lawfully arrested while committing crime and to search the place where the arrest is made in order to find and seize things connected with the crime as its fruits or as the means by which it was committed, as well as weapons and other things to effect an escape from custody, is not to be doubted."

Having recognized the validity of a search incident to a lawful arrest, the scope of such a search raised considerable difficulties for the Court. In *Harris v. United States,* decided in 1947, the Court sustained as valid a five-hour search of a four-room apartment by FBI agents incident to an arrest. In 1948, however, the Court held in *Trupiano v. United States* that a search incident to an arrest was not valid if the officers had had sufficient time to secure a search warrant before the search. Then two years later, in 1950, the Court held in *United States v. Rabinowitz* that a one-and-one-half-hour search of a one-room office, incident to a lawful arrest there, was valid, despite the fact that the officers could have obtained a warrant in advance. *Trupiano* was expressly overruled in *Rabinowitz,* and the Court held that the test of the validity of a search incident to an arrest "is not whether it is reasonable to procure a search warrant, but whether the search was reasonable."

By the 1960s, when the Fourth Amendment was fully applied to the states, it thus appeared that the *Harris* and *Rabinowitz* cases delineated the proper scope of a search incident to a lawful arrest under the amendment. Officers could search not only the person arrested but also the premises where the arrest occurred, up to at least the scope of the search in *Harris,* a four-room apartment,[11] and warrants were not required for searches incident to lawful arrests, even if the officers could reasonably have procured a warrant beforehand. In *Chimel v. California,* decided in 1969, however, the Court enunciated new standards governing searches incident to arrests that substantially reduced their permissible scope under the Fourth Amendment.

Case Study
**THE CASE OF THE
BABBLING BURGLAR:
CHIMEL V. CALIFORNIA**

The California Supreme Court characterized the facts surrounding Ted Steven Chimel's trouble with the law as being "rather bizarre," a characterization that can be viewed as judicial

---

11. Officers could not, however, seize the entire contents of a house where an arrest was made. In *Kremen v. United States,* in 1957, the Court held invalid the FBI's seizure of the entire contents of a cabin where arrests of fugitives had occurred. The articles seized were itemized as an appendix to the opinion of the Court, and this itemization filled eleven printed pages.

understatement. Chimel was a dental technician, a coin collector, and a sometime coin dealer. He was a neighbor of Mr. and Mrs. Vito Louis Pulati, who were also coin collectors, and was a frequent visitor in the Pulatis' home in Santa Ana, California. During the period before February 1965, the Pulatis were engaged in cataloguing their extensive coin collection, and Chimel visited them, discussing coins and the Pulatis' collection.

Chimel and the Pulatis were also members of three coin clubs in the Santa Ana area, but on the night of February 2, 1965, the Pulatis noticed that Chimel was absent from a regular meeting of one of the clubs. Upon returning home, they discovered that their home had been burglarized and part of their coin collection had been stolen. They noticed, however, that the house had not been ransacked, but rather that the burglar appeared to know exactly what items from their collection he wanted and had left undisturbed other coins and valuables. The Pulatis apparently immediately suspected Chimel as the culprit, since he had been absent from the club meeting that night. More importantly, the Pulatis had lived in Santa Ana only a short time, and only Chimel and the real estate broker who had sold them their house were aware that they kept their coin collection on the premises. Chimel had also asked the Pulatis on one occasion whether their collection was insured.

The Pulatis' suspicions were, of course, insufficient as a basis to arrest Chimel, and he appears to have gone unmolested by the police until the summer of 1965. On August 14, however, the Money Vault, a coin shop in Orange, was also burglarized, and again there was evidence linking Chimel to the crime. Indeed, it appears that Chimel himself provided evidence that he was involved in the Money Vault burglary. On the evening before, for example, a neighbor, Thomas Ambrose, visited Chimel and asked if he would like to go bicycle riding. Chimel demurred, saying that he had "a big deal going." He showed Ambrose a walkie-talkie in his car, and attempted to contact Charles (Chuck) Hamburger on the walkie-talkie, indicating he and Hamburger intended to use walkie-talkies on the "big deal." The day following the Money Vault burglary, Chimel told Ambrose that he and Hamburger had broken into the coin shop, but later he telephoned Ambrose to say he had only been joking. Ambrose reported this information to the Orange Police Department after reading an account of the burglary in the newspapers.

B. R. Slocum, the owner of the Money Vault, was also acquainted with Ted Chimel. Chimel had visited the Money Vault, and Slocum later testified that Chimel was one of only two persons who knew where the most valuable coins in the shop were kept. These coins had been taken in the burglary. Slocum also testified that Chimel had asked before the burglary if Slocum was insured and whether or not Slocum would like to have his shop "knocked over." Chimel had, in addition, inquired about the alarm system in the coin shop. After the burglary, Chimel telephoned Slocum and accused him of robbing the store himself for the insurance. When Slocum said the burglary had been sloppy, Chimel excitedly insisted that the job had been "real professional."

Relying on this information linking Chimel to the Money Vault burglary, Officer T. Del Coma, a burglary detective in the Orange Police Department, took Chimel into custody on August 25. Having taken Chimel to the police station, Del Coma and Chimel discussed the Money Vault burglary and the possibility that the stolen coins might be returned, leaving "up in the air" who might return them. Following this discussion, Chimel was released from custody, but on August 30 he returned to the Orange Police Department with Chuck Hamburger and an attorney, Everett Jones, and again discussed with Del Coma the possibility of returning the stolen coins. The discussions were apparently inconclusive because Chimel and Hamburger felt that Slocum, the store owner, was claiming more coins had been stolen than had actually been the case.[12] During the discussions, attorney Jones felt constrained to admonish Chimel to keep quiet on several occasions.

Officer Del Coma had been reporting regularly to Orange County Deputy District Attorney Robert Law on the progress of

12. The purpose of these discussions was apparently to obviate a civil suit by Slocum against Chimel and Hamburger for recovery of the coins. Some of the coins stolen in the Money Vault burglary were later seized by Torrance police officers from the office of attorney Everett Jones. Charles Hamburger was never arrested and apparently became a fugitive.

the investigation of the Money Vault burglary, and on August 30 Del Coma requested that Law authorize issuance of a complaint against Chimel, charging him with burglary. Law refused this request because he doubted there was sufficient evidence against Chimel to constitute probable cause to arrest him. During the first week of September, however, Jack Parsons, the owner of the Lido Coin Shop in Costa Mesa, reported to the police that Chimel had told him he had been involved in the Money Vault burglary. Chimel had alluded to the possibility of being arrested and asked Parsons if he would be willing to sell some coins for him to raise money if he were arrested. This additional evidence convinced Deputy District Attorney Law that a complaint should be issued against Chimel, and he authorized Officer Del Coma to secure a warrant for Chimel's arrest.

On September 13, 1965, Del Coma appeared before Judge David French in the Municipal Court of Santa Ana–Orange Judicial District and swore in a complaint that

> on or about the 14th day of August, 1965, at and within
> Orange County, California, the crime of Felony, to-wit:
> Violation of Section 459 of the Penal Code was committed
> by Ted Steven Chimel who at the time and place last afore-
> said, did then and there willfully, feloniously and burglar-
> iously enter a building known as The Money Vault, located at
> 153 North Glassell Street, Orange, in said County and State,
> with intent to commit theft.

Del Coma then requested "that a warrant may be issued for the arrest of the said Ted Steven Chimel and that he be dealt with according to law."

Judge French issued a warrant for Chimel's arrest for bur- glary. Since Chimel lived in Santa Ana, Officer Del Coma was accompanied by two detectives from the Santa Ana Police Depart- ment when he executed the arrest warrant at about four o'clock in the afternoon of September 13. The officers knocked on the door of Chimel's house, and were admitted by Chimel's wife. Chimel returned from work about ten or fifteen minutes after the officers arrived. Del Coma served him with the arrest warrant in the living room of the house and advised him of his rights. Del Coma asked if it would be all right for the officers to look around the house, but Chimel said, "I'd rather you didn't." Del Coma informed Chimel, however, that incident to the arrest the officers had a right to search the premises, and they proceeded to do so. During the course of the search, the officers seized various coins and medals that they believed had been stolen from the Money Vault coin shop.

About two days after the arrest, Mr. and Mrs. Pulati identified some of the seized coins as among those stolen from their home the previous February. None of the items seized at Chimel's home was ever identified as having been taken from the Money Vault. On the basis of the Pulatis' identification, however, Santa Ana police detectives also obtained a warrant for Chimel's arrest for the burglary of the Pulati home. The warrant was again served on Chimel at his home on September 16, and again a search incident to the arrest was conducted, but no further incriminating evidence was apparently uncovered.

After a preliminary hearing on October 14, 1965, Ted Chimel was bound over for trial on two counts of burglary, and after several continuances, Chimel's case came on for trial in the Superior Court of Orange County on July 5, 1966. The prosecution presented the testimony of the Pulatis, B. R. Slocum, the owner of the Money Vault, Chimel's neighbor Thomas Ambrose, and others, but the crucial evidence against Chimel consisted of the coins and other numismatic items seized at his home by Del Coma on September 13. On the question of whether these seized items were admissible as evidence against Chimel, the prosecution encountered considerable legal difficulty under the Fourth and Fourteenth Amendments.

California law had originally provided that, in order for an officer to procure a warrant for the arrest of a criminal suspect, the officer had to submit affidavits or produce sworn testimony before a magistrate who would then examine the evidence to determine if it established probable cause that a crime had been committed and that the suspect had committed the crime. If the magistrate was thus satisfied, he would issue a warrant for the arrest of the suspect. A similar procedure, requiring a showing of probable cause before a magistrate, was demanded by California law before a search warrant would issue.

Over the years, however, California courts began to uphold arrests as valid even though a warrant had been secured without a showing of probable cause, and in 1951 the legislature passed a statute making the issuance of an arrest warrant by a magistrate an almost automatic process after a complaint against a suspect had been filed. The traditional requirement of a showing of probable cause before a magistrate was, however, retained for search warrants. After 1951, then, it became much easier for California police officers to obtain arrest warrants than to obtain search warrants. This situation undoubtedly affected the limited extent to which search warrants were used by the police; in San Francisco, for example, with 30,000 major crimes reported per year, the police obtained only 20 search warrants in 1968. In Los Angeles, only 1,897 search warrants were issued from 1930 to 1968; in 1968, only 197 search warrants were issued in Los Angeles.[13]

In Chimel's case, Officer Del Coma had complied with the 1951 California Penal Code in securing a warrant for Chimel's arrest. He had simply filed a complaint and stated under oath before a magistrate that he had information and belief that Chimel had committed a burglary. Del Coma did not present any evidence justifying this charge (as traditional probable cause would have required), and under the 1951 revision of the code such evidence was not demanded for an arrest warrant.

By the time of Chimel's arrest in 1965, however, these procedures for issuance of arrest warrants were of very doubtful constitutionality under the Fourth and Fourteenth Amendments of the federal Constitution. In 1961, the Supreme Court had held in *Mapp v. Ohio* that the Fourth Amendment fully applied to the states via the due process clause and had further applied the *Weeks* exclusionary rule to the states, thus making evidence seized in violation of the Fourth Amendment inadmissible in state courts. Federal standards deriving from the Fourth Amendment were

13. Fred P. Graham, *The Self-Inflicted Wound* (New York: Macmillan, 1970), p. 204.

therefore applicable after 1961 to both searches and arrests conducted by state officers.

The Fourth Amendment standard of probable cause for an
arrest or search warrant and the procedures to be followed in
procuring warrants had been enunciated by the Supreme Court in
Giordenello v. United States in 1958 and *Aguilar v. Texas* in 1964.
In *Giordenello,* an agent of the Federal Bureau of Narcotics
obtained a warrant for Giordenello's arrest by swearing before a
United States commissioner that "on or about January 26, 1956,
at Houston, Texas, Veto Giordenello did receive, conceal, etc.,
narcotic drugs, to-wit: heroin hydrochloride with knowledge of
unlawful importation; in violation of Section 174, Title 21, United
States Code. . . . " The agent executed the warrant and seized a
bag of heroin from Giordenello's hand during the course of the
arrest. The bag of heroin was admitted as evidence against Giordenello at his trial, and he was convicted, but he appealed to the
Supreme Court on the ground that the heroin had been illegally
seized because the warrant for his arrest had been illegally issued
in violation of the Fourth Amendment.

The Supreme Court held that the Fourth Amendment
requirement of a showing of probable cause "of course applies to
arrest as well as search warrants." Quoting an earlier case, the
Court said the inferences from the facts in a complaint must be
drawn by a "neutral and detached magistrate instead of being
judged by an officer engaged in the often competitive enterprise of
ferreting out crime." The Court explained,

> The purpose of the complaint, then, is to enable the appro-
> priate magistrate, here a Commissioner, to determine whether
> the "probable cause" required to support a warrant exists.
> The Commissioner must judge for himself the persuasiveness
> of the facts relied on by a complaining officer to show prob-
> able cause. He should not accept without question the
> complainant's mere conclusion that the person whose arrest
> is sought has committed a crime.

The Court held that the complaint on which the arrest
warrant had been issued in the *Giordenello* case had been insufficient, since it contained "no affirmative allegation that the

[officer] spoke with personal knowledge of the matters contained therein; it does not indicate any sources for the complainant's belief; and it does not set forth any other sufficient basis upon which a finding of probable cause could be made." Since Giordenello's arrest on this warrant had been violative of the Fourth Amendment, the Court held that the heroin seized as an incident to the arrest had been illegally seized and should not have been admitted as evidence against him, and his conviction therefore had to be reversed.

In *Aguilar v. Texas,* the Court reaffirmed its decision in *Giordenello,* holding insufficient an affidavit for a search warrant for narcotics. "Although the reviewing court will pay substantial deference to judicial determinations of probable cause," the Supreme Court said, "the court must still insist that the magistrate perform his 'neutral and detached' function and not serve merely as a rubber stamp for the police." In *Aguilar,* a magistrate had issued a search warrant upon the basis of an affidavit filed by two police officers in which they swore that they had "received reliable information from a credible person and do believe" that narcotics were at a certain location. Such an affidavit, the Court said, did not establish probable cause under the Fourth Amendment. "Although an affidavit may be based on hearsay information and need not reflect the direct observations of the affiant . . . ," the Court said, "the magistrate must be informed of some of the underlying circumstances from which the informant concluded the narcotics were where he claimed they were, and some of the underlying circumstances from which the officer concluded that the informant, whose identity need not be disclosed, . . . was 'credible' or his information 'reliable.' "

Under these two cases, it therefore appeared that the procedure under which officer Del Coma had secured the warrant for Ted Chimel's arrest was constitutionally defective. In his complaint, Del Coma had not included any of the "underlying circumstances" that led him to believe Chimel was guilty of burglary and that would allow the judge to perform his "neutral and detached" function of determining whether probable cause existed for the arrest.

Since the arrest warrant for Chimel appeared to have been

unconstitutionally issued, Keith Monroe, Chimel's trial attorney, based a substantial part of his defense on the contentions that (1) Chimel had been illegally arrested, (2) the search of Chimel's home incident to his arrest was thus also illegal, and (3) therefore the coins and other items found during the search had been illegally seized and were inadmissible as evidence against him at his trial, under the doctrine of *Mapp v. Ohio.*

During Chimel's trial, the Fourth and Fourteenth Amendment contentions came to a head when Officer Del Coma testified about the arrest and search. Del Coma, a prosecution witness, was first questioned by Assistant District Attorney James G. Enright. He described how he had procured a warrant for Chimel's arrest and had proceeded to Chimel's home to arrest him. When the witness was questioned about the search of the Chimel residence, defense counsel Monroe objected to the testimony on the ground that the search had violated the Fourth Amendment, but the trial judge overruled Monroe's objection and allowed Del Coma's description of the search to be heard by the jury.

After Del Coma's description, however, the jury was dismissed, and on July 11, out of the presence of the jury, arguments were heard on the validity of the arrest warrant and the search incident to Chimel's arrest. Interestingly, the superior court judge who presided at the trial was the same Judge French who had been sitting as a municipal judge at the time of Chimel's arrest and had issued the arrest warrant. Defense counsel Monroe moved for a mistrial before Judge French at the July 11 hearing, arguing that Chimel had been arrested under an illegally issued warrant, according to *Giordenello* and *Aguilar,* that the subsequent search had thus been illegal, and that the testimony on the arrest and search that the jury had already heard had resulted in substantial prejudice sufficient to deny Chimel a fair trial. Monroe also argued, of course, under *Mapp v. Ohio,* that the evidence unlawfully seized was inadmissible at Chimel's trial.

Assistant District Attorney James Enright argued, on the other hand, that the arrest warrant had been validly issued under the Fourth and Fourteenth Amendments. Moreover, in any case, Officer Del Coma had had sufficient information in his possession at the time of the arrest to constitute probable cause to arrest

Chimel without a warrant. Thus, even if the arrest warrant were invalidly issued, Enright argued, Chimel's arrest was still valid, and the search incident to the arrest was also valid. Therefore the coins and medals seized in Chimel's home should be admitted as evidence against him.

Keith Monroe replied that the

> United States Supreme Court has said squarely that the inferences from the facts which lead to the Complaint must be drawn by a neutral Magistrate, and obviously there must be some facts before this Magistrate before any inference can be drawn. Under the statutes as amended in 1951, the Magistrate's function in this State is a rubberstamp function: Is there a Complaint on file? Yes, there is a Complaint on file. Warrant issued. Obviously this requires no discretion, no evaluation, no nothing. . . . I suggest to Your Honor that this case, this case which is now before the Court, is an excellent example of the Arrest Warrant under what I insist are the presently illegal procedures being used in fact as a Search Warrant. . . .

Judge French, however, announced that he had "heard enough. The motion for a mistrial will be denied." Chimel's trial would continue, and the evidence seized would be admitted into evidence. The judge's cryptic denial of the motion, however, left unclear what the basis for his decision was. Did he feel that the arrest warrant had been legally issued and therefore the search had also been valid, or was he ruling that Del Coma had had probable cause to arrest Chimel even without a warrant, and that both the arrest and search were thus legal? Under prodding by Assistant District Attorney Enright, Judge French clarified that he found Del Coma had had probable cause to arrest Chimel without an arrest warrant, thus making irrelevant the legality of the procedure under which the warrant had been issued.

Judge French had thus accepted the prosecution's argument, and the coins and other items seized from Chimel's house were admitted as evidence. Cross-examining Del Coma, Monroe brought out that not only had the master bedroom and the sewing room been searched but also a cursory search, at least, had been made of the entire house, the attic, the garage, and a small workroom.

Despite persistent questioning by Monroe, however, Del Coma refused to characterize the search as a "ransacking" of Chimel's house.

The trial ended on July 12, 1966, and the jury returned a verdict finding Chimel guilty of one count of first degree burglary and one count of second degree burglary.[14] Chimel's case was appealed to the California Court of Appeal, Fourth District, Second Division, where Monroe again challenged the judgment of the trial court on the grounds that the warrant for Chimel's arrest had been illegally issued and that the items from his home had been illegally seized. But on August 30, 1967, the court of appeal affirmed Chimel's conviction.

The court agreed with Monroe that the arrest warrant had been illegally issued and that the "statutory authority permitting the issuance of a warrant of arrest premised solely upon the formal allegation couched in the language of the charged offense suffers from a defect of constitutional proportions violative of the Fourth Amendment as applicable to the states through the Fourteenth Amendment." The court noted, however, the state's argument that, in the "absence of a valid warrant of arrest, . . . the arrest was justified independent of the warrant based on the personal knowledge of the arresting officer, T. Del Coma, which was sufficient to amount to probable cause for the arrest. . . ." The court of appeal agreed with the state's conclusion, but "not necessarily with its reasoning." Although "the presence of probable cause for the arrest by the personal knowledge of the arrest officers has been held to validate an otherwise invalid arrest, subjected to attack on *Giordenello-Aguilar* grounds," the court found that dependence on this rule might "induce officers to rely entirely upon arrests based upon 'probable cause.' Such a result would negate the Fourth Amendment almost in its entirety," the court warned. "Accordingly, we add that in the instance in which an officer has in good faith obtained a warrant for the arrest of the accused *and,* additionally, personally has knowledge to constitute probable cause for the arrest, otherwise invalid on *Giordenello-*

14. First degree burglary is punishable in California by five years to life in prison; second degree burglary is punishable by imprisonment in the county jail for one year or imprisonment in the state prison for one to fifteen years.

Aguilar . . . grounds, the arrest has been lawfully made and any of the fruits of the lawful search incident to such an arrest are fully admissible in evidence if material and relevant to prove any element of the offenses charged." The court of appeal thus affirmed Chimel's conviction on the basis of somewhat different reasoning than that used by the trial court.

Chimel's case was appealed to the California Supreme Court, which, at the time, was considering another case, *People v. Sesslin,* involving a challenge to the arrest procedures under the California Penal Code. In *Sesslin,* the court held that an "arrest warrant issued solely upon the complainant's 'information and belief' . . . cannot stand if the complaint or an accompanying affidavit does not allege underlying facts upon which the magistrate can independently find probable cause to arrest the accused." The court held, however, that the arrest procedures under the Penal Code would be construed to require such a showing of probable cause and were therefore valid under the Fourth Amendment.

The California Supreme Court's ruling in *Sesslin* clearly invalidated the warrant under which Chimel had been arrested. In its decision in *Chimel,* the court therefore held that the "complaints upon which both the September 13 and the September 16 arrest warrants were issued are the same type of printed form as the complaint held insufficient to support a valid warrant in *People v. Sesslin,*" and, "[f]or the reasons set forth in *Sesslin,* we hold that the warrants here, because of constitutional infirmity under the *Giordenello-Aguilar* standard, cannot support a legal arrest."

The court then held that the "legality of an arrest, however, cannot depend exclusively upon the validity of the warrant pursuant to which the arrest is executed since an arrest without a warrant may stand if based on probable cause." Reviewing the information that Officer Del Coma had at the time of Chimel's arrest, the court held that it was sufficient to constitute probable cause to arrest Chimel. The arrest and subsequent search were both therefore valid under the Fourth Amendment, the court held, despite the fact that the procedure by which the arrest warrant had been obtained was invalid.

The court did not believe

that the search, which occurred incident to an arrest based

upon probable cause, should be invalidated solely because of reliance upon a defective arrest warrant. If we were to rule otherwise, we would not only prevent the introduction of entirely proper evidence but also discourage officers from first presenting to a magistrate the evidence upon which they could later rely in establishing probable cause to justify an arrest and incidental search and seizure. Officers would very likely eschew the warrant that could both fall of its own weight and bring down with it the structure of an otherwise impeccable search and seizure.

Chimel's conviction was therefore affirmed by the California Supreme Court, and the appellate remedies available to Chimel in California were exhausted. The only remaining chance of overturning the conviction lay in a petition for certiorari to the United States Supreme Court. Keith Monroe filed such a petition on May 16, 1968, along with a motion for leave to proceed *in forma pauperis* in the Supreme Court, since Chimel was without funds to finance the appeal.[15] On November 25, the Court granted certiorari in *Chimel v. California.* The motion for leave to proceed *in forma pauperis* was subsequently granted, and the Court appointed Keith Monroe as free counsel for Chimel.

Ted Chimel had remained in jail during the appeal of his case through the California courts, since the trial court had denied bail pending appeal. Attorney Monroe now petitioned Justice Douglas, in his capacity as circuit justice, to order Chimel's release on bail pending the appeal to the Supreme Court. Douglas granted the petition on December 6, 1968, and Chimel was released on a $1,050 bond, after being incarcerated for twenty-eight months.

In arguing before the Supreme Court, Monroe considerably altered the theory upon which he had argued for a reversal of Chimel's conviction by the California courts. The basic defense contention at trial and on appeal in California had been that Chimel's arrest had been invalid. This contention had been rejected by the California courts on the ground that Officer Del Coma had had probable cause to arrest Chimel without a warrant.

---

15. A petition to proceed *in forma pauperis* may be filed with the Court when the defendant is indigent. If it is granted, the normal costs of appealing a case to the Court are waived, and free counsel is appointed for the indigent defendant. In the *Chimel* case, Keith Monroe continued to serve as Chimel's counsel before the Court.

In the face of this rejection, Monroe conceded before the Supreme Court that the arrest had been valid, and he focused instead on the validity of the search of Chimel's home as an incident to the arrest.

In his brief, Monroe reviewed the history of the freedom from unreasonable searches and seizures as it had developed in England up to its inclusion in the Bill of Rights of the United States Constitution. From this historical review, he concluded that under English common law any

> legal right to search a man's home was very, very grudgingly given, and when given it was attended by the strictist safeguards to preclude any arbitrary rummaging through a man's private possessions. And having fought a revolution based in part on the pernicious writs of assistance, it must be assumed that the framers of our own Constitution were fully familiar with the English law and had no intention of [retracting] it an inch.

Monroe thus argued that whenever it was reasonable for a police officer to obtain a warrant before searching a man's home, the Fourth Amendment required that a warrant be secured. The search of Chimel's home had therefore been illegal, he argued, because the search had not been based on a search warrant issued on a showing of probable cause, as required by the Fourth Amendment. Affirmation of Chimel's conviction, Monroe told the Court,

> would irresistibly lead to the conclusion that an officer's right to search a man's home is greater without a search warrant and without antecedent justification than it is with those protections. Resolutely, the foregoing conclusion, once reached, compels the further conclusion that search warrants should not in any case be used. This conclusion is equivalent to repeal of the Fourth Amendment. No Court can do that. Therefore, this case must be reversed.

Monroe suggested that the arrest in *Chimel* had been simply a ruse by which Officer Del Coma could search the house where the arrest had occurred, and that such conduct was encouraged by judicial decisions sustaining wide-ranging searches incident to arrests. Difficulties for Monroe's argument were, of course, posed by the Court's decisions in *Harris v. United States* and *United States v. Rabinowitz.* In those cases, the Court had upheld searches as incidents to lawful arrests, and in *Rabinowitz* it had held that such a search need not be conducted pursuant to a search warrant even if the officers had had a reasonable time to secure a warrant. In *Harris,* the warrantless search of a four-room apartment for several hours had been upheld as an incident to a lawful arrest. Monroe's argument that the search of Chimel's home was invalid under the Fourth Amendment thus necessarily involved the contention that *Harris* and *Rabinowitz* had been wrongly decided by the Court.

The "statement in *United States v. Rabinowitz* that in an otherwise reasonable search, a 'warrant is not required,' is erroneous," Monroe argued. "It is a derelict on the waters of the law and deserves once and for all time to be put to its final rest." He also argued that *Harris* and *Rabinowitz* provided insufficient guidelines for the lower courts to keep the scope of searches within reasonable bounds. In an appendix to his brief, Monroe included the results of research by law students at the University of California at Los Angeles, which indicated that the lower courts were construing the *Harris-Rabinowitz* line of cases expansively and upholding wide-ranging searches without warrants as incidents to arrests. This was another reason urged on the Court for abandoning that line of cases and reversing Chimel's conviction.

In urging the Court to affirm Chimel's conviction, the California attorney general argued that the "right under certain circumstances to conduct a reasonable search incident to arrest is well founded in the common law and this Court's decisions and is an essential technique in day-to-day law enforcement." The search of Chimel's home, the attorney general said, "was clearly reasonable under current standards, the continued validity of which is apparent in light of the necessity of balancing the traditional right of citizens to be free from unreasonable invasions of privacy with the need of citizens for effective law enforcement."

Officer Del Coma, the attorney general argued, had probable cause to arrest Chimel, and the subsequent search was "confined to areas where the arresting officer reasonably expected to find the fruits of the particular burglary for which petitioner had just been arrested." The intensive search of a four-room apartment that the Court had upheld in *Harris,* the attorney general said,

> dwarfs what took place here. Substitution of an inflexible standard for the present guideline of reasonableness under all the circumstances of the particular case would give rise to continued problems of definition and distinction. If the scope of a reasonable search is to be limited to a particular circumference around the suspect, or to the room where the arrest takes place, how large may the circumference or room be? What of hallways, and of a room that actually is no more than an area divided by a partition from the remainder of the room?

Given the reasonableness of the search of Chimel's home, the attorney general contended that it should not be invalidated merely because it was done without a search warrant. He pointed out that the problem of describing the numerous coins and other numismatic items in *Chimel* made it impractical for Officer Del Coma to obtain a search warrant. The attorney general noted studies indicating that it took two hours under ideal conditions to obtain a search warrant; a blanket rule that otherwise reasonable searches were invalid because of the absence of a warrant would impose a tremendous burden on police officers, prosecutors, and judges, he contended. "Nationwide," he said, "in 1967 there were 239,461 arrests for burglary alone (and 1,605,700 reported burglaries committed). A rule requiring a search warrant in all but emergency situations would place an intolerable burden on magistrates, prosecutors, and law enforcement officers without effecting a commensurate advancement of the rights of the individual."

Officer Del Coma had had probable cause to arrest Chimel, the attorney general concluded, and since the arrest was valid, the subsequent search incident to the arrest was also valid. The scope of the search had been reasonable, he argued, under *Harris* and *Rabinowitz,* given Del Coma's reasonable expectation of finding the fruits of Chimel's crime in the area of his home that was searched. The attorney general thus urged the Court to affirm Chimel's conviction.

The oral arguments were presented on March 27, 1969, and three months later, on June 23, 1969, the Court announced its decision. Justice Stewart wrote the majority opinion reversing Chimel's conviction and spelling out new standards that substantially narrowed the permissible scope of searches incident to arrests. Stewart was joined by Chief Justice Warren and Justices Douglas, Marshall, and Brennan; Justice Harlan concurred in the judgment of reversal, while Justice White, joined by Justice Black, dissented.[16]

CHIMEL V. CALIFORNIA
395 U.S. 752, decided June 23, 1969

Mr. Justice Stewart delivered the opinion of the Court.

This case raises basic questions concerning the permissible scope under the Fourth Amendment of a search incident to a lawful arrest. [Stewart then summarized the facts in the case.]

Without deciding the question, we proceed on the hypothesis that the California courts were correct in holding that the arrest of the petitioner was valid under the Constitution. This brings us directly to the question whether the warrantless search of the petitioner's entire house can be constitutionally justified as incident to that arrest. The decisions of this Court bearing upon that question have been far from consistent, as even the most cursory review makes evident.

Approval of a warrantless search incident to a lawful arrest seems first to have been articulated in Weeks v. United States . . . , in which the Court stated:

> What then is the present case? Before answering that inquiry specifically, it may be well by a process of exclusion to state what it is not. It is not an assertion of the right on the part of the Government, always recognized under English and American law, to search the person of the accused when legally arrested to discover and seize the fruits or evidences of crime . . . .

That statement made no reference to any right to search the *place* where an arrest occurs, but was limited to a right to search the "person." Eleven years later the case of Carroll v. United States . . . brought the following embellishment of the Weeks statement:

> When a man is legally arrested for an offense, whatever is found upon his person *or in his control* which it is unlawful for him to have and

16. Justice Abe Fortas had resigned from the Court on May 14, 1969.

which may be used to prove the offense may be seized and held as evidence in the prosecution . . . .

Still, that assertion too was far from a claim that the "place" where one is arrested may be searched so long as the arrest is valid. Without explanation, however, the principle emerged in expanded form a few months later in Agnello v. United States . . . —although still by way of dictum:

> The right without a search warrant contemporaneously to search persons lawfully arrested while committing crime and to search the place where the arrest is made in order to find and seize things connected with the crime as its fruits or as the means by which it was committed, as well as weapons and other things to effect an escape from custody, is not to be doubted. . . .

[In *Harris v. United States*, decided in 1947] officers had obtained a warrant for Harris' arrest on the basis of his alleged involvement with the cashing and interstate transportation of a forged check. He was arrested in the living room of his four-room apartment, and in an attempt to recover two canceled checks thought to have been used in effecting the forgery, the officers undertook a thorough search of the entire apartment. Inside a desk drawer they found a sealed envelope marked "George Harris, personal papers." The envelope, which was then torn open, was found to contain altered Selective Service documents, and those documents were used to secure Harris' conviction for violating the Selective Training and Service Act of 1940. The Court rejected Harris' Fourth Amendment claim, sustaining the search as "incident to arrest." . . .

Only a year after Harris, however, the pendulum swung again. In Trupiano v. United States . . . , agents raided the site of an illicit distillery, saw one of several conspirators operating the still, and arrested him, contemporaneously "seiz[ing] the illicit distillery." . . . The Court held that the arrest and others made subsequently had been valid, but that the unexplained failure of the agents to procure a search warrant—in spite of the fact that they had had more than enough time before the raid to do so—rendered the search unlawful. The opinion stated:

> It is a cardinal rule that, in seizing goods and articles, law enforcement agents must secure and use search warrants wherever reasonably practicable. . . . This rule rests upon the desirability of having magistrates rather than police officers determine when searches and seizures are permissible and what limitations should be placed upon such activities. . . . To provide the necessary security against unreasonable intrusions upon the private lives of individuals, the framers of the Fourth Amendment required adherence to judicial processes wherever possible. And subsequent history has confirmed the wisdom of that requirement. . . .

In 1950, two years after Trupiano, came United States v. Rabinowitz . . . , the decision upon which California primarily relies in the case now before us. In Rabinowitz, federal authorities had been informed that the defendant was dealing in stamps bearing forged overprints. On the basis of that information they secured a warrant for his arrest, which they executed at his one-room business office. At the time of the arrest, the officers "searched the desk, safe, and file cabinets in the office for about an hour and a half," . . . and seized 573 stamps with forged overprints. The stamps were admitted into evidence at the defendant's trial, and this Court affirmed his conviction, rejecting the contention that the warrantless search had been unlawful. The Court held that the search in its entirety fell within the principle giving law enforcement authorities "[t]he right 'to search the place where the arrest is made in order to find and seize things connected with the crime. . . . '" Harris was regarded as "ample authority" for that conclusion. . . . The opinion rejected the rule of Trupiano that "in seizing goods and articles, law enforcement agents must secure and use search warrants wherever reasonably practicable." The test, said the Court, "is not whether it is reasonable to procure a search warrant, but whether the search was reasonable. . . ."

Rabinowitz has come to stand for the proposition, inter alia, that a warrantless search "incident to a lawful arrest" may generally extend to the area that is considered to be in the "possession" or under the "control" of the person arrested. And it was on the basis of that proposition that the California courts upheld the search of the petitioner's entire house in this case. That doctrine, however, at least in the broad sense in which it was applied by the California courts in this case, can withstand neither historical nor rational analysis.

Even limited to its own facts, the Rabinowitz decision was, as we have seen, hardly founded on an unimpeachable line of authority. As Mr. Justice Frankfurter commented in dissent in that case, the "hint" contained in Weeks was, without persuasive justification, "loosely turned into dictum and finally elevated to a decision. . . ."

Nor is the rationale by which the State seeks here to sustain the search of the petitioner's house supported by a reasoned view of the background and purpose of the Fourth Amendment. Mr. Justice Frankfurter wisely pointed out in his Rabinowitz dissent that the Amendment's proscription of "unreasonable searches and seizures" must be read in light of "the history that gave rise to the words"—a history of "abuses so deeply felt by the Colonies as to be one of the potent causes of the Revolution. . . . " The Amendment was in large part a reaction to the general warrants and warrantless searches that had so alienated the colonists and had helped speed the movement for inde-

pendence. In the scheme of the Amendment, therefore, the requirement that
"no Warrant shall issue, but upon probable cause," plays a crucial part. As the
Court put it in McDonald v. United States . . . :

> We are not dealing with formalities. The presence of a search warrant
> serves a high function. Absent some grave emergency, the Fourth
> Amendment has interposed a magistrate between the citizen and the
> police. This was done not to shield criminals nor to make the home a
> safe haven for illegal activities. It was done so that an objective mind
> might weigh the need to invade that privacy . . . deemed too precious to
> entrust to the discretion of those whose job is the detection of crime
> and the arrest of criminals. . . . And so the Constitution requires a
> magistrate to pass on the desires of the police before they violate the
> privacy of the home. We cannot be true to that constitutional require-
> ment and excuse the absence of a search warrant without a showing by
> those who seek exemption from the constitutional mandate that the
> exigencies of the situation made that course imperative. . . .

Only last Term in Terry v. Ohio . . . , we emphasized that "the police
must, whenever practicable, obtain advance judicial approval of searches and
seizures through the warrant procedure," . . . and that "[t]he scope
of . . . search must be 'strictly tied to and justified by' the circumstances
which rendered its initiation permissible. . . . " The search undertaken by the
officer in that "stop and frisk" case was sustained under that test, because it
was no more than a "protective . . . search for weapons. . . . " But in a
companion case, Sibron v. New York . . . , we applied the same standard to
another set of facts and reached a contrary result, holding that a policeman's
action in thrusting his hand into a suspect's pocket had been neither motivated by nor limited to the objective of protection. Rather, the search had
been made in order to find narcotics, which were in fact found.

A similar analysis underlies the "search incident to arrest" principle,
and marks its proper extent. When an arrest is made, it is reasonable for the
arresting officer to search the person arrested in order to remove any weapons
that the latter might seek to use in order to resist arrest or effect his escape.
Otherwise, the officer's safety might well be endangered, and the arrest itself
frustrated. In addition, it is entirely reasonable for the arresting officer to
search for and seize any evidence on the arrestee's person in order to prevent
its concealment or destruction. And the area into which an arrestee might
reach in order to grab a weapon or evidentiary items must, of course, be
governed by a like rule. A gun on a table or in a drawer in front of one who is
arrested can be as dangerous to the arresting officer as one concealed in the
clothing of the person arrested. There is ample justification, therefore, for a
search of the arrestee's person and the area "within his immediate control"—
construing that phrase to mean the area from within which he might gain

possession of a weapon or destructible evidence.

There is no comparable justification, however, for routinely searching any room other than that in which an arrest occurs—or, for that matter, for searching through all the desk drawers or other closed or concealed areas in that room itself. Such searches, in the absence of well-recognized exceptions, may be made only under the authority of a search warrant. The "adherence to judicial processes" mandated by the Fourth Amendment requires no less. . . .

It is argued in the present case that it is "reasonable" to search a man's house when he is arrested in it. But that argument is founded on little more than a subjective view regarding the acceptability of certain sorts of police conduct, and not on considerations relevant to Fourth Amendment interests. Under such an unconfined analysis, Fourth Amendment protection in this area would approach the evaporation point. It is not easy to explain why, for instance, it is less subjectively "reasonable" to search a man's house when he is arrested on his front lawn—or just down the street—than it is when he happens to be in the house at the time of the arrest. . . .

It would be possible, of course, to draw a line between Rabinowitz and Harris on the one hand, and this case on the other. For Rabinowitz involved a single room, and Harris a four-room apartment, while in the case before us an entire house was searched. But such a distinction would be highly artificial. The rationale that allowed the searches and seizures in Rabinowitz and Harris would allow the searches and seizures in this case. No consideration relevant to the Fourth Amendment suggests any point of rational limitation, once the search is allowed to go beyond the area from which the person arrested might obtain weapons or evidentiary items. The only reasoned distinction is one between a search of the person arrested and the area within his reach on the one hand, and more extensive searches on the other.

The petitioner correctly points out that one result of decisions such as Rabinowitz and Harris is to give law enforcement officials the opportunity to engage in searches not justified by probable cause, by the simple expedient of arranging to arrest suspects at home rather than elsewhere. We do not suggest that the petitioner is necessarily correct in his assertion that such a strategy was utilized here, but the fact remains that had he been arrested earlier in the day, at his place of employment rather than at home, no search of his house could have been made without a search warrant. In any event, even apart from the possibility of such police tactics, the general point so forcefully made by Judge Learned Hand in United States v. Kirschenblatt . . . , remains:

> After arresting a man in his house, to rummage at will among his papers in search of whatever will convict him, appears to us to be indistinguishable from what might be done under a general warrant; indeed, the

warrant would give more protection, for presumably it must be issued by a magistrate. True, by hypothesis the power would not exist, if the supposed offender were not found on the premises; but it is small consolation to know that one's papers are safe only so long as one is not at home. . . .

Rabinowitz and Harris have been the subject of critical commentary for many years, and have been relied upon less and less in our own decisions. It is time, for the reasons we have stated, to hold that on their own facts, and insofar as the principles they stand for are inconsistent with those that we have endorsed today, they are no longer to be followed.

Application of sound Fourth Amendment principles to the facts of this case produces a clear result. The search here went far beyond the petitioner's person and the area within which he might have obtained either a weapon or something that could have been used as evidence against him. There was no constitutional justification, in the absence of a search warrant, for extending the search beyond that area. The scope of the search was, therefore, "unreasonable" under the Fourth and Fourteenth Amendments, and the petitioner's conviction cannot stand.

Reversed.

Mr. Justice Harlan, concurring.

I join the Court's opinion with these remarks concerning a factor to which the Court has not alluded. The only thing that has given me pause in voting to overrule Harris and Rabinowitz is that as a result of Mapp v. Ohio . . . and Ker v. California . . . , every change in Fourth Amendment law must now be obeyed by state officials facing widely different problems of local law enforcement. We simply do not know the extent to which cities and towns across the Nation are prepared to administer the greatly expanded warrant system which will be required by today's decision; nor can we say with assurance that in each and every local situation, the warrant requirement plays an essential role in the protection of those fundamental liberties protected against state infringement by the Fourteenth Amendment.

Thus, one is now faced with the dilemma . . . of choosing between vindicating sound Fourth Amendment principles at the possible expense of state concerns, long recognized to be consonant with the Fourteenth Amendment before Mapp and Ker came on the books, or diluting the Federal Bill of Rights in the interest of leaving the States at least some elbow room in their methods of criminal law enforcement. No comparable dilemma exists, of course, with respect to the impact of today's decision within the federal system itself.

This federal-state factor has not been an easy one for me to resolve, but in the last analysis I cannot in good conscience vote to perpetuate bad Fourth Amendment law.

I add only that this case [and other cases applying parts of the Bill of Rights to the states] serve to point up, as few other cases have, the profound changes that the "incorporation doctrine" has wrought both in the workings of our federal system and upon the adjudicative processes of this Court.

Mr. Justice White, with whom Mr. Justice Black joins, dissenting.

Few areas of the law have been as subject to shifting constitutional standards over the last 50 years as that of the search "incident to an arrest." There has been a remarkable instability in this whole area, which has seen at least four major shifts in emphasis. Today's opinion makes an untimely fifth. In my view, the Court should not now abandon the old rule. . . .

The modern odyssey of doctrine in this field is detailed in the majority opinion. . . .

The rule which has prevailed, but for very brief or doubtful periods of aberration, is that a search incident to an arrest may extend to those areas under the control of the defendant and where items subject to constitutional seizure may be found. The justification for this rule must, under the language of the Fourth Amendment, lie in the reasonableness of the rule. . . . In terms, then, the Court must decide whether a given search is reasonable. The Amendment does not proscribe "warrantless searches" but instead proscribes "unreasonable searches" and this Court has never held nor does the majority today assert that warrantless searches are necessarily unreasonable.

Applying this reasonableness test to the area of searches incident to arrests, one thing is clear at the outset. Search of an arrested man and of the items within his immediate reach must in almost every case be reasonable. There is always a danger that the suspect will try to escape, seizing concealed weapons with which to overpower and injure the arresting officers, and there is a danger that he may destroy evidence vital to the prosecution. Circumstances in which these justifications would not apply are sufficiently rare that inquiry is not made into searches of this scope, which have been considered reasonable throughout . . . .

This is not to say that a search can be reasonable without regard to the probable cause to believe that seizable items are on the premises. But when there are exigent circumstances, and probable cause, then the search may be made without a warrant, reasonably. An arrest itself may often create an emergency situation making it impracticable to obtain a warrant before embarking on a related search. Again assuming that there is probable cause to search premises at the spot where a suspect is arrested, it seems to me unreasonable to require the police to leave the scene in order to obtain a search warrant when they are already legally there to make a valid arrest, and when there must almost always be a strong possibility that confederates of the arrested man will in the meanwhile remove the items for which the police have probable cause to search. This must so often be the case that it seems to me as unreasonable to require a warrant for a search of the premises as to require a warrant for search of the person and his very immediate surroundings.

This case provides a good illustration of my point that it is unreasonable to require police to leave the scene of an arrest in order to obtain a search warrant when they already have probable cause to search and there is a clear danger that the items for which they may reasonably search will be removed before they return with a warrant. Petitioner was arrested in his home after an arrest whose validity will be explored below, but which I will now assume was valid. There was doubtless probable cause not only to arrest petitioner, but also to search his house. He had obliquely admitted, both to a neighbor and to the owner of the burglarized store, that he had committed the burglary. In light of this, and the fact that the neighbor had seen other admittedly stolen property in petitioner's house, there was surely probable cause on which a warrant could have issued to search the house for the stolen coins. Moreover, had the police simply arrested petitioner, taken him off to the station house, and later returned with a warrant, it seems very likely that petitioner's wife, who in view of petitioner's generally garrulous nature must have known of the robbery, would have removed the coins. For the police to search the house while the evidence they had probable cause to search out and seize was still there cannot be considered unreasonable. . . .

This line of analysis, supported by the precedents of this Court, hinges on two assumptions. One is that the arrest of petitioner without a valid warrant was constitutional as the majority assumes; the other is that the police were not required to obtain search warrant in advance, even though they knew that the effect of the arrest might well be to alert petitioner's wife that the coins had better be removed soon. Thus it is necessary to examine the constitutionality of the arrest since if it was illegal, the exigent circumstances which it created may not, as the consequences of a lawless act, be used to justify the contemporaneous warrantless search. But for the arrest, the warrantless search may not be justified. And if circumstances can justify the warrantless arrest, it would be strange to say that the Fourth Amendment bars the warrantless search, regardless of the circumstances, since the invasion and disruption of a man's life and privacy which stem from his arrest are ordinarily far greater than the relatively minor intrusions attending a search of his premises.

Congress has expressly authorized a wide range of officials to make arrests without any warrant in criminal cases. United States Marshals have long had this power, which is also vested in the agents of the Federal Bureau of Investigation, and the Secret Service and the narcotics law enforcement agency. That warrantless arrest power may apply even when there is time to get a warrant without fear that the suspect may escape is made perfectly clear by the legislative history of the statute granting arrest power to the FBI. . . .

In light of the uniformity of judgment of the Congress, past judicial decisions, and common practice rejecting the proposition that arrest warrants are essential wherever it is practicable to get them, the conclusion is inevitable that such arrests and accompanying searches are reasonable, at least until experience teaches the contrary. It must very often be the case that by the time probable cause to arrest a man is accumulated, the man is aware of police interest in him or for other good reasons is on the verge of flight. Moreover, it will likely be very difficult to determine the probability of his flight. Given this situation, it may be best in all cases simply to allow the arrest if there is probable cause, especially since that issue can be determined very shortly after the arrest.

Nor are the stated assumptions at all fanciful. It was precisely these facts which moved the Congress to grant to the FBI the power to arrest without a warrant without any showing of probability of flight. . . .

If circumstances so often require the warrantless arrest that the law generally permits it, the typical situation will find the arresting officers lawfully on the premises without arrest or search warrant. Like the majority, I would permit the police to search the person of a suspect and the area under his immediate control either to assure the safety of the officers or to prevent the destruction of evidence. And like the majority, I see nothing in the arrest alone furnishing probable cause for a search of any broader scope. However, where as here the existence of probable cause is independently established and would justify a warrant for a broader search for evidence, I would follow past cases and permit such a search to be carried out without a warrant, since the fact of arrest supplies an exigent circumstance justifying police action before the evidence can be removed, and also alerts the suspect to the fact of the search so that he can immediately seek judicial determination of probable cause in an adversary proceeding, and appropriate redress. . . .

The majority today proscribes searches for which there is probable cause and which may prove fruitless unless carried out immediately. This rule will have no added effect whatsoever in protecting the rights of the criminal accused at trial against introduction of evidence seized without probable cause. Such evidence could not be introduced under the old rule. Nor does the majority today give any added protection to the right to privacy of those whose houses there is probable cause to search. A warrant would still be sworn out for those houses, and the privacy of their owners invaded. The only possible justification for the majority's rule is that in some instances arresting officers may search when they have no probable cause to do so and that such unlawful searches might be prevented if the officers first sought a warrant from a magistrate. Against the possible protection of privacy in that class of cases, in which the privacy of the house has already been invaded by entry to make the arrest—an entry for which the majority does not assert that any warrant is necessary—must be weighed the risk of destruction of evidence for which there is probable cause to search, as a result of delays in obtaining a search warrant. Without more basis for radical change than the Court's opinion reveals, I would not upset the balance of these interests which has been struck by the former decisions of the Court. . . .

An arrested man, by definition conscious of the police interest in him, and provided almost immediately with a lawyer and a judge, is in an excellent position to dispute the reasonableness of his arrest and contemporaneous search in a full adversary proceeding. I would uphold the constitutionality of this search contemporaneous with an arrest since there were probable cause both for the search and for the arrest, exigent circumstance involving the removal or destruction of evidence, and a satisfactory opportunity to dispute the issues of probable cause shortly thereafter. In this case, the search was reasonable.

The Court thus reversed *Harris v. United States* and *United States v. Rabinowitz* and significantly restricted the scope of searches incident to lawful arrests. Such searches, it held, could include only the person of the individual arrested and the immediate surroundings from which he might obtain a weapon or destroy seizable evidence. Since the scope of the search of Ted Chimel's home had far exceeded these limits, the Court reversed his conviction.

Chimel had served more than two years in jail before his release on bond pending appeal to the Court. With the ruling that the evidence seized at Chimel's home had to be excluded from the trial, California prosecuting authorities decided that they had insufficient evidence to justify a retrial of Chimel, and he became a free man once again. In December 1969, however, he was again arrested for possession of stolen goods, this time a stamp collection.

He was subsequently declared legally insane and was committed to the Atascadero State Hospital. After remaining an inmate there for a little more than a year, he was declared sane enough to stand trial. Representing Chimel on the stolen stamp charge, Keith Monroe struck a plea bargain with the prosecution that reduced the charge to receiving stolen property. Chimel was sentenced to one year in jail, but he received credit for the time he had served at Atascadero and in pretrial incarceration, with the result that he went free on three years' probation.

"All went well during almost all of the three years probation," Keith Monroe said, "and I really came to believe that Ted would not follow in the footsteps of Ernesto Miranda and Danny Escobedo by nonetheless winding up in prison. Probation was to expire, of course, on September 20, 1974. An hour or two after midnight on August 18-19, my bedside phone commenced jangling. Ted, according to a friend of his on the wire, had several hours before been arrested while apparently in the course of emptying a parking meter of its contents." The saga of Ted Chimel's troubles with the law therefore continued.

The *Chimel* decision not only narrowed the permissible scope of searches incident to lawful arrests, but also marked the end of an era for the Court. The day the decision was announced, June 23, 1969, was Chief Justice Earl Warren's last day on the Court. Warren had announced in 1968 that he would retire, but his retirement had been postponed by the defeat of President Johnson's nomination of Justice Fortas to succeed him. President Nixon had requested that Warren serve until the end of the 1968-69 Court term, which was June 23, 1969, the day *Chimel* was decided.

In his 1968 campaign for the presidency, Richard Nixon had stressed the "law and order" issue and had blamed the rapid rise in the crime rate on permissive decisions by the Court. As president, Nixon had the opportunity to appoint not only a new chief justice but also three associate justices within his first two years in office, due to the retirement of Chief Justice Warren, the resignation of Justice Fortas in 1969, and the deaths of Justices Black and

Table 4
PERSONNEL OF THE WARREN AND BURGER COURTS

Justices of the Court in 1969	*Justices of the Court in 1975*
Warren, C.J. (retired June 23, 1969)	Burger, C.J. (sworn in June 1969)
Black (died, September 1971)	Powell (sworn in December 1971)
Douglas	Douglas
Harlan (died, December 1971)	Rehnquist (sworn in Dec. 1971)
Brennan	Brennan
Stewart	Stewart
White	White
Fortas (resigned May 14, 1969)	Blackmun (sworn in June, 1970)
Marshall	Marshall

Harlan in 1971. Although Nixon's promise to appoint "strict constructionists" to the Court had not been free of ambiguity, the clear inference had been that his appointees would be less liberal on criminal procedure issues than the majority of the Warren Court had been. This proved to be true of Warren Earl Burger, Harry Blackmun, Lewis Powell, and William Rehnquist. The Court that had sat on June 23, 1969, was soon substantially transformed by the Nixon appointments. (See table 4.)

Despite this transformation, however, the Burger Court has not engaged in dramatic reversals of Warren Court decisions in the field of criminal procedure; rather it has generally limited the principles of the Warren Court decisions, while taking a more generous view of the claims of law enforcement officials than those of criminal defendants.

Nine years after its announcement by the Warren Court, for example, the *Miranda* decision stands unreversed. But the Burger Court did hold in 1971, in *Harris v. New York,* that statements made by a criminal defendant under interrogation without prior *Miranda* warnings could be used by the prosecution for the purpose of impeaching the defendant's credibility if he chose to testify in his own behalf. On the other hand, the Court in 1972 extended the principles of one of the Warren Court's most important decisions, *Gideon v. Wainwright,* by holding in *Argersinger v. Hamlin* that indigent criminal defendants must have appointed counsel in any case involving a potential loss of liberty. It thus extended the *Gideon* rule to misdemeanor cases involving possible jail terms.

In the field of searches and seizures, the Burger Court has also whittled away at some Warren Court decisions without, however, pronouncing any dramatic reversals. Although Chief Justice Burger early announced his opposition to the exclusionary rule (see his 1971 dissent in *Bivens v. Six Unknown Agents*), neither *Mapp* nor *Weeks* has been reversed, and evidence seized in violation of the Fourth Amendment continues to be excluded in both state and federal courts. And the Burger Court in 1972 rejected the Nixon administration's contention that the government could eavesdrop electronically on or wiretap those suspected of "domestic subversion," without prior authorization via the warrant requirements of the Fourth Amendment (*United States v. United States District Court*).

On the other hand, the Burger Court has held that law enforcement officers need not advise an individual of his right against unreasonable searches and seizures before requesting consent for a search (*Schneckloth v. Bustamonte,* decided in 1973), in contrast to the *Miranda* requirement that a suspect be advised of his rights under the self-incrimination clause before interrogation. The Court has also held that demands by grand juries for voice and handwriting exemplars are not "searches and seizures," nor is a subpoena to appear before a grand jury a "seizure," within the meaning of the Fourth Amendment (*United States v. Dionisio,* and *United States v. Mara,* both 1973 decisions). And the Court in 1974 refused to extend the exclusionary rule to prohibit the use of unconstitutionally seized evidence as the basis of questioning before a grand jury (*United States v. Calandra*).

Although *Chimel* has not been reversed, the Court has upheld rather extensive warrantless searches of individuals lawfully arrested for traffic violations. In two 1973 cases, *United States v. Robinson* and *Gustafson v. Florida,* the Court upheld full searches of individuals lawfully arrested for traffic violations, without any showing of probable cause to believe that further evidence of the traffic violations would be discovered. With Justices Douglas,

Brennan, and Marshall dissenting, the Court held that a

> custodial arrest of a suspect based on probable cause is a rea-
> sonable intrusion under the Fourth Amendment; that intrus-
> ion being lawful, a search incident to the arrest requires no
> additional justification. It is the fact of the lawful arrest
> which establishes the authority to search, and we hold that in
> the case of a lawful custodial arrest a full search of the person
> is not only an exception to the warrant requirement of the
> Fourth Amendment, but is also a "reasonable" search under
> that Amendment.

The Court thus upheld the seizure of heroin (in *Robinson*) and
marijuana (in *Gustafson*) on persons lawfully arrested for traffic
violations and rejected claims that these went beyond the valid
scope of searches incident to lawful arrests.

Significant changes in the criminal procedure decisions of the
Warren Court have tended to hinge upon the votes of Justices
White and Stewart. When one of them joins the Nixon appointees
(Burger, Blackmun, Powell, and Rehnquist), a more conservative
majority of the Court is formed. The remnant of the Warren
Court's liberal majority (Douglas, Brennan, and Marshall), on the
other hand, needs the votes of both White and Stewart to form a
majority. Given Justice White's conservative propensities in the
field of criminal procedure, the tendency of the Burger Court has
clearly swung against the claims of criminal defendants. How
permanent this shift in the Court's criminal procedure policy will
be depends substantially upon future personnel changes on the
Court.

Chapter Three

THE SUPREME COURT AND FREEDOM OF EXPRESSION POLICY

Introduction Although the First Amendment guarantees of freedom of speech and of the press were added to the Constitution in 1791, it was not until 1919 that the Supreme Court began systematically to address the question of the scope of these guarantees. Not until the *Gitlow-Fiske-Stromberg-Near* line of cases, decided between 1925 and 1931, were freedom of speech and freedom of the press held to be guaranteed by the due process clause of the Fourteenth Amendment against infringement by the states. As enunciated by the Court, constitutional policy on freedom of expression has therefore been developed during the past fifty years.

One of the perennial problems in this field of policy has been the extent to which freedom of speech and of the press protects the advocacy of unlawful action. In the first authoritative interpretation of freedom of speech, *Schenck v. United States,* in 1919, Justice Holmes, writing for the Court, formulated the "clear and present danger" doctrine as the proper test of the extent to which the First Amendment protected the advocacy of unlawful action.

"The question in every case," Holmes said, "is whether the words used are used in such circumstances and are of such a nature as to create a clear and present danger that they will bring about the substantive evils that Congress has a right to prevent." The clear and present danger doctrine thus suggested that government need not wait until advocacy of unlawful action had actually produced such action, but rather that government could punish speech itself when it created a clear and present danger of unlawful action. It also suggested, on the other hand, that government had to demonstrate that the unlawful action was relatively imminent before speech could be constitutionally proscribed.

While the clear and present danger doctrine is perhaps the most widely known test of the scope of freedom of expression, it has had a checkered history of acceptance by the Court. Although Justice Holmes spoke for a unanimous Court in the *Schenck* case, it soon became apparent that a majority of his colleagues did not accept his formulation of the doctrine. In *Gitlow v. New York,* decided in 1925, a majority of the Court held that a legislature could determine what kinds of expression were likely to create clear and present dangers of unlawful action, and that the Court's only function in passing on the validity of such laws was to decide whether they were reasonable. It was clear from *Gitlow* that the majority was not following the clear and present danger doctrine, since Justice Holmes reiterated and defended the doctrine in an eloquent dissent.

Although the doctrine enjoyed an intermittent revival in Court decisions during the 1940s, the Court again backed away from the doctrine in *Dennis v. United States,* a 1951 case in which the Court sustained the convictions of leaders of the Communist Party for advocating the violent overthrow of the government. Although the government failed to demonstrate in *Dennis* that the defendants' advocacy had produced an imminent attempt to overthrow the government, the Court nonetheless held that the proper test under the First Amendment was "whether the gravity of the 'evil,' discounted by its improbability, justifies such an invasion of free speech as is necessary to avoid the danger." A majority of the Court held that the gravity of the evil in *Dennis*—the possible attempt to overthrow the government—even discounting its improbability, justified punishment of the Communists for advocating violent overthrow. This "gravity of the evil" test was a rather pale and faded replica of the original clear and present danger doctrine. In another case involving prosecution of members of the Communist Party, *Yates v. United States,* in 1957, the Court refined its *Dennis* holding by stating that the First Amendment did protect advocacy of unlawful action in the abstract or as a matter of theoretical discussion. What the First Amendment did not protect, the Court said, was incitement of unlawful action.

Probably the best summary of the Court's contemporary position on the extent to which the First Amendment protects advocacy of unlawful action may be found in *Brandenburg v. Ohio,* decided in 1969. There the Court said that its decisions had "fashioned the principle that the constitutional guarantees of free speech and free press do not permit a State to forbid or proscribe advocacy of the use of force or of law violation except where such advocacy is directed to inciting or producing imminent action and is likely to incite or produce such action." The contemporary policy appears to be, therefore, that the First Amendment protects the advocacy of unlawful action, and, in order for such advocacy to be proscribed, it must be directed at producing imminent unlawful action and be likely to bring such action about.

Another measure of the scope of free expression that the Court has used extensively in recent years is a doctrine enunciated in *Chaplinsky v. New Hampshire* in 1942. Speaking for the Court, Justice Frank Murphy held that there were certain "well-defined and narrowly limited classes of speech, the prevention and punishment of which have never been thought to raise any Constitutional problem. These include the lewd and obscene, the profane, the libelous, and the insulting or 'fighting words'—those which of their very nature inflict injury or tend to incite an immediate breach of the peace." Such forms of expression, Murphy suggested, were not protected by the First Amendment, because they could not be considered as "an essential part of any exposition of ideas and are of such slight social value as a step to truth that any benefit that may be derived from them is clearly outweighed by the social interest in order and morality." In *Chaplinsky,* the

Court thus sustained the conviction of a Jehovah's Witness for calling a police officer a "God damned racketeer" and a "damned Fascist" on the grounds that such expression constituted the use of "fighting words," likely to provoke an immediate violent reaction from those to whom they were addressed, and the expression served no useful purpose in the exposition of ideas.

The *Chaplinsky* decision suggested that the purpose of the guarantee of free expression in the First Amendment was to protect the expression of ideas with socially redeeming value. If certain forms of expression had no socially redeeming value, they were outside the protection of the First Amendment, and Justice Murphy suggested that "fighting words," obscene expressions, and libel had such a nature. The *Chaplinsky* doctrine thus denied First Amendment protection to certain forms of expression, such as obscene and libelous statements, because of their content, regardless of whether they created any imminent danger of unlawful or antisocial action. In recent years, the Court has expanded on the *Chaplinsky* doctrine in decisions attempting to define obscenity and libel as they relate to the First Amendment.

The Court first attempted to define obscenity in *Roth v. United States* and *Alberts v. California* in 1957. Writing for the Court, Justice Brennan again repeated the *Chaplinsky* doctrine that obscene expression was beyond the protection of the First Amendment because it was "utterly without redeeming social importance." A work was obscene, Brennan said, if "to the average person, applying contemporary community standards, the dominant theme of the material taken as a whole appeals to the prurient interests." And in a series of decisions culminating in *A Book (Fanny Hill) v. Attorney General*, decided in 1966, the Court held that the definition of obscenity required that (1) the dominant theme of the material taken as a whole must appeal to a prurient interest in sex; (2) the material must be patently offensive because it affronts contemporary community standards relating to the description or representation of sexual matters; and (3) the material must be utterly without redeeming social value. While still excluding obscenity from First Amendment protection, the Court managed to define obscenity by the late 1960s so that it was rather difficult to condemn any work as obscene, since such a work had to be utterly without social value as well as being patently offensive and appealing to a prurient interest in sex.

The Warren Court, however, was badly divided on the definition of obscenity, and during its later years it did not attempt to further refine its obscenity rulings but rather reversed most obscenity convictions without opinion. The Burger Court, on the other hand, chose to redefine obscenity somewhat in *Miller v. California* in 1973. (Justices Douglas, Brennan, Stewart, and Marshall dissented from the ruling.) Writing for the Court, Chief Justice Burger held that a work was obscene if (1) to the average person, applying contemporary community standards, it appealed to the prurient interest; (2) the work depicted or described, in a patently offensive way, sexual conduct specifically defined by the applicable state law; and (3) the work taken as a whole lacked serious literary, artistic, political, or scientific value. The Court further held that the "community standards" to be applied in testing the question of obscenity are those of the local community rather than "hypothetical and unascertainable" national standards.

Miller thus revised the tests of obscenity that had been generally applicable during the Warren Court period. The principal changes were the Court's rejection of the idea that a work must be utterly without redeeming social value in order to be obscene and its acceptance of local, rather than national, community standards for the test of obscenity. Under *Miller,* a work may be found obscene if it lacks any serious literary, artistic, political, or scientific value, according to local community standards, but it need not be *utterly* without redeeming social value. The *Miller* redefinition would, at least theoretically, allow the suppression of more works as obscene than the Warren Court standards had.

The Court has also used the *Chaplinsky* doctrine in its approach to libel cases. In *New York Times v. Sullivan,* decided in 1964, the Court reaffirmed the *Chaplinsky* doctrine that deliberate lies were beyond the protection of the First Amendment because of their lack of socially redeeming value. But the Court held that a rule allowing libel judgments against the media for unintentional falsehoods about public officials would lead to self-censorship and would unduly inhibit free expression. It therefore held that a public official could not be awarded a libel judgment "for a defamatory falsehood relating to his official conduct unless he proves that the statement was made with 'actual malice'—that is, with knowledge that it was false or with reckless disregard to whether it was false or not."

The *New York Times* test was subsequently extended by the Court to apply to libel actions brought by "public figures" as well as public officials (*Associated Press v. Walker* and *Curtis Publishing Co. v. Butts,* in 1967). Those persons who, although not public officials, "are nevertheless intimately involved in the resolution of important public questions, or, by reason of their fame, shape events in areas of concern to society at large," were held by the Court to come under the *New York Times* test for libel actions.

Subsequently, however, the Court became badly divided on the question of whether the *New York Times* test, with its greater protection for the media from libel actions, should be extended to apply to libel suits brought by private individuals who were neither public officials nor public figures but who became involved in events of public interest. When this problem was addressed in *Rosenbloom v. Metromedia* in 1971, the result was five different opinions from the Court, none of which commanded the support of more than three of the justices.

In 1974, in *Gertz v. Welch,* the Court, divided five to four, held that the *New York Times* test did not apply to libel actions instituted by private individuals. Again affirming the *Chaplinsky* doctrine, the majority held that under "the First Amendment there is no such thing as a false idea. However pernicious an opinion may seem, we depend for its correction not on the conscience of judges and juries but on the competition of other ideas. But there is no constitutional value in false statements of fact. Neither the intentional lie nor the careless error materially advances society's interest in 'uninhibited, robust, and wide-open' debate on public issues." While acknowledging the validity of the *New York Times* rule as applied to public officials and public figures, the Court held that private individuals "are not only more vulnerable to injury [from libel] than public officials and public figures" but "also more deserving of recovery."

The Court concluded that "so long as they do not impose liability without fault, the States may define for themselves the appropriate standard of liability for a publisher or broadcaster of defamatory falsehood injurious to a private individual." The Court further held, however, that damages in libel suits involving private individuals should be limited to compensatory damages; punitive damages should be awarded only on a showing of knowledge of falsity or reckless disregard for the truth.[17]

In addition to the free expression problems raised by the advocacy of unlawful action and those the Court has addressed under the *Chaplinsky* doctrine, the question of the extent to which the First Amendment protects what has been called "expression-plus" has constituted another major policy problem for the Court in recent years. Expression-plus involves conduct that also either serves or is related to the expression of views. The principal question in most expression-plus cases is the extent to which the government may regulate or prohibit conduct or physical action that also involves the expression of views.

The classic example of expression-plus is picketing, which consists of both the expression of views and the physical conduct of parading in a given location. The Court accorded picketing the protection of the First Amendment in 1940, in *Thornhill v. Alabama,* but it soon acknowledged that the conduct element in picketing justified greater governmental regulation than other forms of "pure expression," since the physical conduct aspect of picketing could be the dominant aspect of the activity. The Court subsequently upheld governmental regulation or prohibition of mass picketing, picketing for an illegal purpose, and picketing attended by violence, on the ground that the expression element of picketing in such cases had been overborne and submerged by the physical conduct involved.

In more recent years, the dominant forms of expression-plus have included not only picketing but also demonstrations, street parades, and various forms of "symbolic speech." In *Edwards v. South Carolina,* decided in 1963, the Court recognized that demonstrations protesting racial segregation were protected by the

17. Compensatory damages are damages awarded in libel cases, usually by a jury, to compensate the plaintiff for the actual injuries the libel has caused him; punitive damages are awarded to the plaintiff to punish the perpetrator of the libel and to deter him from such conduct in the future.

First Amendment, but in subsequent cases it held that demonstrations and parading could be legitimately restricted by narrowly drawn statutes regulating the time, place, duration, and manner of these forms of expression-plus. Permits regulating the time and duration of street parades could be required if the permit regulations were administered in a nondiscriminatory manner, the Court held in *Cox v. Louisiana,* in 1965. And demonstrations or picketing that interfered with the proceedings in a courthouse, blocked entrances to public buildings, or interfered with the use to which public property was dedicated could be prohibited altogether (*Cameron v. Johnson,* in 1968; *Adderley v. Florida,* in 1966).

In a leading case involving "symbolic speech," the Court in 1968 refused to accord First Amendment protection to the burning of draft cards, despite the argument that such "symbolic speech" was a form of political protest against the Vietnam War (*United States v. O'Brien*). The Court refused to accept the view "that an apparently limitless variety of conduct can be labeled 'speech' whenever the person engaging in the conduct intends thereby to express an idea." When speech and nonspeech elements were combined, the Court said, and the government demonstrated a sufficiently compelling interest in regulating the conduct or nonspeech element, then "symbolic speech" might be prohibited altogether. In *O'Brien,* the Court held, the governmental interest in the administration of the draft, including the requirement of possession of draft cards by those eligible, was a sufficiently compelling interest to justify the prohibition of the burning of draft cards.

In contrast to *O'Brien,* however, the Court held in *Tinker v. Des Moines Community School District,* in 1969, that the First Amendment protected the wearing of black armbands by students in the public schools as a protest against the Vietnam War. The suppression of such "symbolic speech," the Court held, could not be justified by any compelling governmental interest, since there was no demonstration that school discipline was adversely affected, and the conduct involved was peaceful and nondisruptive.

In 1971, the Court's doctrines regarding the scope of free expression protected by the First Amendment came to be sorely tested in another case involving a protest against the Vietnam War, and the result was a Court opinion in which almost all the doctrines and tests of the scope of freedom of expression were brought to bear. We shall now examine in detail Paul Robert Cohen's trouble with the law in California, and the Court's subsequent decision in *Cohen v. California.*

Case Study

MUST EXPLETIVES BE DELETED?
THE "FUCK THE DRAFT" CASE

Paul Robert Cohen was a nineteen-year-old resident of Los Angeles, California, where he was employed by Ohrbach's Department Store. On the evening of April 25, 1968, he attended a gathering of friends and acquaintances at which opposition to the Vietnam War and the necessity of public opposition to the war and the draft were discussed. During the meeting, someone (Cohen did not know who) wrote the words "Fuck the Draft," "Stop War," and a peace symbol on Cohen's jacket.

Although he was aware that the words were on his jacket, Cohen wore his jacket the following day, because, he said later, the weather was cold and it was the only jacket he owned. He proceeded to the Los Angeles county courthouse and ultimately entered and observed the proceedings in Division 20 of the municipal court. He wore his jacket while in the corridors of the courthouse, but he removed the jacket and held it folded over his arm while in the courtroom.

While in the corridor, however, Cohen and the message his jacket bore were observed by Police Sergeant Huston Splawn and other officers. Sergeant Splawn saw Cohen entering the courtroom of the municipal court, and the sergeant sent a message to the presiding judge of Division 20 requesting that Cohen be arrested for contempt of court, but the judge refused the request. When Cohen left the courtroom, however, Sergeant Splawn arrested him and advised him of his rights.

On April 29, 1968, a complaint was filed in the Municipal Court of the Los Angeles Judicial District charging that Cohen "did wilfully and unlawfully and maliciously disturb the peace and quiet" by "engaging in tumultuous and offensive conduct" in violation of section 415 of the California Penal Code. Represented by a deputy public defender, Cohen was arraigned on this charge on May 1, and upon his plea of not guilty, his bail was set at $625.

Paul Cohen's case did not come on for trial until September, but in the meantime his cause attracted rather significant support. The Southern California Civil Liberties Union was made aware of the case, and it concluded that Cohen's expression of views on the Vietnam War and the draft via the message on his jacket constituted a form of constitutionally protected expression under the First Amendment. The organization therefore undertook to finance Cohen's defense and provide an attorney at his trial. Melville B. Nimmer, chairman of the Lawyers' Committee of the SCCLU and a professor at UCLA Law School, became Cohen's counsel.

The trial was held in the municipal court before Judge James Harvey Brown. Three police officers testified that they had observed Cohen in the courthouse and had observed the words on his jacket. They also testified that women and children were present in the corridors of the courthouse during Cohen's presence, but, on cross-examination by Nimmer, they conceded that Cohen had not engaged in any acts of violence, nor had any persons been incited by his conduct to threaten or commit any acts of violence. The officers also testified that they had not observed Cohen causing the emission of any loud or unusual noises. Cohen testified in his own behalf and related how the messages had come to be on his jacket. He had worn the jacket because it was cold, he said, but he had also worn it to inform the public of the depth of his feelings against the war and the draft.

Judge Brown ruled during the trial that section 415 of the Penal Code, which prohibited "tumultuous or offensive" conduct, should be construed to prohibit written words even if unaccompanied by any actual or threatened violence and that Cohen could be convicted under the section for using "vulgar, profane, or indecent language" within the presence of women or children in a loud and boistrous manner, even if the language was written rather than oral. Attorney Nimmer objected to this ruling to no avail. Judge Brown also rejected Nimmer's contention that Cohen's expression of his views was protected by the First and Fourteenth Amendments, and ruled that the words "Fuck the Draft" were within the constitutional definition of obscenity. Cohen was found guilty of violating section 415 by the judge, and he was sentenced to thirty days in the county jail.

Nimmer appealed Cohen's conviction to the Appellate Department of the Los Angeles County Superior Court, and on January 20, 1969, that court reversed the trial judge, ruling that Cohen's wearing of the jacket and message had not constituted "tumultuous and offensive" conduct. "There was no evidence that the conduct of the appellant was tumultuous, and conduct that is merely offensive is insufficient," the appellate department held. "Appellant may have been guilty of other offenses, but he was not guilty of the offense of which he was convicted."

A petition for a rehearing of the appellate department's reversal was filed by the Los Angeles city attorney, and the court granted a rehearing on February 13. After reargument, however, the appellate department on May 23 again announced its reversal of Cohen's conviction. The court noted that Cohen's conduct had not incited any actual or threatened violence and that his counsel had contended that the trial court's construction of section 415 violated the First and Fourteenth Amendment guarantees of freedom of expression. The court concluded, however, that this constitutional question need not be reached, since it construed section 415 to prohibit tumultuous *and* offensive conduct, although the statute said tumultuous *or* offensive. Its construction of section 415 was justified, the court said, because the section was part of a general disturbance of the peace statute that prohibited offenses involving "noise, disturbance, or conflict." Unless section 415 were read to prohibit "tumultuous *and* offensive conduct," it said, an individual could be convicted for "offensive conduct" alone even though the conduct was quiet and peaceful.

If section 415 did allow a conviction for quiet and peaceful offensive conduct, the court concluded that the section would be vulnerable to constitutional attack on the grounds that it was vague and indefinite, since it failed "to indicate in what respect the conduct must be 'offensive.' For example, if one is engaged in such offensive conduct as picking his nose in public or failing to use the proper deodorant, could he be held guilty of disturbing the peace? These uncertainties could be avoided by limiting the 'offensive' conduct to that which is also 'tumultuous.' " Cohen's conduct had been "reprehensible," but "quiet and peaceful," the court continued. "He neither engaged in, threatened, nor incited any acts of violence. Moreover, it is conceded by the prosecution that appellant's conduct was not 'tumultuous.' In the absence of conduct that was 'tumultuous *and* offensive,' the appellant was not guilty of disturbing the peace in violation of Section 415 of the Penal Code." The appellate department also ruled that the trial judge had erred in holding that Cohen could be convicted for using "vulgar, profane, or indecent language within the presence of women and children, in a loud and boisterous manner," since Cohen had not been charged with that offense. Once again, therefore, the decision of the municipal court was reversed.

On June 5, 1969, however, the appellate department certified the *Cohen* case to the California Court of Appeal, Second Appellate District, Division Two, on the question of whether the appellate department's construction of section 415 had been correct. On October 22, the court of appeal announced a decision reversing the appellate department and reinstating Cohen's conviction. The court construed section 415 to prohibit either tumultuous or offensive conduct and held that the kind of offensive conduct prohibited was the use of "fighting words" that were likely to provoke others to violence. "Thus under Section 415," the court of appeal said, "a person who engages in offensive behavior which has a tendency to provoke *others* to acts of violence or to in turn disturb the peace and quiet is guilty of disturbing the peace although his own conduct, while offensive, was not in itself violent." It should have been reasonably foreseeable by Cohen, the court continued, that his "conduct might cause others to rise up to commit a violent act against the person of the defendant or attempt to forcibly remove his jacket. The fact that the police intervened and that the defendant was arrested before violence occurred does not make his conduct any the less provocative. We think it also a reasonable inference from the time and place of defendant's act that he intended to provoke disorder."

As Cohen's counsel, Melville Nimmer had argued before the court of appeal that section 415 was vague and indefinite if construed to prohibit "offensive conduct" and that, as applied in Cohen's case, the section violated the freedom of expression guaranteed by the First and Fourteenth Amendments. The court rejected these contentions, holding instead that the kind of offensive conduct prohibited was conduct "which incites violence or has a tendency to incite others to violence or a breach of the peace," and that by restricting offensive conduct to embrace only such "fighting words" section 415 was not vague or indefinite. On the freedom of expression argument, the court of appeal held that Cohen's actions had been primarily conduct or at most expression-plus, such as the draft card burning in *United States v. O'Brien,* and that here, as in *O'Brien,* the government had a compelling interest in regulating or prohibiting that conduct, which overrode any communicative element in the conduct. The court additionally held that the "Fuck the Draft" message on Cohen's jacket constituted "fighting words" and was thus beyond the scope of protection of the First and Fourteenth Amendments under the doctrine of *Chaplinsky.*

Cohen's offense, the court said, "was his selection of the public corridors of the county courthouse as the place to parade before women and children who were involuntarily subjected to unprintable language. The expression used by the defendant to propagate his views is one of the most notorious four-letter words in the English language. Despite its ancient origins, it has yet to gain sufficient acceptance to appear in any standard dictionary." The court noted, "The defendant has not been subjected to prosecution for expressing his political views. His right to speak out against the draft and war is protected by the First Amendment. However, no one has the right to express his views by means of printing lewd and vulgar language which is likely to cause others to breach the peace to protect women and children from such exposure." In the court's view, "based on our interpretation of the decisions of the United States Supreme Court . . . the defendant's conduct in this case went beyond the permissive ambit of the First Amendment's protection."[18]

18. The court of appeal did hold that the trial judge had erred in ruling that Cohen could be convicted for using profanity within the presence of women and children in a loud and boisterous manner. Cohen had not been loud or boisterous and

Melville Nimmer petitioned for a rehearing in the court of appeal, but the court denied the petition on November 13, 1969. The California Supreme Court, dividing four to three, refused to hear the *Cohen* case on December 17. Having exhausted all state remedies, Nimmer filed an appeal and a motion to proceed *in forma pauperis* in the United States Supreme Court, and the Court noted probable jurisdiction on June 22, 1970.

While *Cohen* was pending before the Supreme Court, it engendered an interesting controversy about the proper strategy to pursue. The case had been sponsored almost from the beginning by the Southern California Civil Liberties Union and had been fought in the California courts primarily on the issue of freedom of expression. While the litigation was proceeding in the California courts, however, Chief Justice Warren retired on June 23, 1969, and Justice Abe Fortas resigned from the Court under fire in May of the same year. By the time *Cohen* came before the Court, Warren had been replaced by Chief Justice Burger, and Justice Blackmun had replaced Fortas.

Despite the changed personnel on the Court, Melville Nimmer and the Southern California CLU felt that the key issue in the case and the one that the arguments before the Court should focus on was the free expression issue. When the Supreme Court granted the appeal, however, the Northern California Civil Liberties Union also became interested in the case and decided to file an *amicus curiae* brief. Counsel for the Northern California CLU, notably Professor Anthony Amsterdam of Stanford Law School, concluded that *Cohen* could not be won on the freedom of expression issue, presumably because of the changed makeup of the Court. Indeed, the Northern California CLU felt that if the *Cohen* case were decided on that issue, the Court would probably affirm Cohen's conviction and in the process create a negative precedent in the field of freedom of expression. In its *amicus* brief, therefore, the Northern California CLU sought to convince the Court that section 415 of the California Penal Code was invalid primarily

was not charged with that offense, it said. But the trial judge's error on this point was a harmless one, the court ruled, since Cohen was guilty of "offensive conduct," and a "decision which is right in result will not be reversed on appeal although the reason stated is wrong."

because of its vagueness and indefiniteness, and it urged the Court not to decide the case on the freedom of expression issue on the grounds that that issue was not properly presented in the case.

Because Nimmer and the Southern California CLU remained convinced that the free expression issue should be the focus of the arguments, the SCCLU refused to consent to the filing of the NCCLU *amicus* brief, while, ironically, counsel for the State of California did consent. The Court itself, however, granted the NCCLU permission to file, and its position was thus presented to the Court despite the opposition of the southern branch.[19]

Cohen v. California thus raised a conflict over strategy between the two California Civil Liberties Unions and two professors of law. At the heart of the conflict were differing predictions and expectations of how the Burger Court would react to freedom of expression claims. Uncertainty about the performance of the Burger Court was, of course, not limited to *Cohen* but affected the planning of strategy in other civil liberties litigation, especially in the field of criminal procedure.

Despite the conflict over proper strategy in *Cohen,* Melville Nimmer focused his arguments to the Court squarely on the freedom of expression issue. "We begin with the incontrovertible fact that Appellant was engaging in speech," Nimmer told the Court. "Since his expression was formulated in words, and since he was arrested because of his words . . . , there is presented in this case, at least *prima facie,* an abridgment of Appellant's freedom of speech in violation of the First and Fourteenth Amendments." Since freedom of speech was involved, Cohen's expression of views regarding the draft could be validly prohibited only (1) if the expression constituted "fighting words" that would provoke others to violence; (2) if the expression fell within the constitutional definition of obscenity; (3) if the expression involved "expression-plus" and the government had a compelling interest in regulating the conduct involved that was sufficient to merit suppressing the communicative element in Cohen's action; or (4) if

19. Under the Supreme Court's rules, a party wishing to file an *amicus curiae* brief must secure the permission of both of the principal parties in the case, or, absent such permission, obtain the consent of the Court itself. The Court's consent is rather freely given to parties wishing to enter cases as *amici.*

Cohen's expression of views had constituted a major invasion of the privacy of others by inflicting unwanted and offensive views upon them.

On the first point, Nimmer noted that there had been no evidence of actual or threatened violence as a result of Cohen's expression of his views. The California court of appeal had simply assumed that the words of Cohen's message would provoke violence, although no evidence in the record supported such an assumption. Certainly, Nimmer argued, there was no evidence that Cohen had used the words with the intent to incite violence, or that such violence was imminent or likely. Under *Brandenburg v. Ohio,* this was the test of when advocacy of unlawful action could be suppressed under the First Amendment. "If a speaker's right to express himself could be constitutionally obliterated because his audience so strongly disagrees with the words he speaks that they are willing to resort to violence," Nimmer continued, "this would in effect limit First Amendment rights to expressions which are not sharply controversial."

Cohen's expression also did not constitute "fighting words" within the meaning of *Chaplinsky v. New Hampshire,* Nimmer argued, since the phrase "Fuck the Draft" was not directed at any given person or persons. "These words did not criticize, even less verbally attack those who viewed the sign. It is the institution of the draft, and not persons who viewed the sign, that was being attacked. If the concept of 'fighting words' can be so broadly interpreted as to be applied here, then any expression with which an audience strongly disagrees constitutes 'fighting words' susceptible of abridgment."

Nor was Cohen's expression obscene, Nimmer argued, since under the Court's decisions, obscene material had to appeal to the prurient interest in sex, be patently offensive in the description or portrayal of sexual matters, and be utterly without redeeming social value. "It hardly requires scholarly erudition or citation of authority," he said, "to establish the obvious fact that the phrase 'Fuck the Draft' does not arouse sexual thoughts, nor appeal to a prurient interest in sex. It is true that in its origin the word 'fuck' did have a sexual connotation, and currently one meaning of the word relates to sexual intercourse." But Nimmer cited dictionary definitions of the word to indicate that it could also mean to cheat, trick, take advantage of, or deceive, it could mean confused or disorganized, or it could express "dismay and annoyance."

In Cohen's case, Nimmer argued, "the phrase 'Fuck the Draft' was intended to express . . . dismay and annoyance with the Selective Service System, generally known as 'the draft.' " He commented, "No one could possibly have believed that Appellant was suggesting sexual intercourse with the Selective Service System." Cohen's use of the phrase had also not been patently offensive, he continued, since, in order to be patently offensive, material must relate to the depiction of sexual matters. And Cohen's expression had not been utterly without redeeming social importance or value, since it had involved the expression of legitimate political views regarding the war and the draft.[20]

Nimmer also denied that Cohen's expression of views could be classified as expression-plus, justifying greater governmental regulation in the First Amendment field. Even assuming his message had constituted expression-plus, however, Cohen had had the right to be where he was, and California had not demonstrated any compelling interest in regulating or prohibiting any nonspeech element that might have been involved. Simply because a political expression contained profanity it was not deprived of First Amendment protection, Nimmer contended. Indeed, profanity served the purpose of expressing deep feelings and was a means of attacking the establishment that was used especially by young people. In any case, the word "fuck" was being used increasingly in society, as evidenced by the fact that, of the ten bestselling hardcover works of fiction in 1969, seven repeatedly used the word.

Finally, Nimmer argued that Cohen had not invaded any major right of privacy of other individuals, as might be the case if he had insisted on inflicting his views on people in the privacy of their homes. "If persons who do not wish to hear speech which they think they may oppose to the point of finding it highly offensive were to be insulated by law from any such speech," he

20. This argument was, of course, made before the Court's 1973 redefinition of obscenity to require a lack of serious literary, artistic, political or scientific value, rather than an utter lack of social value, in *Miller v. California.*

said, "then freedom of speech would amount to little more than the right to address audiences who already agree with the speaker. In that event commerce in the marketplace of ideas would be frozen, and the democratic dialogue silenced." Cohen had not inflicted offensive views on a captive audience, Nimmer concluded, and "if fleeting exposure to unwelcome speech deprives Appellant of his First Amendment rights, then the same principle would be applicable to street-corner speakers, and even to radio and television programs, and the central core would be cut out of the First Amendment."

Defending the validity of section 415 on behalf of California were the city attorney and deputy city attorney of Los Angeles. They argued two principal points: (1) that Cohen's message had constituted "fighting words" that were likely to provoke violent reactions, and (2) that Cohen's chosen means of expression constituted both conduct and expression, that is, expression-plus, and that the state had a sufficiently compelling interest in regulating Cohen's conduct to justify the suppression of any communicative element that might have been involved.

On the first point, California counsel argued that the fact that Cohen had not engaged in violent or tumultuous conduct was no defense to a charge of disturbing the peace by offensive conduct, since it should have been reasonably foreseeable by Cohen that the message on his jacket "would cause others to commit violent acts or disturb the peace." A person "may be guilty of the offense of breach of the peace," they argued, "if he commits acts likely to provoke violence or disturbance of good order, even though no such eventuality be intended."

Cohen had inflicted his offensive message on a "captive audience" in the Los Angeles county courthouse, counsel argued, invading the privacy of others and, by the language he chose, producing the likelihood of provoking "the average person to retaliation, and thereby [causing] a breach of the peace." If Cohen's form of expression were held to be constitutionally protected, it was argued,

> then one need merely imagine the type of signs that will be
> publicly displayed against private citizens. ('Fuck Catholics';

'Fuck Negroes'; 'Fuck Whites'; 'Fuck Jews';—signs carried in protest by opponents of these 'groups'); against public institutions (a 'Fuck the United States Congress' sign in protest over enactments of the National Legislature); or against public officials (a 'Fuck Nixon' sign carried by an opponent of the war policies of the President of the United States; a 'Fuck the Justices of the United States Supreme Court' sign displayed in protest of decisions rendered by this Honorable Court).

The display of such horrible signs in public places, California counsel contended, would "tend to incite an immediate breach of the peace by observers of the signs."

In addition to the contention that Cohen's message had constituted "fighting words," California counsel argued that Cohen's "Fuck the Draft" message was expression-plus, comparable to the burning of a draft card in *United States v. O'Brien.* "This Court has held that when 'speech' and 'nonspeech' elements are combined in the same course of conduct, a sufficiently important governmental interest in regulating the nonspeech element can justify incidental limitations on First Amendment freedoms. The California Court of Appeal determined that appellant's conduct consisted of 'speech' and 'nonspeech' elements." Cohen's act of walking through a public building with "Fuck the Draft" on his jacket, it was argued, was conduct justifying governmental intervention and regulation despite whatever communicative element had been involved, since the privacy of the observing individuals had been invaded.

The conviction of Cohen for "offensive conduct" that disturbed the peace, California counsel therefore argued, did not infringe on the freedom of expression protected by the First and Fourteenth Amendments. "No one has the right to express his views by means of printing lewd and vulgar language, which is likely to cause others to breach the peace to protect women and children from exposure to such language," they concluded.

The Northern California Civil Liberties Union, hoping to divert the Court from the free expression issue, contended in its *amicus curiae* brief that the case did not "present the question whether, consistently with the First and Fourteenth Amendments, a State may punish the utterance of a class of non-obscene 'profane' speech." Cohen had been convicted for "offensive conduct" not for profanity, the NCCLU argued, and the question was thus whether section 415 was invalidly overbroad because it prohibited conduct that could not rationally be said to provoke unlawful acts.

"If we undertook to fight every man who said or displayed the word 'fuck' or equally embarrassing words in public, we would be fighting most of the time," the NCCLU said. "Only gallantry or irascibility of pathological proportions could inspire such a crusade." The conclusion of the California courts that Cohen's expression would provoke breaches of the peace was irrational, the NCCLU concluded, and such an application of a breach of the peace statute, allowing the suppression of free expression on the basis of "vagrant fears of unreasonable, hostile reaction," violated the First Amendment.

A decision of the California Supreme Court, *In re Bushman* rendered while *Cohen* was pending, also tended to prompt the Court not to reach the merits in the case. On January 27, 1970, the California court construed section 415 to prohibit "willful and malicious conduct that is violent and endangers public safety and order or creates a clear and present danger that others will engage in violence of that nature." It was doubtful that Cohen could have been validly convicted under such a construction of section 415, and the *Bushman* decision therefore opened up the possibility that the United States Supreme Court might simply vacate the judgment in *Cohen* and remand it for consideration by the California Supreme Court in light of *Bushman*.

Cohen was nonetheless argued orally before the Court on February 22, 1971. Just before Melville Nimmer began his argument, Chief Justice Burger suggested to him that, "as in most cases, the Court is thoroughly familiar with the factual setting of this case and it will not be necessary for you, I am sure, to dwell on the facts." Nimmer said later that he took the Chief Justice's remarks as a suggestion "that I avoid the word 'fuck' in the Court's chambers. It seemed to me, however, that if I followed this suggestion I would in effect concede the State's case by acknowledging that I was dealing with an unspeakable word. I, therefore, responded by stating that I could sum up the facts very briefly, and then in a terse summation did mention the fact that the defendant was convicted for wearing a jacket bearing the words 'Fuck the Draft.' "

Nimmer's insistent focus on the free expression issue paid off on June 7, 1971, when the Court announced its decision reversing Cohen's conviction. Justice Harlan wrote the majority opinion, joined by Justices Douglas, Brennan, Stewart, and Marshall. Justice Blackmun, joined by Chief Justice Burger, Justice Black, and in part by Justice White filed a dissenting opinion.

COHEN V. CALIFORNIA
403 U.S. 15, decided June 7, 1971

Mr. Justice Harlan delivered the opinion of the Court.

This case may seem at first blush too inconsequential to find its way into our books, but the issue it presents is of no small constitutional significance.

[Harlan quoted the facts of the case from the court of appeal's opinion and traced the history of the litigation. He then settled that the Court had jurisdiction of the appeal.]

In order to lay hands on the precise issue which this case involves, it is useful first to canvass various matters which this record does *not* present.

The conviction quite clearly rests upon the asserted offensiveness of the *words* Cohen used to convey his message to the public. The only "conduct" which the State sought to punish is the fact of communication. Thus, we deal here with a conviction resting solely upon "speech," . . . not upon any separately identifiable conduct which allegedly was intended by Cohen to be perceived by others as expressive of particular views but which, on its face, does not necessarily convey any message and hence arguably could be regulated without effectively repressing Cohen's ability to express himself. Cf. United States v. O'Brien . . . . Further, the State certainly lacks power to punish Cohen for the underlying content of the message the inscription conveyed. At least so long as there is no showing of an intent to incite disobedience to or disruption of the draft, Cohen could not, consistently with the First and Fourteenth Amendments, be punished for asserting the evident position on the inutility or immorality of the draft his jacket reflected. Yates v. United States . . . .

Appellant's conviction, then, rests squarely upon his exercise of the "freedom of speech" protected from arbitrary governmental interference by the Constitution and can be justified, if at all, only as a valid regulation of the manner in which he exercised that freedom, not as a permissible prohibition on the substantive message it conveys. This does not end the inquiry, of course, for the First and Fourteenth Amendments have never been thought to give absolute protection to every individual to speak whenever or wherever he pleases, or to use any form of address in any circumstances that he chooses. In this vein, too, however, we think it important to note that several issues typically associated with such problems are not presented here.

In the first place, Cohen was tried under a statute applicable throughout the entire State. Any attempt to support this conviction on the ground that the statute seeks to preserve an appropriately decorous atmosphere in the courthouse where Cohen was arrested must fall in the absence of any language in the statute that would have put appellant on notice that certain kinds of otherwise permissible speech or conduct would nevertheless, under California law, not be tolerated in certain places. See Edwards v. South Carolina .... Cf. Adderley v. Florida .... No fair reading of the phrase "offensive conduct" can be said sufficiently to inform the ordinary person that distinctions between certain locations are thereby created.

In the second place, as it comes to us, this case cannot be said to fall within those relatively few categories of instances where prior decisions have established the power of government to deal more comprehensively with certain forms of individual expression simply upon a showing that such a form was employed. This is not, for example, an obscenity case. Whatever else may be necessary to give rise to the States' broader power to prohibit obscene expression, such expression must be, in some significant way, erotic. Roth v. United States .... It cannot plausibly be maintained that this vulgar allusion to the Selective Service System would conjure up such psychic stimulation in anyone likely to be confronted with Cohen's crudely defaced jacket.

This Court has also held that the States are free to ban the simple use, without a demonstration of additional justifying circumstances, of so-called "fighting words," those personally abusive epithets which, when addressed to the ordinary citizen, are, as a matter of common knowledge, inherently likely to provoke violent reaction. Chaplinsky v. New Hampshire .... While the four-letter word displayed by Cohen in relation to the draft is not uncommonly employed in a personally provocative fashion, in this instance it was clearly not "directed to the person of the hearer" .... No individual actually or likely to be present could reasonably have regarded the words on appellant's jacket as a direct personal insult. Nor do we have here an instance of the exercise of the State's police power to prevent a speaker from intentionally provoking a given group to hostile reaction. . . . There is, as noted above, no showing that anyone who saw Cohen was in fact violently aroused or that appellant intended such a result.

Finally, in arguments before this Court much has been made of the claim that Cohen's distasteful mode of expression was thrust upon unwilling or unsuspecting viewers, and that the State might therefore legitimately act as it did in order to protect the sensitive from otherwise unavoidable exposure to appellant's crude form of protest. Of course, the mere presumed presence of unwitting listeners or viewers does not serve automatically to justify curtailing all speech capable of giving offense. . . . While this Court has recognized that government may properly act in many situations to prohibit intrusion into the privacy of the home of unwelcome views and ideas which cannot be totally banned from the public dialogue, . . . we have at the same time consistently stressed that "we are often 'captives' outside the sanctuary of the home and subject to objectionable speech" . . . . The ability of government, consonant with the Constitution, to shut off discourse solely to protect others from hearing it is, in other words, dependent upon a showing that substantial privacy interests are being invaded in an essentially intolerable manner. Any broader view of this authority would effectively empower a majority to silence dissidents simply as a matter of personal predilections.

In this regard, persons confronted with Cohen's jacket were in a quite different posture than, say, those subjected to the raucous emissions of sound trucks blaring outside their residences. Those in the Los Angeles courthouse could effectively avoid further bombardment of their sensibilities simply by averting their eyes. And, while it may be that one has a more substantial claim to a recognizable privacy interest when walking through a courthouse corridor than, for example, strolling through Central Park, surely it is nothing like the interest in being free from unwanted expression in the confines of one's own home. . . . Given the subtlety and complexity of the factors involved, if Cohen's "speech" was otherwise entitled to constitutional protection, we do not think the fact that some unwilling "listeners" in a public building may have been briefly exposed to it can serve to justify this breach of the peace conviction, where, as here, there was no evidence that persons powerless to avoid appellant's conduct did in fact object to it, and where that portion of the statute upon which Cohen's conviction rests evinces no concern, either on its face or as construed by the California courts, with the special plight of the captive auditor, but, instead, indiscriminately sweeps within its prohibitions all "offensive conduct" that disturbs "any neighborhood or person" . . . .

Against this background, the issue flushed by this case stands out in bold relief. It is whether California can excise, as "offensive conduct," one particular scurrilous epithet from the public discourse, either upon the theory of the court below that its use is inherently likely to cause violent reaction or upon a more general assertion that the States, acting as guardians of public morality, may properly remove this offensive word from the public vocabulary.

The rationale of the California court is plainly untenable. At most it reflects an "undifferentiated fear or apprehension of disturbance [which] is not enough to overcome the right to freedom of expression." Tinker v. Des Moines Indep. Community School Dist. . . . . We have been shown no evidence that substantial numbers of citizens are standing ready to strike out physically at whoever may assault their sensibilities with execrations like that uttered by Cohen. There may be some persons about with such lawless and violent proclivities, but that is an insufficient base upon which to erect, consistently with constitutional values, a governmental power to force persons who wish to ventilate their dissident views into avoiding particular forms of expression. The argument amounts to little more than the self-defeating proposition that to avoid physical censorship of one who has not sought to provoke such a response by a hypothetical coterie of the violent and lawless, the States may more appropriately effectuate that censorship themselves. . . .

Admittedly, it is not so obvious that the First and Fourteenth Amendments must be taken to disable the States from punishing public utterance of this unseemly expletive in order to maintain what they regard as a suitable level of discourse within the body politic. We think, however, that examination and reflection will reveal the shortcomings of a contrary viewpoint.

At the outset, we cannot overemphasize that, in our judgment, most situations where the State has a justifiable interest in regulating speech will fall within one or more of the various established exceptions, discussed above but not applicable here, to the usual rule that governmental bodies may not prescribe the form or content of individual expression. Equally important in our conclusion is the constitutional backdrop against which our decision must be made. The constitutional right of free expression is powerful medicine in a society as diverse and populous as ours. It is designed and intended to remove governmental restraints from the arena of public discussion, putting the decision as to what views shall be voiced largely into the hands of each of us, in the hope that use of such freedom will ultimately produce a more capable citizenry and more perfect polity and in the belief that no other approach would comport with the premise of individual dignity and choice upon which our political system rests. . . .

To many, the immediate consequence of this freedom may often appear to be only verbal tumult, discord, and even offensive utterance. These are, however, within established limits, in truth necessary side effects of the broader enduring values which the process of open debate permits us to achieve. That the air may at times seem filled with verbal cacophony is, in this sense not a sign of weakness but of strength. We cannot lose sight of the fact that, in what otherwise might seem a trifling and annoying instance of individual distasteful abuse of a privilege, these fundamental societal values are truly implicated. That is why "[wholly] neutral futilities . . . come under the protection of free speech as fully as do Keats' poems or Donne's sermons," . . . and why "so long as the means are peaceful, the communication need not meet standards of acceptability" . . . .

Against this perception of the constitutional policies involved, we discern certain more particularized considerations that peculiarly call for reversal of this conviction. First, the principle contended for by the State seems inherently boundless. How is one to distinguish this from any other offensive word? Surely the State has no right to cleanse public debate to the point where it is grammatically palatable to the most squeamish among us. Yet no readily ascertainable general principle exists for stopping short of that result were we to affirm the judgment below. For, while the particular four-letter word being litigated here is perhaps more distasteful than most others of its genre, it is nevertheless often true that one man's vulgarity is another's lyric. Indeed, we think it is largely because governmental officials cannot make principled distinctions in this area that the Constitution leaves matters of taste and style so largely to the individual.

Additionally, we cannot overlook the fact, because it is well illustrated by the episode involved here, that much linguistic expression serves a dual communicative function: it conveys not only ideas capable of relatively precise, detached explication, but otherwise inexpressible emotions as well. In fact, words are often chosen as much for their emotive as their cognitive force. We cannot sanction the view that the Constitution, while solicitous of the cognitive content of individual speech, has little or no regard for that emotive function which, practically speaking, may often be the more important element of the overall message sought to be communicated. Indeed, as Mr. Justice Frankfurter has said, "[one] of the prerogatives of American citizenship is the right to criticize public men and measures—and that means not only informed and responsible criticism but the freedom to speak foolishly and without moderation" . . . .

Finally, and in the same vein, we cannot indulge the facile assumption that one can forbid particular words without also running a substantial risk of suppressing ideas in the process. Indeed, governments might soon seize upon the censorship of particular words as a convenient guise for banning the expression of unpopular views. We have been able, as noted above, to discern little social benefit that might result from running the risk of opening the door to such grave results.

It is, in sum, our judgment that, absent a more particularized and compelling reason for its actions, the State may not, consistently with the First and Fourteenth Amendments, make the simple public display here involved of this single four-letter expletive a criminal offense. Because that is the only arguable sustainable rationale for the conviction here at issue, the judgment below must be

Reversed.

Mr. Justice Blackmun, with whom The Chief Justice and Mr. Justice Black join.

I dissent, and I do so for two reasons:

1. Cohen's absurd and immature antic, in my view, was mainly conduct and little speech. . . . The California Court of Appeal appears so to have described it . . . , and I cannot characterize it otherwise. Further, the case appears to me to be well within the sphere of Chaplinsky v. New Hampshire, . . . where Mr. Justice Murphy, a known champion of First Amendment freedoms, wrote for a unanimous bench. As a consequence, this Court's agonizing [over] First Amendment values seems misplaced and unnecessary.

2. I am not at all certain that the California Court of Appeal's construction of Sec. 415 is now the authoritative California construction. The Court of Appeal filed its opinion on October 22, 1969. The Supreme Court of California declined review by a four-to-three vote on December 17. . . . A month later, on January 27, 1970, the State Supreme Court in another case construed Sec. 415, evidently for the first time. . . . Chief Justice Traynor, who was among the dissenters to his court's refusal to take Cohen's case, wrote the majority opinion. He held that Sec. 415 "is not unconstitutionally vague and overboard" and further said:

"[That] part of Penal Code section 415 in question here makes punishable only wilful and malicious conduct that is violent and endangers public safety and order or that creates a clear and present danger that others will engage in violence of that nature. . . . [It] does not make criminal any nonviolent act unless the act incites or threatens to incite others to violence. . . ." Inasmuch as this Court does not dismiss this case, it ought to be remanded to the California Court of Appeal for reconsideration in the light of the subsequently rendered decision by the State's highest tribunal. . . .

Mr. Justice White concurs in Paragraph 2 of Mr. Justice Blackmun's dissenting opinion.

The Court majority had applied most of its available doctrines and tests to determine whether Cohen's message was constitutionally protected under the First and Fourteenth Amendments, and it had concluded that it was. Despite the uncertainties generated by the transition from the Warren Court to the Burger Court, Melville Nimmer and the Southern California Civil Liberties Union had been vindicated, albeit by the narrowest of margins, in their determination to press the freedom of expression issue.

In the period since *Cohen,* the Court has invalidated numerous breach of the peace statutes or ordinances as applied to various forms of expression. It has struck down statutes or ordinances prohibiting the use of "opprobrious words or abusive language, tending to cause a breach of the peace" (*Gooding v. Wilson,* in 1972); prohibiting abuse of another person by "menacing, insulting, slanderous or profane language" (*Plummer v. Columbus,* in 1973); prohibiting willful conduct in a "noisy, boisterous, rude, insulting or other disorderly manner with intent to annoy or abuse another" (*Norwell v. Cincinnati,* in 1973); and forbidding a person "wantonly to curse or revile or to use obscene or opprobrious language toward or with reference to any member of the city police while in the actual performance of his duties" (*Lewis v. New Orleans,* in 1974). In each of these cases, the Court found that the state courts had failed to construe the laws to prohibit only "fighting words." Unless confined to the prohibition of "fighting words," the Court held, such laws were susceptible to being applied to constitutionally protected expression, in violation of the First and Fourteenth Amendments.

In a case similar to *Cohen,* the Court has ruled that the University of Missouri could not validly dismiss a student for distributing a publication that contained a cartoon depicting the Statue of Liberty and the Goddess of Justice being raped by policemen, and containing an article headlined, "Motherfucker Acquitted." Such expression was not obscene, the Court ruled, and the university's dismissal of the student for "indecent conduct and speech" was invalid under the First Amendment (*Papish v. University of Missouri,* decided in 1973).

In addition to rather rough language, political expression in recent years has often involved use of the United States flag in ways that have run afoul of various laws prohibiting the desecration or misuse of the flag. The Court, however, invalidated a Massachusetts statute prohibiting treating the flag "contemptuously" in a 1974 case involving a defendant who wore a small flag on the seat of his pants. The Court held that the Massachusetts statute was void for vagueness, since it inadequately defined what contemptuous treatment of the flag consisted of (*Smith v. Goguen*). And, finally, in *Spence v. Washington,* decided in 1974, the Court held that the State of Washington could not validly punish a person for flying a flag upside down with a peace symbol attached to it from his apartment window in protest against the invasion of Cambodia and the Kent State University killings. Spence's use of the flag was a form of constitutionally protected political expression, the Court held, and his conviction had violated the First Amendment.

As *Cohen* and these more recent "breach of the peace" cases indicate, the Court is adhering to the *Chaplinsky* doctrine that the First Amendment protects only the expression of socially redeeming ideas and does not therefore protect "fighting words," obscenity, or libel. Such an approach to the amendment's scope of protection opens up the danger that legitimate expression may be rendered unprotected by attaching labels such as "fighting words" or "obscenity" to it. Such a danger can be avoided to an extent by precision in the definition of what such unprotected forms of expression constitute, but judging by the Court's obscenity decisions, its attempts at definitional precision have been considerably less than successful. Consequently there remains a considerable danger to free expression from manipulation of the concept of constitutionally unprotected expression that was spawned by the *Chaplinsky* doctrine.

Chapter Four

RELIGION
AND THE STATE

Introduction The First Amendment contains dual protections for
religious freedom by providing that "Congress shall
make no law respecting an establishment of religion, or prohibiting
the free exercise thereof." The establishment clause prohibits
governmental support for an established religion or religions and
compulsion on the individual to support beliefs he does not hold.
The free exercise clause guarantees the right of the individual to
entertain whatever religious beliefs or nonbeliefs he chooses, free
of governmental interference. Although the religion clauses of the
First Amendment were originally limitations on the federal government only, the Supreme Court held in 1940, in *Cantwell v.
Connecticut,* that the free exercise clause was applicable to the
states via the due process clause of the Fourteenth Amendment,
and in 1947 it similarly applied the establishment clause to the
states in *Everson v. Board of Education.*

     In its first authoritative interpretation of the establishment
clause in *Everson,* the Court held that neither "a state nor the

Federal government can set up a church. Neither can pass laws which aid one religion, aid all religions, or prefer one religion over another." Neither the states nor the federal government, the Court continued, could force or influence

> a person to profess a belief or disbelief in any religion. No person can be punished for entertaining or professing religious beliefs or disbeliefs, for church attendance or non-attendance. No tax in any amount, large or small, can be levied to support any religious activities or institutions, whatever they may be called or whatever form they may adopt to teach or practice. Neither a state nor the Federal Government, can openly or secretly, participate in the affairs of any religious organization or groups and vice versa.

Despite the Court's acceptance of the view that the establishment clause creates a "wall of separation between church and state," the wall has proved somewhat more porous than the Court's absolutist language in *Everson* would indicate. Even in *Everson*, the Court upheld public financing of free bus transportation for students attending parochial schools. Such a public policy, it held, was primarily for the health, safety, and welfare of children and was not aimed at benefiting the church operating the parochial school the children attended. This "child benefit theory" was also later used to justify public provision of free textbooks for parochial school students (*Board of Education v. Allen*, decided in 1968).

The Court has also upheld released time for religious instruction of public school students, Sunday closing laws, tax exemptions for church property used for religious purposes, public financing of buildings to be used for instruction in secular subjects at church colleges and universities, and the granting of conscientious objector status under the draft laws to opponents of all wars, although conscientious objectors to only certain wars are denied such status. On the other hand, the Court has relied on the establishment clause to invalidate public school prayers and Bible readings, religious proselytizing in public school buildings, state prohibition of teaching the theory of evolution in the public schools, and recent attempts to grant public subsidies to parochial schools. (For a summary of the Court's major establishment clause decisions, see table 5.)

It is thus clear, as Justice Powell acknowledged for the Court in *Committee for Public Education v. Nyquist* in 1973, that "this Nation's history has not been one of entirely sanitized separation between Church and State." The Court insists, however, that in order for public policies to pass muster under the establishment clause, they must (1) reflect a clearly secular legislative purpose, (2) have as their primary effect neither the advancement nor the inhibition of religion, and (3) avoid excessive governmental entanglement with religion.

Under the free exercise clause, on the other hand, the central problem of interpretation has been the extent to which religious objections to valid secular policies may be upheld and the extent to which the government may prohibit religiously inspired activities in order to protect the general welfare. The free exercise clause, as the Court said in *Cantwell v. Connecticut,* embraces two aspects—freedom to believe and freedom to act. "The first is absolute but, in the nature of things, the second cannot be. Conduct remains subject to regulation for the protection of society."

In dealing with religious freedom, therefore, the traditional rule developed by the courts has been that religious objections may not be sustained against a governmental policy enacted for secular purposes in the interest of the general welfare. Applying this valid secular policy rule, the Court sustained a congressional prohibition of polygamy as practiced by the Mormons in Utah Territory in *Reynolds v. United States,* as early as 1878. Under the free exercise clause, Chief Justice Waite said,

> Congress was deprived of all legislative power over mere opinion, but was left free to reach actions which were in violation of social duties or subversive of good order. Laws are made for the government of actions, and while they cannot interfere with mere religious belief and opinions, they may with practices. Suppose one believed that human sacrifice were a necessary part of religious worship, would it be seriously contended that the civil government under which he lived could not interfere to prevent a sacrifice?

Table 5

SUMMARY OF IMPORTANT SUPREME COURT ESTABLISHMENT
CLAUSE DECISIONS

Case	*Policy*	*Decision*
Everson v. Board of Education (1947)	Free bus transportation for parochial school students	Upheld
McCollum v. Illinois (1948)	Religious proselytizing in public school buildings	Invalidated
Zorach v. Clauson (1952)	Release of public school students for attendance at religion classes off school property	Upheld
Sunday Closing Cases (1961)	Laws requiring closing of certain businesses on Sundays	Upheld
Engel v. Vitale (1962)	State-composed prayer recited in public schools	Invalidated
Murray v. Curlett (1963) *School District of Abington v. Schempp* (1963)	Prayer and Bible-reading in public schools	Invalidated
Board of Education v. Allen (1968)	Free textbooks for parochial school students	Upheld
Epperson v. Arkansas (1968)	State prohibition of teaching theory of evolution	Invalidated
Walz v. Tax Commission (1970)	Tax exemptions for church property used for religious purpose	Upheld
Lemon v. Kurtzman (1971)	State subsidies for teachers and materials in "secular" subjects taught in parochial schools	Invalidated
Tilton v. Richardson (1971)	Government grants for construction of buildings for "secular" uses at church colleges and universities*	Upheld
Gillette v. United States (1971)	Exemption from draft of conscientious objectors to all wars but not objectors to particular wars	Upheld

Levitt v. Committee for Public Education (1973)	State subsidy for record-keeping and testing in parochial schools	Invalidated
Hunt v. McNair (1973)	State credit used to construct buildings for "secular" purposes at church college	Upheld
Sloan v. Lemon (1973)	Reimbursement of parents of parochial school children for tuition expenses	Invalidated
Committee for Public Education v. Nyquist (1973)	State grants for maintenance and repairs at parochial schools; state reimbursement for tuition at parochial schools; tax relief for parents with children in parochial schools	Invalidated

* This was a federal government program, and one provision, giving the government only a twenty-year interest in the buildings constructed with federal funds, was invalidated.

Using the valid secular policy rule, the Court has also sustained public policies requiring compulsory vaccination despite objections by some religious groups that vaccinations violate their religious convictions (*Jacobson v. Massachusetts,* decided in 1905). And in *Prince v. Massachusetts,* a 1944 case, the Court upheld a child labor law that prohibited children under certain ages from engaging in occupations on the streets at night, despite an objection by Jehovah's Witnesses that such activities by their children were a part of the exercise of their faith. Neither "rights of religion nor rights of parenthood are beyond limitation," the Court said in *Prince.*

Acting to guard the general interest in youth's well being, the state as parens patriae may restrict the parent's control by requiring school attendance, regulating or prohibiting the child's labor, and in many other ways. Its authority is not nullified merely because the parent grounds his claim to control the child's course of conduct on religion or conscience. Thus, he cannot claim freedom from compulsory vaccination for the child more than himself on religious grounds.

"It is too late in the day," the Court concluded, "now to doubt that legislation appropriately designed to reach such evils [as child labor] is within the state's police power, whether against the parent's claim to control of the child or one that religious scruples dictate contrary action."

Despite the Court's acceptance and application of the valid secular policy rule in cases such as *Prince,* it has opened loopholes in the rule in several of its decisions. For example, in *Minersville School District v. Gobitis,* in 1940, the court initially sustained the compulsory flag salute in public schools as applied to Jehovah's Witness students whose religious scruples would not permit their participation in such a ceremony. The inculcation of patriotism through the ceremony, the Court held, was a valid secular policy that the states could pursue despite religious objections to it. Then, in 1943, in *West Virginia Board of Education v. Barnette,* the Court reversed itself and held the compulsory salute invalid under the First and Fourteenth Amendments. Although it rejected its earlier reliance on the valid secular policy rule in *Gobitis,* Justice Jackson's opinion for the Court held that by requiring the compulsory flag salute the states had transcended "constitutional limitations on their powers" and invaded "the sphere of intellect and spirit which it is the purpose of the First Amendment to our Constitution to reserve from all official control." Instead of recognizing the religious objections to the compulsory flag salute as valid, the Court thus held in *Barnette* that the ceremony was not a valid policy that the states might pursue, because it invaded rights of the "intellect and spirit" guaranteed by the First and Fourteenth Amendments.

In the *Sunday Closing Cases,* decided in 1961, the Court sustained state laws requiring the closing of certain businesses on Sundays against the claim that such laws violated the establishment clause. Although originally enacted from religious motives, the Court held that Sunday closing laws could be construed to embody a valid secular policy—the policy of guaranteeing one day of rest per week for working people. In one of the *Sunday Closing Cases, Braunfeld v. Brown,* however, a Jewish merchant argued that Sunday closing laws penalized his exercise of religious beliefs.

He was required by his religion to close his business on Saturday, the Jewish Sabbath, while the law required him also to close on Sunday. Because of his religious beliefs, he argued, he was penalized economically in relation to his non-Jewish competitors who were required to close their businesses only on Sundays.

The Court in *Braunfeld* nonetheless rejected the free exercise clause arguments by applying the valid secular policy rule. It conceded that, "if the purpose or effect of a law is to impede the observance of one or all religions or is to discriminate invidiously between religions, that law is constitutionally invalid even though the burden may be characterized as being only indirect." But, if a state enacts a policy such as the Sunday closing laws, the Court said, "the purpose and effect of which is to advance the State's secular goals, the statute is valid despite its indirect burden on religious observance unless the State may accomplish its purposes by means which do not impose such a burden." The Sunday closing law was validly applied to a Jewish merchant, the Court concluded, because such a law had a valid secular purpose, it was not discriminatorily aimed at any religion, and its burden on the free exercise of religion was only indirect.

In *Braunfeld,* however, the Court had opened a possible loophole in the valid secular policy rule with its statement that "indirect" burdens upon the free exercise of religion could be imposed by valid secular policies unless "the State may accomplish its purpose by means which do not impose such a burden." This statement opened up the possibility that claims under the free exercise clause could be raised against a governmental policy if its purpose could be accomplished by other means that would not inhibit religious freedom.

The Court's rejection of the free exercise claim in *Braunfeld* was also seriously undermined by its subsequent decision in *Sherbert v. Verner* in 1963. In *Sherbert,* South Carolina denied unemployment compensation to a Seventh-Day Adventist because she refused to accept employment on Saturday, the Sabbath in her religion. The state required that, in order to be eligible for unemployment benefits, a person must be willing to accept suitable employment if it is available. Mrs. Sherbert's religious objections to Saturday work, the state decided, made her ineligible for unemployment benefits because they made her unavailable for suitable employment.

The Court held, however, that this South Carolina policy violated the free exercise clause. It distinguished previous cases in which it had applied the valid secular policy rule, because they invariably involved religiously motivated conduct posing "some substantial threat to public safety, peace or order." The Court held that Mrs. Sherbert's religious objections to Saturday work constituted "no conduct prompted by religious principles of a kind within the reach of state legislation." The burden imposed on her free exercise of religion by South Carolina, the Court thus held, had to be justified by a "compelling state interest in the regulation of a subject within the State's constitutional power to regulate." The state had contended that recognition of Mrs. Sherbert's religious claims would permit possibly fraudulent claims of objections to Saturday work by others, thus diluting the unemployment compensation fund and hindering employers in scheduling Saturday work. Such possibilities were held by the Court not to constitute a "compelling state interest," since "even if the possibility of spurious claims did threaten to dilute the fund and disrupt the scheduling of work, it would plainly be incumbent upon the [state] to demonstrate that no alternative forms of regulation would combat such abuses without infringing First Amendment rights."

As the concurring opinion of Justice Stewart and the dissenting opinion of Justice Harlan, joined by Justice White, pointed out, not only had the Court in *Sherbert* carved out an exception to the valid secular policy rule, but its decision also raised serious establishment clause issues. Under the Court's ruling, South Carolina was constitutionally required to extend unemployment benefits to persons whose objections to Saturday work were religiously motivated, but the state was not required to extend such exemptions to those whose objections to Saturday work were based on secular, nonreligious grounds. The result of the Court's holding in *Sherbert* was thus to require a state to give preferential treatment to religious beliefs. As Justice Harlan said in dissent, South Carolina under the Court's decision "must *single out* for financial assistance those whose behavior is religiously motivated, even though it denies such assistance to others whose identical behavior (in this case, inability to work on Saturdays) is not religiously motivated." Yet the establishment clause, as construed by the Court, required governmental neutrality toward religion and prohibited legislation that either advanced or inhibited religion.

The *Sherbert* case demonstrated that litigation involving religious issues often raised intertwined problems under both the free exercise and the establishment clauses, and, indeed, that the constitutional policies mandated by the religion clauses sometimes collided. The Court again faced problems of this sort in *Gillette v. United States,* in 1971. The case involved a challenge of the provision of the Selective Service Act exempting from the draft any person "who, by reason of religious training and belief, is conscientiously opposed to participation in war in any form." This provision was construed to apply only to those who opposed all wars on religious grounds, but it did not exempt those who conscientiously objected only to particular wars. Such an application of the provision, it was argued in *Gillette,* constituted both an establishment of religion, because it singled out specific religious beliefs for preferential treatment, and a violation of the free exercise of religion, because it burdened particular religious beliefs.

The Court sustained the conscientious objector provision of the Selective Service Act in *Gillette,* however. The exemption from the draft of objectors to all wars, but not objectors to particular wars, the Court held, was nondiscriminatory in that it did not favor or disfavor any particular religious sects. The policy of the act was also held to have the valid secular purpose of providing for respect for conscience while at the same time insuring ease and fairness in the administration of the law. Rejecting the establishment clause argument, the Court held that the purposes underlying the conscientious objector provisions were "neutral and secular," that "valid neutral reasons exist for limiting the exemption to objectors to all war, and that the section therefore cannot be said to reflect a religious preference."

In rejecting the argument based on the free exercise clause, the Court applied the valid secular policy rule and held that the decisions of the Court interpreting freedom of religion "do not at their farthest reach support the proposition that a stance of conscientious opposition relieves an objector from any colliding duty fixed by a democratic government." The "impact of conscription on objectors to particular wars is far from unjustified," the Court held. "The conscription laws, applied to such persons as to others, are not designed to interfere with any religious ritual or practice, and do not work a penalty against any theological position."

From the Court's decisions in *Sherbert* and *Gillette,* several general propositions appeared reasonably clear. First, although the valid secular policy rule was subject to important exceptions, if the public interest in uniform application of a valid secular policy was judged by the Court to be sufficiently weighty or enough to constitute a "compelling governmental interest," religious objections to such a policy would be rejected. Compulsory vaccinations and the enforcement of the draft law were clearly policies of this nature. Absent a compelling governmental interest in the uniform application of a particular policy, free exercise claims could validly be raised against a policy imposing burdens on religious values. And despite the Court's interpretation of the establishment clause to require governmental neutrality in the field of religion, exemptions from otherwise valid secular policies for those objecting to them on grounds of religious conscience could be granted, or even constitutionally required, as in the *Sherbert* case. In such instances, the establishment clause's strictures were clearly being relaxed by the Court in favor of free exercise clause values.

The extent to which the free exercise clause required an exemption from what was clearly a valid secular policy came before the Court again in *Wisconsin v. Yoder* in 1972. The power of the states to compel school attendance of children had long been recognized as a valid policy to ensure a reasonably educated citizenry. The Court itself, in *Brown v. Board of Education* in 1954, had recognized that education "is perhaps the most important function of state and local governments. Compulsory school attendance laws and the great expenditures for education both demonstrate our recognition of the importance of education to our democratic society. . . . It is the very foundation of good citizenship." Despite the importance of education, however, the Old Order Amish refused on religious grounds to send their children to school beyond the eighth grade. As a consequence, Amish parents were fined and jailed in state after state. The conflict between the Amish and the compulsory school attendance policy came to a head in *Yoder,* and once again the Court was required to consider the validity of religious objections to this "most important function." We shall now examine in detail the *Yoder* litigation and how the Court resolved the conflict between the Amish and the policy of compulsory school attendance.

Case Study
THE GOOD GUYS IN THE BLACK HATS: RELIGIOUS LIBERTY AND THE AMISH IN WISCONSIN

The Amish are a product of the Reformation. Their development as a sect may be traced to the Anabaptist movement of the 1600s, which emphasized a return to what was conceived of as a more pure, primitive form of Christianity. The Swiss Anabaptists were usually referred to as the Swiss Brethren and were centered in Zurich. It was among them that the followers of Jacob Ammann established a separate sect between 1693 and 1697, called the Amish after their leader. Because of religious persecution in Europe, the first Amish came to America and settled in Pennsylvania as early as 1727. They presently number approximately 50,000 and are primarily concentrated in Pennsylvania, Ohio, Indiana, and New York, with smaller settlements in other states.

The most conservative of the Amish are the Old Order Amish who eschew most of the technology of the twentieth century because of their belief that a relatively isolated, rural farm life is the true path to salvation. Probably the most well-known characteristic of the Old Order Amish is their reliance on the horse and buggy as their principal means of transportation in lieu of the automobile. Other characteristic practices include the refusal to have electricity, radio, television, and other modern appliances in their farm homes, the wearing of broad-brimmed black hats and beards by Amish men (mustaches are forbidden), and the wearing of rather somber black or dark clothing by Amish men, women, and children—making the name the "Plain People" an appropriate one.

The Amish believe that the training of their young people is primarily a task of the church-community rather than of the state, although it was not until the twentieth century that they began to have serious clashes with public authorities about the compulsory education system. As long as the public schools that Amish children attended were typically isolated, rural one-room schools, and children were required to attend school until only the eighth grade, the Amish had few serious objections to public schooling for their young people. As compulsory school attendance came to be required beyond the eighth grade, and the one-room school gave way to large consolidated schools in rural areas, however, the religious beliefs of· the Amish and the compulsory education system headed increasingly for a collision.

Although an eighth-grade education for their children is acceptable to the Amish, they believe that further education leads to the breakdown of values they cherish and to "worldly" influences on their children. Abiding by their interpretation of the Biblical injunction that believers not "conform to the World, . . . [and] not be unequally yoked together with unbelievers," the Amish insist that in order to preserve their simple, rural communities, young people of adolescent age must be instructed in the values of the Amish community and learn the kinds of skills they will need in order to lead a relatively self-sufficient farm existence. The objection of the Amish to education beyond the eighth grade is therefore based not on opposition to further training of their young people but rather on a belief that the public school system beyond grade school prepares young people for a world the Amish do not share—a modern, competitive, technological society. Opposition to high school educations for their adolescent youth is, as perceived by the Amish, necessary to the preservation of their way of life and the values of their church-communities.

Such beliefs naturally led to sporadic conflicts between the

Amish and the public school authorities, since compulsory school attendance laws in most states require school attendance until age sixteen, seventeen, or sometimes eighteen. In enforcing such laws, public authorities were enforcing an American value perhaps as strongly held by most Americans as the Amish objections to it—that is, the belief that education is essential not only for individual success but also for the maintenance of free institutions. Such faith in education is traceable to Thomas Jefferson, who urged his friends to mount a "crusade against ignorance; establish and improve the law for educating the common people." For, as Jefferson also said, if "a nation expects to be ignorant and free, in a state of civilization, it expects what never was and never will be."[21]

In Pennsylvania, for example, the compulsory school attendance law required school attendance until age seventeen but allowed fifteen-year-olds to apply for work permits excusing them from school for the performance of farm work. Amish children in Pennsylvania often repeated the eighth grade to insure that they would be fifteen when they completed their formal schooling and then applied for work permits. In the 1950s, school officials began to refuse to allow children to repeat eighth grade and began to deny work permits to Amish children. The Amish then withheld their children from school, were charged with violations of the compulsory school attendance law, and were convicted and fined. Many Amish refused to pay their fines, and some were jailed. Arrests of Amish parents occurred as many as ten times. Finally, the governor intervened and worked out a compromise whereby Amish children could perform household and farm tasks and attend Amish vocational schools several hours a week in lieu of attending school beyond the eighth grade.

When such clashes between the religious beliefs of the Amish and the school attendance laws were the subject of litigation, however, the courts uniformly rejected the argument that compelling Amish children to attend school beyond the eighth grade

21. It should also be noted, however, that on the subject of compulsory education, Jefferson said that it was "better to tolerate the rare instance of a parent refusing to let his child be educated, than to shock the common feelings and ideas by the forcible asportation and education of the infant against the will of the father."

violated the religious liberty of the Amish. Compulsory school attendance, the courts held, was a valid secular policy enforced by the state for the general welfare and could not therefore be successfully challenged on the grounds of religious freedom. In litigation arising from the clash, *Commonwealth v. Beiler,* a Pennsylvania court in 1951 thus acknowledged that the "Amish are our 'plain people,' a quiet, pious, industrious, thrifty people, whose vitalizing contributions to the welfare, and especially to the development of the agricultural resources, of the Commonwealth have always been gratefully recognized." But, the court continued,

> there is no interference with religious liberty when the State reasonably restricts parental control, or compels parents to perform their natural and civil obligations to educate their children. They may be educated in the public schools, in private or denominational schools, or by approved tutors; but educated they must be within the age limits and in the subjects prescribed by law. The life of the Commonwealth—its safety, its integrity, its independence, its progress—and the preservation of the democratic way of life, depend upon the enlightened intelligence of its subjects.

A clash between the Amish and Ohio authorities that resulted in litigation also led to a similar ruling by the Ohio courts. The Amish in Ohio had established their own schools, but they were one-room affairs, and the Amish teachers had only eighth-grade educations or less themselves. The Ohio courts upheld the prosecution of the Amish for failure to send their children to adequate schools with certified teachers. "No question of religious freedom is presented in this case," an Ohio court held in *Ohio v. Hershberger,* decided in 1955. "By requiring the defendant to provide for the proper education of his children, his right to worship according to the dictates of his conscience is in no way abridged, and his right to instruct his children in the tenets of his chosen faith is unquestioned."

Despite such decisions against them, the Amish continued to resist the compulsory school attendance laws, and an important further clash occurred in Buchanan County, Iowa, in 1965. The Amish had established their own schools in the county, but they were taught by Amish girls who were uncertified and had only elementary school educations. Following a political dispute in the county in which the Amish had voted in favor of an unpopular position, school inspectors were dispatched to the Amish schools and declared them unfit. The Amish were convicted and fined in local courts for sending their children to unfit schools, and for several weeks Amishmen were haled into court and fined on a daily basis. They refused to pay the fines on religious grounds, and the public authorities threatened to sell Amish farms to satisfy the judgments against them.

The Amish children continued to attend their own schools, but on November 19, 1965, public school authorities arrived with a school bus at the Amish school and attempted to force the children onto the bus for transportation to the consolidated public school. Some of the children fled into cornfields with school officials in hot pursuit. Twenty-eight Amish children were eventually rounded up and sent to the public school. The procedure was repeated on November 22, but, when the school officials arrived at the Amish school, the children began screaming and singing "Jesus Loves Me," and the school officials retreated. News reports and pictures of the school officials pursuing Amish children through cornfields had, in the meantime, produced a national outcry against the officials and aroused widespread sympathy for the Amish.

Iowa Governor Harold E. Hughes ordered a truce in the dispute, a halt to attempts to take the Amish children to the public schools, and an end to the fines being levied against Amish parents. Ultimately, the Iowa legislature exempted the Amish from the compulsory school attendance law for two years, an exemption that could be renewed. A private foundation also contributed money to pay the salaries of certified teachers in the Amish schools. Governor Hughes summed up the Iowa clash when he said, "I am more willing to bend laws and logic than human beings. I will always believe that Iowa and America are big enough in space and spirit to provide a kindly place for all good people, regardless of race, or creed."

Despite such sentiments, the law as interpreted by the courts remained unreceptive to the Amish objections to compulsory education beyond the eighth grade. An important consequence of the 1965 Iowa clash was that it had spotlighted the plight of the Amish for a nationwide audience and aroused sympathetic supporters to action on their behalf. As a direct result, a group of ministers, bankers, lawyers, and professors formed a group called the National Committee for Amish Religious Freedom, which had as its purpose the defense of the right of the Amish to pursue their way of life free from official harassment. The NCARF was chaired by the Reverend William C. Lindholm, a Lutheran minister from Livonia, Michigan, and it included leading Jews (such as Edwin J. Lucan, general counsel of the American Jewish Committee), Catholics (such as the Reverend Robert F. Drinan, S.J., dean of the Boston University Law School), and Protestants (such as the Reverend Dean M. Kelley, executive director of the Commission on Religious Liberty of the National Council of Churches). The committee also received strong support from the Religious Liberty Association of the Seventh-Day Adventist Church, including favorable editorials and publicity in its publication, *Liberty*. The efforts of the national committee were directed "toward gaining liberty for the Amish and helping people understand the tremendous anguish these simple Christians must endure when their religious liberty is threatened," Chairman Lindholm said.

One of the principal purposes of the committee was to win recognition by the courts of the legitimacy of the Amish objections to compulsory schooling on religious liberty grounds. Such a non-Amish organization was necessary for the support of the Amish cause in the courts, since the Amish generally refused to defend themselves in litigation. Without a non-Amish group, such as the NCARF, therefore, the religious freedom interests of the Amish would not be adequately presented in litigation, especially appellate litigation.

The national committee's first undertaking was to test the religious liberty issue in regard to compulsory attendance laws before the United States Supreme Court in *Garber v. Kansas,* a case that had gone against the Amish in the Kansas courts. Amishman LeRoy Garber had refused to send his fifteen-year-old daughter to school, and he was convicted and fined for violation of the Kansas school attendance law requiring education until the age of sixteen. In 1966 the Kansas Supreme Court sustained his conviction on appeal. "Failure to comply with reasonable requirements in the exercise of the police power for the general welfare," the Kansas Supreme Court said, "has never been condoned in the name of religious freedom." The court maintained that "[t]he question of how long a child should attend school is not a religious one," and it held, "No matter how sincere he may be the individual cannot be permitted upon religious grounds to be the judge of his duty to obey laws enacted in the public interest."

The NCARF mustered funds to appeal the *Garber* case to the United States Supreme Court. The American Civil Liberties Union also supported the appeal, and Melvin Wulf of the ACLU filed the brief on behalf of Garber, while Leo Pfeffer, who frequently appears as counsel for the American Jewish Congress, filed an *amicus curiae* brief on behalf of the NCARF urging the Court to hear the case. On October 23, 1967, however, over the dissents of Chief Justice Warren and Justices Douglas and Fortas, the Court refused to hear *Garber*. The supporters of the Amish had come within only one vote of obtaining a hearing on the merits before the Court, since it requires the votes of only four justices for an appeal to be granted. This was a major defeat for the Amish and their supporters, since state court rulings that were uniformly adverse to the Amish remained in full force and effect.

In 1964, Amish from Iowa, Illinois, and Ohio began to settle in the area of New Glarus, in Green County, Wisconsin, a community of approximately 1,200 residents twenty-five miles southwest of Madison. The Amish built their own one-room school for the education of their young people up to the eighth grade, and when the school opened in the fall of 1968, thirty-eight Amish children who had been attending the New Glarus public elementary school transferred to it. The school administrator of the New Glarus public schools, Kenneth J. Glewen, requested that the Amish children not be withdrawn until after the third Friday in September when a school population count was to be conducted, since state aid to the public schools was based on that count, and the withdrawal of the Amish children would cost the New Glarus public schools approximately $18,000 in state aid.

The Amish, however, refused to delay the withdrawal of their children. Kenneth Glewen thereupon filed criminal complaints charging Jonas Yoder, Adin Yutzy, and Wallace Miller with failure to send their children to school after their graduation from eighth grade. The children were Frieda Yoder, age fifteen, Barbara Miller, age fifteen, and Vernon Yutzy, age fourteen. Jonas Yoder and Adin Yutzy were Amishmen, while Wallace Miller was a member of the Conservative Amish Mennonite Church. The complaints charged that Yoder, Yutzy, and Miller were violating the Wisconsin compulsory school attendance law, which required that children be educated until age sixteen.

The Amish were thus once again in trouble with the school attendance laws, but on this occasion the National Committee for Amish Religious Freedom was prepared, and it intervened in defense of the Amish at the trial court level. The NCARF furnished William B. Ball of Harrisburg, Pennsylvania, as defense counsel for the Wisconsin Amish, and Ball, in association with a local lawyer, Thomas C. Eckerle, of Madison, filed a motion to dismiss the charges on April 2, 1969. The Wisconsin compulsory school attendance law as applied to the defendants, they argued, violated the religious freedom guarantees of both the Wisconsin constitution and the First and Fourteenth Amendments of the United States Constitution.

Judge Roger L. Elmer of the Green County Court reserved a ruling on the motion to dismiss until a trial on the merits, and the trial of Yoder, Yutzy, and Miller was held early in April 1969. The NCARF supplied expert witnesses who testified on behalf of the Amish, including Temple University Professor John A. Hostetler, a member of the national committee and author of the leading work on Amish culture.[22] Hostetler described the nature of Amish life to the court and explained the group's religious objections to high school education for their youth. Compelling the attendance of Amish youth in high school, he said, would destroy the Amish church-community, since it would entail the forcible imposition of modern values on Amish children at an age when they needed to receive Amish values by training at home.

22. John A. Hostetler, *Amish Society*, rev. ed. (Baltimore: Johns Hopkins University Press, 1968).

Hostetler also testified that under a grant from the United States Office of Education, Amish children were given IQ and other tests, and that they scored above or at least equal to children in the public schools in regard to nonverbal skills. The Amish children also demonstrated a high degree of social awareness on the tests, with the typical Amish child being described as "quiet, friendly, responsible and conscientious. Works devotedly to meet his obligations and serve his friends and school. Thorough and painstaking, accurate with figures, but needs time to master technical subjects as reasoning is not his strong point. Loyal, considerate, concerned with how other people feel even when they are in the wrong."

Another member of the NCARF who testified at the trial was Professor Donald A. Erickson of the Department of Education at the University of Chicago. Erickson pointed out to the court that the education of Amish children did not stop with the eighth grade, but rather, despite the lack of further formal schooling, intensive training was continued in both the skills and values that the children would require as fully functioning members of the Amish church-community. The training that Amish children thus received at home and on the farm after the eighth grade suited them for the kinds of tasks they would be required to perform as adults, Erickson testified, and this was an accomplishment that the public education system did not always achieve. "The simple elementary school for the Amish performs a fairly important function, helping them in communication and to conduct marketing in the outside world," Erickson continued. "It fits them to deal with people on the high education level to the extent that they need to. But we must recognize that Amish society is a society geared to the notion of a degree of isolation. These people aren't purporting to be learned people, and the self-sufficiency of the Amish community is the best evidence I can point to: whatever is being done seems to function well."

The self-sufficiency and peaceable nature of the Amish was also attested to by another defense witness, Wilbur E. Deiniger, who had previously been sheriff of Green County. Deiniger testified that he had never known an Amish teenager to commit a crime or otherwise be in trouble with the law. "In my opinion," he said, "the Amish people of Green County present no threat to the community." The director of the Department of Social Services of Green County also testified that the Amish did not contribute to either the public assistance or unemployed rolls of the county, nor did the Amish require any public assistance for problems associated with illegitimate births, alcoholism, or mental illness. The lack of education beyond grade school for Amish youths, he said, did not therefore add in any way to the social or tax burdens of Green County.

The testimony produced by the defense was, however, largely beside the point as far as the prosecution was concerned. The law of Wisconsin was that children had to be educated until age sixteen, and it was clear that Jonas Yoder, Adin Yutzy, and Wallace Miller had violated that law. Deputy Attorney General Robert D. Martinson said the state was willing to stipulate that "the defendants are sincere in their religious beliefs," but the fact remained that they had violated the law. The compulsory school attendance law had been enacted in pursuit of a valid secular purpose and for the benefit of the general welfare, the prosecution contended, and religious beliefs, no matter how sincere, could not invalidate a legal policy of that kind.

The defense and prosecution filed briefs in the case, and oral argument was held on June 13. Judge Elmer issued his opinion on August 15, 1969. The judge acknowledged that because of their religious beliefs, the Amish defendants had "a strong conviction that they cannot send their children to high school or any school of academic or secular learning after the children have completed the basic equivalent of an 8th grade education. They feel so strongly in this respect that they are convinced that not only do they jeopardize their own relationships with God, but also those of their children, if they permit such attendance."

Despite the obvious sincerity of these religious objections, Judge Elmer said, the primary purpose of the compulsory school attendance law was to ensure that children had sufficient education to compete in the modern world, and it appeared that an appreciable number of Amish youth subsequently left the faith and were constrained to compete with those in the outside community. The judge concluded that, while "the Wisconsin compulsory school law does interfere with the freedom of the Defendants to act in accordance with their sincere religious beliefs," it was nonetheless "a reasonable and constitutional exercise of the governmental function of the State."

"No one has questioned the exceptional morality of these Defendants as Amish people, their history in relation to their admirable record of lawful conduct in areas other than school laws," Judge Elmer said. The prosecution had not been vindictive, nor had the defendants been treated "in the usual sense as alleged 'criminals.' " But, he concluded, "it is one of the realities of the law here invoked that to enforce what the Legislature has determined to be a proper statute for carrying out its duties to all Wisconsin youth it has logically found it necessary to determine non-compliance to be a misdemeanor and provide for a penalty in conviction thereof. Regretfully, this court feels that, in order to fulfill its function, under the circumstances it must impose at least a symbolic penalty upon this conviction." Judge Elmer therefore fined each defendant five dollars, but waived court costs.

The NCARF immediately appealed this decision to the circuit court, but on November 13, 1969, Circuit Judge Arthur L. Luebke affirmed Judge Elmer's ruling. He was acutely aware "of the fact that the Old Order Amish is a sect admired and respected by all who know them for their integrity, rugged self-reliance, high moral character, and ability to support and care for their brothers, while living and practicing the simple life without the 'benefit' of a formal high school or higher education, all in accordance with the dictates of their religious beliefs." Nevertheless the judge was obliged to conclude "that the compulsory school statute still represents a reasonable and constitutional exercise of the governmental function of the state." The convictions of Yoder, Yutzy, and Miller were thus affirmed.

Chairman Lindholm of the NCARF denounced the circuit court decision and declared that, unless it were reversed, "Amish parents [would] face continued harassment." Although "the penalty against the defendants is light—a 'symbolic' five dollars each, court costs waived," Lindholm said, "the finding of guilty is a very serious matter." The fine, he continued, "symbolizes all we are fighting against—namely the so-called right of the State to come between a parent and his child and dictate what kind of education is best for him. And by so doing to violate the religious convictions of both parent and child." Defense attorney William Ball also charged that there were "disturbing doubts raised concerning the motives of those initiating this prosecution," since the criminal complaints against the Amish had quickly followed the withdrawal of the Amish children from the New Glarus school, which had cost the district $18,000 in state aid.

The Seventh-Day Adventist publication *Liberty* appealed for funds to finance taking the case further. Roland R. Hegstad, editor of *Liberty* and a member of the NCARF, noted that the "case of the Wisconsin Amish is now on appeal to the state supreme court. If, as we hope, the issue goes to the United States Supreme Court, expenses could run as high as $8,000 to $10,000. Even with some legal services donated, a substantial balance will remain to be paid."

Under the sponsorship of the NCARF, an appeal of the case was then pursued to the Wisconsin Supreme Court. The state argued that the compulsory school attendance law was a valid secular policy enacted to assure that each Wisconsin child received an education sufficient to allow him to compete in modern society. Religious objections to such a policy, it was argued, could not validly be urged against its enforcement, and for the court to accept the arguments of the Amish would destroy the uniform application of the compulsory schooling policy. The state also noted that many Amish young people chose to leave their faith and church-communities on reaching maturity, and, unless their parents were compelled to abide by the compulsory school attendance law, these young adults would enter the outside world unprepared to maintain a reasonable existence.

The Wisconsin Supreme Court, however, on January 8, 1971, handed the NCARF and the Amish a major victory. For the first time, a state court upheld the religious freedom claims of the Amish and ruled that the compulsory school attendance laws were invalid as applied to them. No "liberty guaranteed by our Constitution is more important or vital to our free society than is the religious liberty protected by the Free Exercise Clause of the First Amendment," said the court. To uphold the burden imposed on the religious beliefs of the Amish by the compulsory school law, the state had to show that it was justified by a "compelling state interest," as the United States Supreme Court had required in *Sherbert v. Verner.*

Examining whether there was such a compelling state inter- est, the Wisconsin Supreme Court noted that the kind of edu- cation being imposed on the Amish under the law was "for a world which is not theirs; that their cultural values are different; that their life requires no professional training and that two years of high school education does not help Amish children to adjust normally to their Amish environment. The Amish claim, with compelling merit, that their education produces as good a product as two additional years' compulsory high school education does." Some of the Wisconsin Amish, the court noted, had settled in the state after the Iowa clash, "and they sought religious freedom here, in a spirit and with a hope not unlike the Pilgrim Fathers who came to America." If compulsory school laws were to be applied to the Amish in state after state, so that they no longer had anywhere in the United States to flee to, the court concluded, "the impact may result in the extermination of their religious community."

Given such serious burdens on the free exercise of religion, the court said, the state could not validly justify the application of the compulsory school attendance law to the Amish on the ground of a compelling state interest. A compelling interest was not established either by the argument that the state would be put to expense or administrative inconvenience or by the argument that some Amish children left their church-communities after reaching maturity. The state inconvenience attendant on an exemption of the Amish from compulsory schooling would be less than that imposed upon South Carolina as a result of the *Sherbert* decision on unemployment benefits, the court held, and to "force a worldly education upon all Amish children, the majority of whom do not want or need it, in order to confer a dubious benefit upon the few who might later reject their religion is not a compelling interest."

The court concluded "that although education is a subject within the constitutional power of the state to regulate, there is not such a compelling state interest in two years high school compulsory education as will justify the burden it places upon the appellants' free exercise of their religion." It held that "the Wisconsin Compulsory School Attendance Law . . . is unconstitutional as applied to these Amish appellants, and the convictions must be reversed."

The NCARF attorney, William Ball, praised the Wisconsin Supreme Court's decision for coming "right smack down on the constitutional issue of religious liberty," and noted that this was the "first state court to uphold the Amish constitutional liberty." He felt that the decision would be "widely respected throughout the country, where there are numerous religious groups which do not have great economic, political, or numerical strength."

The fight was not over, however, since on April 1, 1971, Wisconsin Attorney General Robert W. Warren petitioned for review of the decision by the United States Supreme Court. This move posed a dilemma for the NCARF and its counsel. To preserve the victory it had achieved in the Wisconsin Supreme Court, the NCARF should argue that the Supreme Court ought to deny certiorari. Yet rulings adverse to the Amish remained on the books in other states and could be affected only by a ruling from the United States Supreme Court. William Ball and the NCARF ultimately filed a brief opposing a grant of certiorari in *Yoder* but admitting that, because of the decisions contrary to that of the Wisconsin court in other states, "the Court may be disposed to grant the writ." If certiorari were granted, Ball urged the Court to affirm the "principle of liberty declared by the Supreme Court of Wisconsin, based on the specific facts of this case." The Supreme Court granted certiorari on May 24, 1971.

In the Supreme Court, the Wisconsin attorney general again argued that the education of children was not only a primary responsibility of the state but also absolutely essential to ensure the enlightened citizenry needed to maintain free, democratic institutions. "It is a self-evident truth that our nation, indeed our civilization, including freedom of worship, was not conceived nor has it survived in ignorance," he stated. "That Wisconsin and the nation have a compelling interest in the establishment and maintenance of a system of education," he said, "is clear beyond all doubt. It is likewise clear beyond all doubt that this interest overrides the religious interest of the parents of children whose attendance at some school, public or private, is required." The state thus had "a right under its police power and the doctrine of *parens patriae* to compel school attendance." [23]

The decision of the Wisconsin Supreme Court, the attorney general argued, had upheld the religious beliefs of Amish parents by ignoring substantial interests of Amish children. Children had the fundamental right to education, he said, and the consequence of the Wisconsin decision was to allow denial of this fundamental right to the Amish child "by the theocratic society into which he was born. Any desire for knowledge is stifled and deviation incurs the punishment of 'shunning.' Regardless of his ability or desires, the young adult Amish has only two alternatives: To join the Amish church at the age of between sixteen and twenty, or to make his way in the other world with only an eighth grade education." Under the Constitution, the Amish were free to establish their own parochial schools, the attorney general continued, but they refused to do so insofar as high schools were concerned. "If the Amish do not want to establish secondary schools for their children," he argued, "then their children should be required to go to a more 'worldly' public secondary school. In failing to provide for secondary education for their children, the Amish are neglecting a parental duty and obligation to their children and neglecting their duty as citizens of a democracy from which they have reaped ample benefit."

The attorney general relied especially on the United States Supreme Court's decision in *Prince v. Massachusetts,* sustaining the Massachusetts child labor law over the objections of Jehovah's Witnesses. "The child labor laws referred to in Prince," the attorney general said, "and the compulsory attendance laws are correlative and spring from the same concern for the welfare of the child." Additionally, he noted, the state's paramount power to compel school attendance had been sustained over religious objec-

23. *Parens patriae* is a well-established legal doctrine that recognizes the power of the state to protect the health, safety, morals, and welfare of children. This power may be exercised even over the objections of parents, if that is deemed reasonably necessary to protect a minor.

tions in every other state court in which the issue had been adjudicated.

Finally, the attorney general argued that for the Court to exempt the Amish from the compulsory school attendance laws would violate not only its own recent pronouncements on such issues but also the establishment clause of the First Amendment. In *Gillette v. United States,* he noted, the Court had rejected the concept of selective conscientious objection to the draft laws, and the arguments of the Amish amounted essentially to a contention that certain groups should, because of their religious beliefs, be exempted from school attendance laws that were as legitimate as the selective service law. If the exemption were granted, it would give preference to the religious beliefs of the Amish at the expense of a valid secular policy and in preference to those who might object to compulsory school laws for nonreligious reasons.

On behalf of the Amish, William Ball argued that, contrary to the state's contentions, the Amish did not favor ignorance for their children. They trained their youth beyond the eighth grade, he noted, and "the Amish system of education beyond the eighth grade of 'learning by doing' in the agricultural life of crop-raising, animal husbandry, farm maintenance and management—coupled with living as a helping and responsible family man and neighbor in the self-sustaining Amish faith-community—may be regarded as ideal education." The enforcement of the compulsory school attendance law against the Amish posed a cruel and impossible dilemma for the group, Ball said. Their choice was either "to obey the State and thereby violate their religion, or to follow their religion and thereby suffer criminal penalty." As a consequence, the "Amish could very soon have no place to go in this country, nowhere to be themselves, and there would take place in America another tragic example of the forced extinction of a culture," similar to the destruction of so many Indian cultures.

Such a burden on the exercise of religious freedom by the Amish could be justified, Ball argued, only by a showing of a "compelling state interest" by Wisconsin in the enforcement of its compulsory school attendance law. Again relying heavily on *Sherbert v. Verner,* he argued that a compelling interest had not been demonstrated by the state. At most, he said, Wisconsin was contending that one or two years' additional schooling for Amish children was so vital as to justify serious invasion of the religious convictions of Amish parents. "What threat to any State interest is avoided by the enforcing of *two* years, or of *one* year, of high schooling upon Amish children?" Ball asked. "It is the position of the State that it not only must, but can, in so brief a span of time, confer its presumed enlightenment of the young Amish man or woman, the insulating of them from 'the disease of ignorance,' and the opening up to them of myriad gateways of 'opportunity' and 'achievement' in the American society."

Ball further argued that the state had failed to demonstrate that any important disruption of the compulsory school system was posed by an exemption of the Amish from its operation. The record demonstrated that the Amish system of training beyond the eighth grade produced useful, functioning members of Amish society who did not commit crimes, were rarely unemployed, and did not add to the welfare costs of society. A compelling state interest in imposing one or two years of high school education on Amish children had not been demonstrated, he argued, although such an imposition would entail a serious intrusion on religious liberty.

Finally, Ball denied that exemption for the Amish would violate the establishment clause. Such an exemption, he said, places "no burden or disadvantage upon any other group or in any way limits free exercise rights of others." On the contrary, reasoning that would deny the Amish an exemption from compulsory school laws would also have justified a denial of the free exercise claims in *Sherbert v. Verner* and *West Virginia Board of Education v. Barnette*. "The Amish require and deserve now," Ball concluded, "explicit recognition by this Court of their liberty to follow the will of God in their earthly pilgrimage, as Amish folk in the Amish community of faith."

The cause of the Amish was also supported by *amicus curiae* briefs filed by organizations representing almost the full spectrum of American religious belief—the General Conference of Seventh-Day Adventists, the National Council of Churches of Christ in the

United States, the Synagogue Council of America,[24] the American Jewish Congress, the National Jewish Commission on Law and Public Affairs, and the Mennonite Central Committee. All of the *amici* supported exemption of the Amish from the compulsory school attendance laws. As one brief said, they sought not only "the maximizing of religious liberty" but also "the preservation of the Amish as a living embodiment of an ancient alternative understanding of the good life."

Wisconsin v. Yoder was argued before the Supreme Court on December 8, 1971, and the decision was announced on May 15, 1972. In it the Court sustained the religious objections of the Amish to the compulsory school attendance laws. Chief Justice Burger wrote the opinion, while concurring opinions were filed by Justices Stewart and White, joined by Justice Brennan. Justice Douglas dissented in part from the Court's decision. Because they had not been on the Court when the *Yoder* case was considered, Justices Powell and Rehnquist did not participate.

WISCONSIN V. YODER
406 U.S. 205, decided May 15, 1972

Mr. Chief Justice Burger delivered the opinion of the Court. [Burger first summarized the proceedings in the Wisconsin courts and the facts in the case.]

Formal high school education beyond the eighth grade is contrary to Amish beliefs, not only because it places Amish children in an environment hostile to Amish beliefs with increasing emphasis on competition in class work and sports and with pressure to conform to the styles, manners, and ways of the peer group, but also because it takes them away from their community, physically and emotionally, during the crucial and formative adolescent period of life. During this period, the children must acquire Amish attitudes favoring manual work and self-reliance and the specific skills needed to perform the adult role of an Amish farmer or housewife. They must learn

---

24. The Synagogue Council of America is an umbrella organization that includes the Central Conference of American Rabbis, the Rabbinical Assembly of America, the Rabbinical Council of America, the Union of American Hebrew Congregations, the Union of Orthodox Jewish Congregations of America, and the United Synagogue of America.

to enjoy physical labor. Once a child has learned basic reading, writing, and elementary mathematics, these traits, skills, and attitudes admittedly fall within the category of those best learned through example and "doing" rather than in a classroom. And, at this time in life, the Amish child must also grow in his faith and his relationship to the Amish community if he is to be prepared to accept the heavy obligations imposed by adult baptism. In short, high school attendance with teachers who are not of the Amish faith—and may even be hostile to it—interposes a serious barrier to the integration of the Amish child into the Amish religious community. Dr. John Hostetler, one of the experts on Amish society, testified that the modern high school is not equipped, in curriculum or social environment, to impart the values promoted by Amish society.

The Amish do not object to elementary education through the first eight grades as a general proposition because they agree that their children must have basic skills in the "three R's" in order to read the Bible, to be good farmers and citizens, and to be able to deal with non-Amish people when necessary in the course of daily affairs. They view such a basic education as acceptable because it does not significantly expose their children to worldly values or interfere with their development in the Amish community during the crucial adolescent period. While Amish accept compulsory elementary education generally, wherever possible they have established their own elementary schools in many respects like the small local schools of the past. In the Amish belief higher learning tends to develop values they reject as influences that alienate man from God.

On the basis of such considerations, Dr. Hostetler testified that compulsory high school attendance could not only result in great psychological harm to Amish children, because of the conflicts it would produce, but would also, in his opinion, ultimately result in the destruction of the Old Order Amish church community as it exists in the United States today. The testimony of Dr. Donald A. Erickson, an expert witness on education, also showed that the Amish succeed in preparing their high school age children to be productive members of the Amish community. He described their system of learning through doing the skills directly relevant to their adult roles in the Amish community as "ideal" and perhaps superior to ordinary high school education. The evidence also showed that the Amish have an excellent record as law-abiding and generally self-sufficient members of society.

Although the trial court in its careful findings determined that the Wisconsin compulsory school-attendance law "does interfere with the freedom of the Defendants to act in accordance with their sincere religious belief" it also concluded that the requirement of high school attendance until age 16 was a "reasonable and constitutional" exercise of governmental power, and therefore denied the motion to dismiss the charges. The Wisconsin Circuit Court affirmed the convictions. The Wisconsin Supreme Court, however, sustained respondents' claim under the Free Exercise Clause of the First Amendment and reversed the convictions. A majority of the court was of the opinion that the State had failed to make an adequate showing that its interest in "establishing and maintaining an educational system overrides the defendants' right to the free exercise of their religion. . . . "

There is no doubt as to the power of a State, having a high responsibility for education of its citizens, to impose reasonable regulations for the control and duration of basic education. . . . [A] State's interest in universal education, however highly we rank it, is not totally free from a balancing process when it impinges on fundamental rights and interests, such as those specifically protected by the Free Exercise Clause of the First Amendment, and the traditional interest of parents with respect to the religious upbringing of their children. . . .

It follows that in order for Wisconsin to compel school attendance beyond the eighth grade against a claim that such attendance interferes with the practice of a legitimate religious belief, it must appear either that the State does not deny the free exercise of religious belief by its requirement, or that there is a state interest of sufficient magnitude to override the interest claiming protection under the Free Exercise Clause. Long before there was general acknowledgment of the need for universal formal education, the Religion Clauses had specifically and firmly fixed the right to free exercise of religious beliefs, and buttressing this fundamental right was an equally firm, even if less explicit, prohibition against the establishment of any religion by government. The values underlying these two provisions relating to religion have been zealously protected, sometimes even at the expense of other interests of admittedly high social importance. The invalidation of financial aid to parochial schools by government grants for salary subsidy for teachers is but one example of the extent to which courts have gone in this regard, notwithstanding that such aid programs were legislatively determined to be in the public interest and the service of sound educational policy by States and by Congress. . . .

The essence of all that has been said and written on the subject is that only those interests of the highest order and those not otherwise served can overbalance legitimate claims to the free exercise of religion. We can accept it as settled, therefore, that, however strong the State's interest in universal compulsory education, it is by no means absolute to the exclusion or subordination of all other interests. . . .

We come then to the quality of the claims of the respondents concerning the alleged encroachment of Wisconsin's compulsory school-attendance statute on their rights and the rights of their children to the free exercise of the religious beliefs they and their forebears have adhered to for almost three centuries. In evaluating those claims we must be careful to determine whether the Amish religious faith and their mode of life are, as they claim, inseparable and interdependent. A way of life, however virtuous and admirable, may not be interposed as a barrier to reasonable state regulation of education if it is based on purely secular considerations; to have the protection of the Religion Clauses, the claims must be rooted in religious belief. Although a determination of what is a "religious" belief or practice entitled to constitutional protection may present a most delicate question, the very concept of ordered liberty precludes allowing every person to make his own standards on matters of conduct in which society as a whole has important interests. Thus, if the Amish asserted their claims because of their subjective evaluation and rejection of the contemporary secular values accepted by the majority, much as Thoreau rejected the social values of his time and isolated himself at Walden Pond, their claims would not rest on a religious basis. Thoreau's choice was philosophical and personal rather than religious, and such belief does not rise to the demands of the Religion Clauses.

Giving no weight to such secular considerations, however, we see that the record in this case abundantly supports the claim that the traditional way of life of the Amish is not merely a matter of personal preference, but one of deep religious conviction, shared by an organized group, and intimately related to daily living. . . .

The conclusion is inescapable that secondary schooling, by exposing Amish children to worldly influences in terms of attitudes, goals, and values contrary to beliefs, and by substantially interfering with the religious development of the Amish child and his integration into the way of life of the Amish faith community at the crucial adolescent stage of development, contravenes the basic religious tenets and practice of the Amish faith, both as to the parent and the child.

The impact of the compulsory-attendance law on respondents' practice of the Amish religion is not only severe, but inescapable, for the Wisconsin law affirmatively compels them, under threat of criminal sanction, to perform acts undeniably at odds with fundamental tenets of their religious beliefs. . . . Nor is the impact of the compulsory-attendance law confined to grave interference with important Amish religious tenets from a subjective point of view. It carries with it precisely the kind of objective danger to the free exercise of religion that the First Amendment was designed to prevent. As the record shows, compulsory school attendance to age 16 for Amish children carries with it a very real threat of undermining the Amish community and religious practice as they exist today; they must either abandon belief and be assimilated into society at large, or be forced to migrate to some other and more tolerant region.

In sum, the unchallenged testimony of acknowledged experts in education and religious history, almost 300 years of consistent practice, and strong evidence of a sustained faith pervading and regulating respondents' entire mode of life support the claim that enforcement of the State's requirement of compulsory formal education after the eighth grade would gravely endanger if not destroy the free exercise of respondents' religious beliefs. . . .

Wisconsin concedes that under the Religion Clauses religious beliefs are absolutely free from the State's control, but it argues that "actions," even though religiously grounded, are outside the protection of the First Amendment. But our decisions have rejected the idea that religiously grounded conduct is always outside the protection of the Free Exercise Clause. It is true that activities of individuals, even when religiously based, are often subject to regulation by the States in the exercise of their undoubted power to promote the health, safety, and general welfare, or the Federal Government in the exercise of its delegated powers. . . . But to agree that religiously grounded conduct must often be subject to the broad police power of the State is not to deny that there are areas of conduct protected by the Free Exercise Clause of the First Amendment and thus beyond the power of the State to control, even under regulations of general applicability. . . . This case, therefore, does not become easier because respondents were convicted for their "actions" in refusing to send their children to the public high school; in this context belief and action cannot be neatly confined in logic-tight compartments. . . .

Nor can this case be disposed of on the grounds that Wisconsin's requirement for school attendance to age 16 applies uniformly to all citizens of the State and does not, on its face, discriminate against religions or a particular religion, or that it is motivated by legitimate secular concerns. A regulation neutral on its face may, in its application, nonetheless offend the constitutional requirement for governmental neutrality if it unduly burdens the free exercise of religion. . . . The Court must not ignore the danger that an exception from a general obligation of citizenship on religious grounds may run afoul of the Establishment Clause, but that danger cannot be allowed to prevent any exception no matter how vital it may be to the protection of values promoted by the right of free exercise. By preserving doctrinal flexibility and recognizing the need for a sensible and realistic application of the Religion Clauses "we have been able to chart a course that preserved the autonomy and freedom of religious bodies while avoiding any semblance of established religion. This is a 'tight-rope' and one we have successfully traversed" . . . .

The State advances two primary arguments in support of its system of compulsory education. It notes, as Thomas Jefferson pointed out early in our history, that some degree of education is necessary to prepare citizens to participate effectively and intelligently in our open political system if we are to preserve freedom and independence. Further, education prepares individuals to be self-reliant and self-sufficient participants in society. We accept these propositions.

However, the evidence adduced by the Amish in this case is persuasively to the effect that an additional one or two years of formal high school for Amish children in place of their long-established program of informal vocational education would do little to serve those interests. . . .

The State attacks respondents' position as one fostering "ignorance" from which the child must be protected by the State. No one can question the State's duty to protect children from ignorance but this argument does not square with the facts disclosed in the record. Whatever their idiosyncrasies as seen by the majority, this record strongly shows that the Amish community has been a highly successful social unit within our society, even if apart from the conventional "mainstream." Its members are productive and very law-abiding members of society; they reject public welfare in any of its usual modern forms. . . .

The State argues that if Amish children leave their church they should not be in the position of making their way in the world without the education available in the one or two additional years the State requires. However, on this record, that argument is highly speculative. There is no specific evidence of the loss of Amish adherents by attrition, nor is there any showing that upon leaving the Amish community Amish children, with their practical agricultural training and habits of industry and self-reliance, would become burdens on society because of educational shortcomings. . . .

Insofar as the State's claim rests on the view that a brief additional period of formal education is imperative to enable the Amish to participate effectively and intelligently in our democratic system, it must fall. The Amish alternative to formal secondary school education has enabled them to function effectively in their day-to-day life under self-imposed limitations on relations with the world, and to survive and prosper in contemporary society as a separate, sharply identifiable and highly self-sufficient community for more than 200 years in this country. In itself this is strong evidence that they are capable of fulfilling the social and political responsibilities of citizenship without compelled attendance beyond the eighth grade at the price of jeopardizing their free exercise of religious belief. . . .

Finally, the State, on authority of Prince v. Massachusetts, argues that a decision exempting Amish children from the State's requirement fails to recognize the substantive right of the Amish child to a secondary education, and fails to give due regard to the power of the State as parens patriae to extend the benefit of secondary education to children regardless of the wishes of their parents. Taken at its broadest sweep, the Court's language in Prince, might be read to give support to the State's position. However, the Court was not confronted in Prince with a situation comparable to that of the Amish as revealed in this record; this is shown by the Court's severe characterization of the evils that it thought the legislature could legitimately associate with child labor, even when performed in the company of an adult. . . . The Court later took great care to confine Prince to a narrow scope in Sherbert v. Verner. . . .

This case, of course, is not one in which any harm to the physical or mental health of the child or to the public safety, peace, order, or welfare has been demonstrated or may be properly inferred. The record is to the contrary, and any reliance on that theory would find no support in the evidence.

Contrary to the suggestion of the dissenting opinion of Mr. Justice Douglas, our holding today in no degree depends on the assertion of the religious interest of the child as contrasted with that of the parents. It is the parents who are subject to prosecution here for failing to cause their children to attend school, and it is their right of free exercise, not that of their children, that must determine Wisconsin's power to impose criminal penalties on the parent. The dissent argues that a child who expresses a desire to attend public high school in conflict with the wishes of his parents should not be prevented from doing so. There is no reason for the Court to consider that point since it is not an issue in the case. . . .

Indeed it seems clear that if the State is empowered, as parens patriae, to "save" a child from himself or his Amish parents by requiring an additional two years of compulsory formal high school education, the State will in large measure influence, if not determine, the religious future of the child. Even more markedly than in Prince, therefore, this case involves the fundamental interest of parents, as contrasted with that of the State, to guide the religious future and education of their children. The history and culture of Western civilization reflect a strong tradition of parental concern for the nurture and upbringing of their children. This primary role of the parents in the upbringing of their children is now established beyond debate as an enduring American tradition. . . .

In the face of our consistent emphasis on the central values underlying the Religion Clauses in our constitutional scheme of government, we cannot accept a parens patriae claim of such all-encompassing scope and with such sweeping potential for broad and unforeseeable application as that urged by the State.

For the reasons stated we hold, with the Supreme Court of Wisconsin, that the First and Fourteenth Amendments prevent the State from compelling respondents to cause their children to attend formal high school to age 16. . . .

It cannot be overemphasized that we are not dealing with a way of life and mode of education by a group claiming to having recently discovered some "progressive" or more enlightened process for rearing children for modern life.

Aided by a history of three centuries as an identifiable religious sect and a long history as a successful and self-sufficient segment of American society, the Amish in this case have convincingly demonstrated the sincerity of their religious beliefs, the interrelationship of belief with their mode of life, the vital role that belief and daily conduct play in the continued survival of Old Order Amish communities and their religious organization, and the hazards presented by the State's enforcement of a statute generally valid as to others. Beyond this, they have carried the even more difficult burden of demonstrating the adequacy of their alternative mode of continuing informal vocational education in terms of precisely those overall interests that the State advances in support of its program of compulsory high school education. In light of this convincing showing, one that probably few other religious groups or sects could make, and weighing the minimal difference between what the State would require and what the Amish already accept, it was incumbent on the State to show with more particularity how its admittedly strong interest in compulsory education would be adversely affected by granting an exemption to the Amish. Sherbert v. Verner . . . .

Nothing we hold is intended to undermine the general applicability of the State's compulsory school-attendance statutes or to limit the power of the State to promulgate reasonable standards that, while not impairing the free exercise of religion, provide for continuing agricultural vocational education under parental and church guidance by the Old Order Amish or others similarly situated. The States have had a long history of amicable and effective relationships with church-sponsored schools, and there is no basis for assuming that, in this related context, reasonable standards cannot be established concerning the content of the continuing vocational education of Amish children under parental guidance, provided always that state regulations are not inconsistent with what we have said in this opinion.

Affirmed.

Mr. Justice Stewart, with whom Mr. Justice Brennan joins, concurring.

... This case in no way involves any questions regarding the right of the children of Amish parents to attend public high schools, or any other institutions of learning, if they wish to do so. As the Court points out, there is no suggestion whatever in the record that the religious beliefs of the children here concerned differ in any way from those of their parents. . . .

It is clear to me, therefore, that this record simply does not present the interesting and important issue discussed in Part II of the dissenting opinion of Mr. Justice Douglas. With this observation, I join the opinion and judgment of the Court.

Mr. Justice White, with whom Mr. Justice Brennan and Mr. Justice Stewart join, concurring.

Cases such as this one inevitably call for a delicate balancing of important but conflicting interests. I join the opinion and judgment of the Court because I cannot say that the State's interest in requiring two more years of compulsory education in the ninth and tenth grades outweighs the importance of the concededly sincere Amish religious practice to the survival of that sect. . . .

The importance of the state interest asserted here cannot be denigrated, however. . . . In the present case, the State is not concerned with the maintenance of an educational system as an end in itself, it is rather attempting to nurture and develop the human potential of its children, whether Amish or non-Amish: to expand their knowledge, broaden their sensibilities, kindle their imagination, foster a spirit of free inquiry, and increase their human understanding and tolerance. It is possible that most Amish children will wish to continue living the rural life of their parents, in which case their training at home will adequately equip them for their future role. Others, however, may wish to become nuclear physicists, ballet dancers, computer programmers, or historians, and for these occupations, formal training will be necessary. There is evidence in the record that many children desert the Amish faith when they come of age. A State has a legitimate interest not only in seeking to develop the latent talents of its children but also in seeking to prepare them for the life style that they may later choose, or at least to provide them with an option other than the life they have led in the past. In the circumstances of this case, although the question is close, I am unable to say that the State has demonstrated that Amish children who leave school in the eighth grade will be intellectually stultified or unable to acquire new academic skills later. The statutory minimum school attendance age set by the State is, after all, only 16.

Decision in cases such as this and the administration of an exemption for Old Order Amish from the State's compulsory school-attendance laws will inevitably involve the kind of close and perhaps repeated scrutiny of religious practices, as is exemplified in today's opinion, which the Court has heretofore been anxious to avoid. But such entanglement does not create a forbidden establishment of religion where it is essential to implement free exercise values threatened by an otherwise neutral program instituted to foster some permissible, nonreligious state objective. I join the Court, because the sincerity of the Amish religious policy here is uncontested, because the potentially adverse impact of the state requirement is great, and because the State's valid interest in education has already been largely satisfied by the eight years the children have already spent in school.

Mr. Justice Douglas, dissenting in part.

I agree with the Court that the religious scruples of the Amish are opposed to the education of their children beyond the grade schools, yet I disagree with the Court's conclusion that the matter is within the dispensation of parents alone. The Court's analysis assumes that the only interests at stake in the case are those of the Amish parents on the one hand, and those of the State on the other. The difficulty with this approach is that, despite the Court's claim, the parents are seeking to vindicate not only their own free exercise claims, but also those of their high-school age children. . . .

If the parents in this case are allowed a religious exemption, the inevitable effect is to impose the parents' notions of religious duty upon their children. Where the child is mature enough to express potentially conflicting desires, it would be an invasion of the child's rights to permit such an imposition without canvassing his views. . . .

This issue has never been squarely presented before today. Our opinions are full of talk about the power of the parents over the child's education. . . . And we have in the past analyzed similar conflicts between parent and State with little regard for the views of the child. See Prince v. Massachusetts . . . . Recent cases, however, have clearly held that the children themselves have constitutionally protectible interests.

These children are "persons" within the meaning of the Bill of Rights. . . .

On this important and vital matter of education, I think the children should be entitled to be heard. While the parents, absent dissent, normally speak for the entire family, the education of the child is a matter on which the child will often have decided views. He may want to be a pianist or an astronaut or an oceanographer. To do so he will have to break from the Amish tradition.

It is the future of the student, not the future of the parents, that is imperiled by today's decision. If a parent keeps his child out of school, then the child will be forever barred from entry into the new and amazing world of diversity that we have today. The child may decide that that is the preferred course, or he may rebel. It is the student's judgment, not his parents', that is essential if we are to give full meaning to what we have said about the Bill of Rights and of the right of students to be masters of their own destiny. If he is harnessed to the Amish way of life by those in authority over him and if his education is truncated, his entire life may be stunted and deformed. The child, therefore, should be given an opportunity to be heard before the State gives the exemption which we honor today.

The views of the two children in question were not canvassed by the Wisconsin courts. The matter should be explicitly reserved so that new hearings can be held on remand of the case. . . .

I think the emphasis of the Court on the "law and order" record of this Amish group of people is quite irrelevant. A religion is a religion irrespective of what the misdemeanor or felony records of its members might be. I am not at all sure how the Catholics, Episcopalians, the Baptists, Jehovah's Witnesses, the Unitarians, and my own Presbyterians would make out if subjected to such a test. . . .

The Court rightly rejects the notion that actions, even though religiously grounded, are always outside the protection of the Free Exercise Clause of the First Amendment. In so ruling, the Court departs from the teaching of Reynolds v. United States . . . , where it was said concerning the reach of the Free Exercise Clause of the First Amendment, "Congress was deprived of all legislative power over mere opinion, but was left free to reach actions which were in violation of social duties or subversive of good order." In that case it was conceded that polygamy was a part of the religion of the Mormons. . . .

Action, which the Court deemed to be antisocial, could be punished even though it was grounded on deeply held and sincere religious convictions. What we do today, at least in this respect, opens the way to give organized religion a broader base than it has ever enjoyed; and it even promises that in time Reynolds will be overruled.

In another way, however, the Court retreats when in reference to Henry Thoreau it says his "choice was philosophical and personal rather than religious, and such belief does not rise to the demands of the Religion Clauses." That is contrary to what we held in United States v. Seeger . . . where we were concerned with the meaning of the words "religious training and belief" in the Selective Service Act, which were the basis of many conscientious objector claims. We said: "Within that phrase would come all sincere religious beliefs which are based upon a power or being, or upon a faith, to which all else is subordinate or upon which all else is ultimately dependent. The test might be stated in these words: A sincere and meaningful belief which occupies in the life of its possessor a place parallel to that filled by the God of those admittedly qualifying for the exemption comes within the statutory definition. This construction avoids imputing to Congress an intent to classify different religious beliefs, exempting some and excluding others, and is in accord with the well-established congressional policy of equal treatment for those whose opposition to service is grounded in their religious tenets. . . . "

I adhere to these exalted views of "religion" and see no acceptable alternative to them now that we have become a Nation of many religions and sects, representing all of the diversities of the human race. . . .

Although the Amish had finally won a significant victory in the Supreme Court, the decision raised some serious questions under the religion clauses of the First Amendment, as the concurring opinions, and especially the partial dissent by Justice Douglas indicated. As Douglas correctly pointed out, only Frieda Yoder had testified at the trial and asserted that her religious beliefs and attitude toward education beyond the eighth grade conformed to those of her parents. Douglas's concern for protecting the wishes not only of Amish parents but also of Amish children in regard to education was probably well taken.

Chief Justice Burger's opinion was also disturbing in other respects. His emphasis on the 300-year history of the Amish as a religious group in justification for the validity of their objections to compulsory school attendance laws was understandable in light of the record, but his opinion could be read to deny the protection of the free exercise clause to individual beliefs of short duration. The history of religious belief is replete with sudden conversions, and it would seem unjustifiable to read the free exercise clause to protect only those held in common with a group, or to gauge the sincerity of a belief by the length of time it has been held.

In addition, Burger asserted that a claim of conscience against a governmental policy must be "rooted in religious belief" before it can be validly asserted under the free exercise clause. Not only did this appear to narrow the category of beliefs embraced by the free exercise clause, as Douglas noted in dissent, but it also indicated that the Court was quite willing to declare what were and were not religious beliefs and to give preference to those it proclaimed to be "genuine." Should the Court take such a course, it would raise more serious establishment clause problems than Burger's opinion seemed to recognize.

Such considerations could not, however, overshadow the immediate victory for the Amish that had been achieved by the NCARF and William Ball, who was himself a Roman Catholic. The *Yoder* "ruling should stop all harassment of the Amish on the educational issue in any state," Ball felt. "In this case," he said, "a small, unprotected, lobbyless people had only one basic protection—the United States Constitution—against a state law that would have destroyed their culture. The Court met the issues head on and decided on grounds of religious freedom and not on narrower grounds. The decision is an excellent defense of religious liberty."

Because they lacked television, radio, or telephones, the Wisconsin Amish at New Glarus who had won in the Supreme Court were informed of the decision in *Yoder* by neighbors and reporters. Adin Yutzy had moved from New Glarus, but Wallace Miller was working on a windmill that supplied power to his farm when informed of the Supreme Court's decision. "I'm happy it went that way, but I don't have anything to say," Miller said. "I knew it was coming, but I didn't worry too much about it either way."

Jonas Yoder was also busy on his 145-acre dairy farm when informed of the Supreme Court victory that bore his name. He appeared embarrassed by all the publicity surrounding the case, and at first said that he did not "feel like making words." In response to questions, however, he replied "I'm really glad to have it over with. It was a long struggle. I wish it had been anybody else." Yoder concluded, "This is a miracle of God," and he added, "Now I just want to get back to farming."

Chapter Five

EQUALITY
AND THE COURT

Introduction Equality as a constitutional policy is provided for in two major provisions of the Constitution, the equal protection clause of the Fourteenth Amendment and the due process clause of the Fifth Amendment. Since the Fourteenth Amendment is a restriction on the powers of the states, challenges to discriminatory state policies are based on the equal protection clause. There is, of course, no equal protection clause that applies to the federal government, but the Supreme Court has held that the due process clause of the Fifth Amendment enforces principles of equality against the federal government that parallel those applicable to the states via the equal protection clause. A state policy involving racial discrimination prohibited by the equal protection clause, for example, would, if embodied in a federal policy, be invalid under the due process clause of the Fifth Amendment, according to the Court's decisions in *Hurd v. Hodge* in 1948 and *Bolling v. Sharpe* in 1954. The Court has therefore read into the due process clause of the Fifth Amendment principles of equality that are, for all practical purposes, identical to those enforced against the states via the Fourteenth Amendment.

Although equal protection principles played a relatively restricted role in constitutional litigation until the 1930s, since then equalitarianism has become a major constitutional value. Indeed, some of the most far-reaching societal changes required by decisions of the Supreme Court in recent years have been based on equal protection principles, such as the desegregation cases (*Brown v. Board of Education* in 1954) and the apportionment cases (*Baker v. Carr* in 1962 and *Reynolds v. Sims* in 1964). And, although the equal protection clause was initially intended to prohibit racial discrimination, the Court has expanded the constitutional policy of equality to prohibit discrimination because of national origin (*Yick Wo v. Hopkins,* in 1886; *Hernandez v. Texas,* in 1954), geographical residence (*Reynolds v. Sims,* in 1964), poverty (*Griffin v. Illinois,* in 1956; *Shapiro v. Thompson,* in 1969), and sex (*Reed v. Reed,* in 1971), as well.

Under both the equal protection clause and the principles of equality guaranteed by the due process clause of the Fifth Amendment, a central problem is that most governmental policies require lines to be drawn and individuals or groups to be classified for the application of the policies. In confronting this commonplace situation, the Court long ago recognized that varying classifications must be judged by different standards under the constitutional principles of equality, depending on the kind of policy the government is enforcing and the nature of the rights being affected. What have evolved in decisions of the Court are three separate tests by which the constitutional validity of governmental policies are determined.

(1) *The "traditional" equal protection test.* The Court has long recognized that governmental policy may legitimately classify individuals or groups for various purposes in enforcing socioeconomic programs without offending the constitutional principles of equality. When the Court perceives that a socioeconomic program is under challenge, it applies a very lenient equal protection standard that imposes a heavy burden on those challenging the policy to demonstrate that the classification involved has no

"rational basis" and no conceivable rational relation to a legitimate governmental objective.

A good recent example of the application of this test arose in
Dandridge v. Williams, decided by the Court in 1970. *Dandridge*
involved a challenge to Maryland's system of Aid to Families with
Dependent Children (AFDC), which granted decreased benefits to
families as the number of children increased and imposed a maximum limit on AFDC payments of $240 or $250 per month,
depending on the family's place of residence. Rejecting an argument that such a state policy violated the equal protection clause
because it discriminated against larger families, the Court held that
Maryland could validly tailor its AFDC program to encourage
gainful employment, to maintain an equitable balance between
welfare families and those supported by a wage earner, to encourage family planning, and to allocate scarce state resources to meet
the needs of the largest possible number of families.

In a classic summary of the traditional equal protection test,
the Court said:

> [In] the area of economics and social welfare, a State does
> not violate the Equal Protection Clause merely because the
> classifications made by its laws are imperfect. If the classifi-
> cation has some "reasonable basis," it does not offend the
> Constitution simply because the classification "is not made
> with mathematical nicety or because in practice it results in
> some inequality . . . . " "The problems of government are
> practical ones and may justify, if they do not require, rough
> accommodations—illogical, it may be, and unscien-
> tific . . . . " "A statutory discrimination will not be set aside
> if any state of facts reasonably may be conceived to justify
> it . . . . " Under this long-established meaning of the Equal
> Protection Clause, it is clear that the Maryland maximum
> grant regulation is constitutionally valid. . . . [The] Equal
> Protection Clause does not require that a State must choose
> between attacking every aspect of a problem or not attacking
> the problem at all. . . . It is enough that the State's action be
> rationally based and free from invidious discrimination.

In an important recent case, *San Antonio School District v.
Rodriguez,* decided in 1973, the Court applied the traditional

equal protection test and upheld the Texas system of financing public schools, despite the fact that it allowed a wide disparity between the dollar amounts spent per pupil in poor school districts and in wealthy districts. Such disparities were caused by the fact that the value of property, on which school taxes were levied, varied considerably from district to district. Although the Texas system therefore resulted in less money being spent in poorer districts than in wealthier ones, the Court concluded that it could not "say that such disparities are the product of a system that is so irrational as to be invidiously discriminatory." It held that the "constitutional standard under the Equal Protection Clause is whether the challenged state action rationally furthers a legitimate state purpose or interest" and "that the Texas plan abundantly satisfies this standard."

If the Court decides that the principles of the traditional test apply to a governmental policy, the challenger thus carries a heavy burden of proof: he or she must show that the classifications used are patently and demonstrably arbitrary and without any rational basis. The Court has enunciated other tests of equality, however, that shift the burden from those challenging governmental policies to the government to demonstrate the legitimacy of the policies.

(2) *The compelling governmental interest test.* If a governmental policy involves a classification that penalizes a recognized constitutional right, then the Court does not apply the traditional (rational basis) test, but rather it insists that the government demonstrate a compelling governmental interest in using the challenged classificiation. Under the "compelling governmental interest" test, therefore, the burden of justification for a given classification shifts to the government, and the classification is subjected to "strict judicial scrutiny."

An example of the Court's application of the "compelling governmental interest" test is *Shapiro v. Thompson,* a 1969 case, in which the Court invalidated a one-year state residence requirement for individuals to be eligible for welfare benefits. Such a policy, the Court held, inhibited the right of poor persons to travel interstate, a right long held to be protected by the Constitution. Any classification that serves to penalize the right to travel interstate, "unless shown to promote a *compelling* governmental interest, is unconstitutional," said the Court. Since the residence requirement did not promote such a compelling governmental interest, it was invalid under the equal protection clause.

(3) *The "suspect" classification test.* The Court has also held that there are certain classifications that are inherently "suspect" and presumptively invalid under constitutional principles of equality. In defending a "suspect" classification, the government carries a very heavy burden of justification, since the Court presumes that the classification is invalid.

Suspect classifications have traditionally been those based on the race, national origin, or ancestry of the individuals affected. In *Loving v. Virginia,* for example, a 1967 case, the Court rejected Virginia's argument that its statute prohibiting interracial marriages was valid because the penalties fell equally on whites and blacks who violated it and because there was a rational basis for the statute. Refusing to apply the traditional equal protection test, the Court held that "the fact of equal application does not immunize the statute from the very heavy burden of justification which the Fourteenth Amendment has traditionally required of state statutes drawn according to race." Classifications based on race or national origin, the Court held, were "odious to a free people whose institutions are founded upon the doctrine of equality," and such classifications had to be subjected to the "most rigid scrutiny" by the courts.

Given these three different tests, a considerable part of the argument before the Court in equal protection cases involves an attempt by one party or the other to persuade the Court that this or that test should apply to a governmental policy. The parties challenging policies usually seek to persuade the Court to apply either the "compelling governmental interest" test or the "suspect classification" test, since the government must shoulder a heavier burden of justifying the policy under these tests, and the chances are greater that the Court will invalidate the policy. The government, on the other hand, often seeks to persuade the Court that the "traditional" test should apply, since the government then need only demonstrate that the policy has a rational basis and is in furtherance of a legitimate governmental objective, while those challenging the policy carry a heavier burden of demonstrating its invalidity.

In recent years, the issue of sexual classifications has been increasingly raised in constitutional litigation. The central focus of the arguments in these cases has been on the question of which test is applicable. At stake, of course, is the extent to which the equal protection clause and the Fifth Amendment due process clause can be used to attack alleged sexual discrimination. A good recent example of this litigation is *Frontiero v. Richardson,* decided by the Court in 1973, which we shall now examine in detail.

Case Study
THE CHAUVINISTS IN BLUE: FRONTIERO V. RICHARDSON

The legal status of women in American society throughout much of our history has been compared to the status of blacks under slavery. Before the Civil War, women possessed few of the legal rights ordinarily associated with American citizenship. Married women, for example, could not hold property or serve as guardians of their children, and women could not vote, hold public office, serve on juries, or even bring suit in the courts in their own names. Thomas Jefferson, usually considered a champion of democracy and equality, reflected the prevailing pre-Civil War attitude when he wrote that even were "our state a pure democracy there would still be excluded from our deliberations women, who, to prevent deprivation of morals and ambiguity of issues, should not mix promiscuously in gatherings of men."

Although the legal status of women began to change slowly after the Civil War, gross sexual discrimination continued to be a commonplace of American society. Perhaps symbolic of the post-Civil War conditions was the case of Myra Bradwell, who sought a license to practice law in Illinois, but whose request was rejected by the Illinois Supreme Court. She challenged this denial in the United States Supreme Court, arguing in *Bradwell v. Illinois* that the state had denied her a privilege and immunity of national citizenship in violation of the privileges and immunities clause of the recently adopted Fourteenth Amendment. A unanimous Court rejected her argument in 1873, however, holding that the Fourteenth Amendment left the power to grant or withhold law licenses in the hands of the states. Justice Bradley, joined by Justices Field and Swayne, concurred in the decision with an opinion that is a classic expression of what would now be called male chauvinism:

> [T]he civil law, as well as nature herself, has always recognized a wide difference in the respective spheres and destinies of man and woman. Man is, or should be, woman's protector and defender. The natural and proper timidity and delicacy which belongs to the female sex evidently unfits it for many of the occupations of civil life. The constitution of the family organization, which is founded in the divine ordinance, as well as in the nature of things, indicates the domestic sphere as that which properly belongs to the domain and functions of womanhood. The harmony, not to say identity, of interests and views which belong or should belong to the family institution, is repugnant to the idea of a woman adopting a distinct and independent career from that of her husband. . . . It is true that many women are unmarried and not affected by any of the duties, complications, and incapacities arising out of the married state but these are exceptions to the general rule. The paramount destiny and mission of woman are to fulfill the noble and benign offices of wife and mother. This is the law of the Creator. And the rules of civil society cannot be based on exceptional cases.

Myra Bradwell was the editor of a highly regarded professional publication, the *Chicago Legal News,* and, although the Illinois legislature later enacted a law admitting women to legal practice, she did not again seek admission to the bar. Two years before her death in 1894, however, the Supreme Court of Illinois on its own motion issued her a law license.

Mrs. Belva Ann Lockwood was another pioneer in the legal profession who encountered difficulties in winning acceptance as a professional woman. Mrs. Lockwood applied for admission to practice before the United States Supreme Court in 1876, but Chief Justice Waite denied her application, holding that "none but men are permitted to practice before [the Court] as attorneys and counsellors." In 1879, however, Congress passed legislation permitting women to practice before the Court, and, on March 3 of the same year, Mrs. Lockwood became the first woman admitted to the Supreme Court bar.

In 1875, the Fourteenth Amendment was the basis for another attempt to assert women's rights, this time the right to vote. Missouri, like all other states at the time, limited the right to vote to males. Virginia Minor contended that denying her the right to vote deprived her of a privilege and immunity of national citizenship in violation of the privileges and immunities clause of the Fourteenth Amendment. In 1875, the Supreme Court rejected her claim in *Minor v. Happersett,* just as it had that of Myra Bradwell. The privileges and immunities clause, Chief Justice Waite said for a unanimous Court, did not guarantee a right to vote, and if "the law is wrong, it ought to be changed; but the power for that is not with us." The chief justice noted,

> The arguments addressed to us bearing upon such a view of the subject may, perhaps, be sufficient to induce those having the power to make the alteration, but they ought not to be permitted to influence our judgment in determining the present rights of the parties now litigating before us. No argument as to woman's need of suffrage can be considered. We can only act upon her rights as they exist. It is not for us to look at the hardship of withholding. Our duty is at an end if we find it is within the power of a State to withhold.

The arguments addressed to the Court in *Minor* were, of course, persistently addressed to those who had "the power to make the alteration," but without avail for more than a generation after Virginia Minor lost her case before the Court. Wyoming was the pioneer in women's suffrage, granting women the right to vote when it became a territory in 1869 and continuing the policy after it became a state in 1890. Efforts at convincing other states to follow suit nevertheless proved disappointing, and by 1914 only ten other states had done so. The women's suffrage movement then focused on an amendment to the federal Constitution and was finally successful in this regard when the Nineteenth Amendment was ratified by the requisite three-fourths of the states in 1920.

Despite the efforts of Virginia Minor, Myra Bradwell, and others to assert women's rights under the Fourteenth Amendment, until recent years there was little litigation in which sexual equality was asserted. Indeed, until very recently, the most important line of Supreme Court decisions dealing with women were cases in which the principal argument centered on the special, weak status of women, which, it was said, justified greater governmental protection and solicitude, particularly for working women. Louis Brandeis made famous his "Brandeis brief" in such a case, *Muller v. Oregon* in 1908, persuading the Supreme Court to uphold maximum hour legislation for women workers.

A similar argument justifying minimum wage legislation for women was rejected by the Court, however, in *Adkins v. Children's Hospital* in 1923. Justice Sutherland, writing for the Court, there rejected an argument that women occupied a unique societal position sufficient to justify governmental fixing of minimum wages for those who worked. Whatever differences in legal status had existed in the past between men and women, Sutherland said, given "the great—not to say revolutionary—changes which have taken place . . . in the contractual, political, and civil status of women, culminating in the 19th Amendment, it is not unreasonable to say that these differences have now come almost, if not quite, to the vanishing point." Dissenting in *Adkins,* Justice Holmes indicated he felt women did require special protection, and he protested that it would take "more than the 19th Amendment to convince me that there are no differences between men and women, or that legislation cannot take those differences into account." Holmes' reasoning was vindicated in 1937 when the Court finally sustained governmental power to regulate minimum wages in *West Coast Hotel v. Parrish,* another case on behalf of women workers.

Contentions that women had a special status in society that justified policies of greater governmental solicitude and protection were therefore quite often the rationale for progressive labor legislation in the United States. More recently, however, many governmental policies that purport to be "protective" of women have come to be regarded as barriers to equal opportunities for women because they operate in practice to exclude women from certain occupational roles. What were once regarded as "progressive" policies have thus come under attack in recent years as policies involving sexual discrimination.

Although the Supreme Court has long indicated that classifications based on race or national origin are constitutionally "suspect," only in the 1970s has the Court begun to demonstrate some skepticism of classifications based on sex. Typical of the Court's approach to sexual classifications before the 1970s, was its decision in *Goesaert v. Cleary,* a 1948 case, upholding a Michigan statute that prohibited women, except wives and daughters of bar owners, from being licensed as bartenders. Rejecting an attack on the Michigan statute based on the equal protection clause of the Fourteenth Amendment, Justice Frankfurter stated for the Court that the "fact that women may now have achieved the virtues that men have long claimed as their perogatives and now indulge in vices that men have long practiced, does not preclude the States from drawing a sharp line between the sexes, certainly in such matters as the regulation of the liquor traffic." In the Court's view, the "Constitution does not require legislatures to reflect sociological insight, or shifting social standards, any more than it requires them to keep abreast of the latest scientific standards."

Also indicative of the Court's past insensitivity to sexual discrimination was its decision in *Hoyt v. Florida* in 1961. Gwendolyn Hoyt killed her husband by assaulting him with a baseball bat, and she was convicted by a jury of second degree murder. Florida law provided that no female would be called for jury duty "unless said person has registered with the clerk of the circuit court her desire to be placed on the jury list." As a result of the law, most Florida juries were composed of males, and Mrs. Hoyt challenged her conviction by such a jury on the grounds that Florida was unconstitutionally excluding women from jury service.

Applying traditional equal protection tests, rather than those applicable to "suspect classifications," the Court held that the "relevant inquiry is whether the exemption itself is based on some reasonable classification and whether the manner in which it is exercisable rests on some rational foundation." In *Hoyt,* the Court said:

> In neither respect can we conclude that Florida's statute is not 'based on some reasonable classification,' and that it is thus infected with unconstitutionality. Despite the enlightened emancipation of women from the restrictions and protections of bygone years, and their entry into many parts of community life formerly reserved to men, woman is still regarded as the center of home and family life. We cannot say that it is constitutionally impermissible for a State, acting in pursuit of the general welfare, to conclude that a woman should be relieved from the civic duty of jury service unless she herself determines that such service is consistent with her own special responsibilities.[25]

Despite decisions such as *Hoyt,* sexual discrimination has been the subject of increased attacks since the 1960s, not only through stepped up litigation, but also through legislative policy changes. Title VII of the 1964 Civil Rights Act outlawed discrimination on the basis of sex as well as race and national origin in employments that come under its provisions. The Equal Pay Act of 1963 also outlawed sexual discrimination in wages under the Fair Labor Standards Act.

At the executive branch level, the President's Commission on the Status of Women reported in 1963 that "equality of rights under the law for all persons, male or female, is so basic to democracy and its commitment to the ultimate value of the individual that it must be reflected in the fundamental law of the land." The commission expressed the hope that the Supreme Court would clarify the "remaining ambiguities with respect to the constitutional protection of women's rights" under the guarantees of equality embraced by the Fifth and Fourteenth Amendments.

---

25. In 1975, however, the Court finally held in *Taylor v. Louisiana* that exclusion of women from juries violates the Sixth and Fourteenth Amendments, which require juries to be composed of "a fair cross section of the community."

As the commission's report indicated, the Court had not used these guarantees to condemn sexual discrimination, and supporters of equal rights for women therefore pressed for congressional passage of the Equal Rights Amendment in order to make sexual equality a constitutional mandate. Although for many years the ERA was treated as a congressional joke, it was approved by the requisite two-thirds majorities in both houses of Congress on March 22, 1972.[26]

In addition to these developments, litigation in the field of women's rights increased significantly in the 1970s. Women's organizations began to resort to the judicial process with increasing frequency and to establish litigating organizations, such as the Legal Defense and Educational Fund of the National Organization for Women. The American Civil Liberties Union announced in 1972 that "women's rights" would be its top priority program for that year, and it created a Women's Rights Project to coordinate litigation to invalidate sexual discrimination under the Fifth and Fourteenth Amendments. Even before this announced program of concentration, however, the ACLU had sponsored a Supreme Court case that resulted in the first major breakthrough regarding the constitutional invalidity of sexual discrimination.

Reed v. Reed, decided by the Court in 1971, challenged an Idaho statute that, as construed, required the appointment of a male administrator of an estate of a deceased person in preference to a similarly situated female. On the death of Richard Lynn Reed, the minor adopted son of Cecil and Sally Reed, the father was appointed administrator of his son's estate in preference to the mother, Sally Reed. The Reeds had separated, and both parents filed applications to be administrators of their son's estate, but the Idaho courts enforced the statutory policy of preferring male administrators to female administrators of estates.

The Supreme Court, however, in a unanimous opinion by Chief Justice Burger, declared the Idaho policy invalid and for the first time condemned sexual discrimination as a violation of the equal protection clause of the Fourteenth Amendment. Counsel

26. At this writing, thirty-three of the required thirty-eight states have ratified the ERA.

for Idaho had argued that the statute was justified because it reduced the workload in the state's probate courts. When both a male and a female applied to be administrators, it was argued, and they were equally entitled to be appointed, the policy of male preference eliminated the necessity of a hearing and an evaluation of the respective merits of the two applicants by the Idaho probate courts, thus reducing their work and increasing their efficiency.

"The question presented by this case, then," Chief Justice Burger said, "is whether a difference in the sex of competing applicants for letters of administration bears a rational relationship to a state objective that is sought to be advanced by the operation of [the Idaho statute]." The objective of relieving the workload of the probate courts was "not without some legitimacy," Burger said, but the Court nonetheless held that the Idaho statute violated the equal protection clause. "To give a mandatory preference to members of either sex over members of the other, merely to accomplish the elimination of hearings on the merits," Burger concluded, "is to make the very kind of arbitrary legislative choice forbidden by the Equal Protection Clause of the Fourteenth Amendment; and whatever may be said as to the positive values of avoiding intrafamily controversy, the choice in this context may not lawfully be mandated solely on the basis of sex."

While Reed was a major victory for those challenging sexual discrimination in the judicial process, the principal objective of the ACLU in sponsoring the case was not achieved. It had sought a ruling by the Court that any governmental policy that classified individuals according to their sex created an inherently "suspect" classification similar to a racial classification, which would require strict judicial scrutiny and the demonstration of a compelling governmental interest to sustain the classification. In Reed, however, the Court had used the traditional equal protection test, holding that the Idaho statute was patently arbitrary and had no rational relationship to a legitimate governmental interest.

While the ACLU's attempt to persuade the Court that sexual classifications should be considered in the same light as racial or national origin classifications was being litigated, Air Force Lieu-

tenant Sharron Frontiero, began a fight against what she considered to be sexual discrimination. Her case would also become a
major effort to convince the Court that sexual classifications fell
within the inherently suspect category.

Mrs. Frontiero had enlisted in the United States Air Force on
October 1, 1968, when she was single, and was assigned as a
physical therapist at Maxwell Air Force Base Hospital in Montgomery, Alabama. In December 1969, she married Joseph
Frontiero, who was a student at Huntington College in Montgomery. He was a veteran and received $205 per month in GI Bill
education benefits, but otherwise Sharron was the sole support
of both of them.

Under the congressional statutes providing benefits for military personnel, a married male member of the Air Force who
lived off base was entitled to a Basic Allowance for Quarters
(BAQ) regardless of whether his wife also worked and regardless of
how much income she might earn. The wife of a male member of
the Air Force was also eligible for certain medical benefits regardless of whether she was in fact dependent on her husband for her
support. Since Sharron and Joseph Frontiero were living off base
in Montgomery, in October 1970, Lt. Frontiero informed her
commanding officer in the Physical Therapy Unit at the Maxwell
Air Force Base Hospital that she wanted to receive a Basic Allowance for Quarters. The commanding officer, Lt. Mary Schmid,
advised Lt. Frontiero to consult the Base Legal Office.

Several days later, Lt. Frontiero consulted the Base Legal
Office and was informed that female members were not entitled to
a BAQ unless their husbands were physically or mentally incapable
of self-support and were in fact dependent on their wives for more
than half of their support. Joseph Frontiero was not of course
physically or mentally incapable of supporting himself. His
monthly expenses totaled $354, but he received $205 per month
in GI Bill benefits and was not therefore dependent on his wife for
more than half his support.

After her discussion with the Base Legal Office, Lt. Frontiero
advised Colonel George Jernigan, the Maxwell Air Force Base
Hospital Commander, that she wanted a BAQ, but Colonel
Jernigan told her that regulations would not permit her to obtain

one. In November, she discussed the situation with Colonel Royal Connell, a member of the Inspector General's staff, who advised her to file a formal complaint. Lt. Frontiero subsequently did so, stating:

> I am married to [a] civilian man who is a full time pre-med student at Huntington College. He receives G.I. benefits which just barely cover the cost of his education. All other expenses (food, rent, insurance, car, etc.) are covered by my salary alone. My husband does not hold a job.
>
> Because I am married, I am not entitled to a housing allowance (according to the AF pay manual) unless my husband can be proven to be mentally or physically incapacitated (which he is not). I was given a BOQ [Bachelor Officer's Quarters] room in which my husband and I cannot possibly live together. Therefore, I maintain an apartment off base at my own expense. Recently I gave up my BOQ room altogether because I had no use for it.
>
> I feel that it is unrealistic to deny a housing allowance to a woman who is supporting her husband, when married men are allowed a housing allowance whether or not they are completely supporting their wives.
>
> I suggest that the Air Force revise their regulations to either:
>
> 1. Award house allowance on the basis of need (taking into account the combined expenses and salaries of both husband and wife.)
>
> OR:
>
> 2. Award married women a housing allowance on the same basis as it is now awarded to men.

Lt. Frontiero's complaint was filed with a personnel inspector, who stated that he informed her on "24 Nov. 70 that no further action could be taken on her complaint. Nothing has changed since the last time I talked to her." He went on, "Lt. Frontiero informed me, that she had contacted personnel from the Civil Liberties Union. They told her that they felt she had a valid complaint. They told the Lt. that after they caught up with some of their back cases they would get in touch with her."

Sharron and Joseph Frontiero also consulted with attorneys Joseph J. Levin, Jr., and Morris S. Dees, Jr., whom the Frontieros knew to be interested in civil rights litigation. Levin and Dees also agreed that the Frontieros had a valid complaint against the Air Force, based on sexual discrimination. The attorneys were preparing at the time to establish an organization specializing in class action litigation in the federal courts in behalf of economically deprived persons. During the course of the *Frontiero* case, they established the Southern Poverty Law Center in Montgomery, and *Frontiero* was financed by the center. This was appropriate, Joseph Levin said later, because "I cannot think of a larger class of persons who are discriminated against economically than women."

On December 23, 1970, Levin and Dees filed a class action complaint in the United States District Court for the Middle District of Alabama on behalf of Sharron and Joseph Frontiero and all other armed service personnel and their spouses similarly situated. The complaint alleged that the federal statutes and military regulations relating to Basic Allowances for Quarters and other benefits for spouses and dependents of military personnel denied female members of the military the equal protection of the laws in violation of the due process clause of the Fifth Amendment.[27] The complaint noted that married male members of the Air Force were entitled not only to a BAQ regardless of their wives' incomes, but also to certain medical benefits for their dependents. Married female members of the Air Force, the complaint noted on the other hand, were entitled to neither a BAQ nor medical benefits for their husbands unless their husbands were dependent on their wives for more than half their support. The "distinctions drawn by the . . . statutes and regulations insofar as they require different treatment for male and female members of the Armed Services . . . are arbitrary and unreasonable, in that they deny equal protection of the laws to [the plaintiffs]," the complaint said. "Each is thereby unconstitutional as being in violation of the due process clause of the fifth amendment to the Constitution of the United States."

27. Since *Frontiero* involved a challenge to a policy of the federal government, the equal protection clause of the Fourteenth Amendment, applicable only to the states, could not be invoked; rather, the principles of equal protection embraced by the due process clause of the Fifth Amendment were the constitutional basis of the case.

The complaint requested the convening of a three-judge district court and a declaratory judgment that the challenged statutes and regulations were unconstitutional.[28] The complaint also sought an injunction prohibiting the Air Force from continued enforcement of these allegedly discriminatory policies and an order awarding back pay and allowances to Lt. Frontiero from December 27, 1969.

A three-judge district court was convened by the chief judge of the Fifth Circuit Court of Appeals on January 7, 1971. Judge Richard T. Rives of the Fifth Circuit and United States District Judges Frank M. Johnson and Frank H. McFadden were assigned to serve on the court. Not until April 5, 1972, was their decision in *Frontiero v. Richardson* announced.[29]

Rives and McFadden, with Johnson dissenting, held that the different treatment of male and female members of the armed forces under the challenged statutes and regulations did not violate the due process clause of the Fifth Amendment. Refusing to hold that classifications by sex were inherently suspect, the court instead applied the traditional equal protection test. It therefore held that in "determining the constitutionality of the statutory scheme which plaintiffs attack, the Court must ask whether the classification established in the legislation is reasonable and not arbitrary and whether there is a rational connection between the classification and a legitimate governmental end." The court continued, "the statute must be upheld 'if any state of facts rationally justifying it is demonstrated to *or perceived by* the courts.' "

The rational basis for the sexual classification in *Frontiero,* the court held, was that Congress sought to avoid imposing on the

28. Since 1937, Congress has provided that suits challenging federal statutes and seeking injunctions against their enforcement require the convening of three-judge district courts, with direct appeals from the judgments of such courts to the Supreme Court.

29. The principal defendant in the case was the secretary of defense, who, at the time the original complaint was filed, was Melvin Laird. The case was thus styled *Frontiero v. Laird* at the district court level, but, while the case was pending before the Supreme Court, Laird was replaced by Elliot Richardson as secretary of defense. The case was thus decided by the Court as *Frontiero v. Richardson,* and for convenience it is referred to here by that name.

armed forces the administrative burden of requiring each married male to demonstrate that his wife was in fact dependent on him for half her support, since this would require "actual proof from some 200,000 male officers and over 1,000,000 enlisted men that their wives were actually dependent upon them." The court found the classification "burdensome for a female member who is not actually providing over one-half the support for her claimed husband only to the extent that were she a man she could receive dependency benefits in spite of the fact that her spouse might not be actually dependent, as that term has been defined by Congress." In the court's view, "the alleged injustice of the distinction lies in the possibility that some married service men are getting 'windfall' payments, while married service women are denied them. Sharron Frontiero is one of the service women thus denied a windfall."

The court also distinguished the Supreme Court's decision in *Reed v. Reed* because the statute there had the effect of excluding "certain qualified females from serving as administrators, whereas the classification present here does not exclude qualified female members. They merely have to show actual dependency." The court was compelled to the conclusion "that the challenged statutes are not in conflict with the Due Process Clause of the Fifth Amendment and that they are in all respects constitutional. The relief prayed for is therefore denied."

In dissent, Judge Johnson argued that if the "administrative convenience" of assuming wives to be dependent justified the statutory classification being challenged, such convenience would be enhanced by requiring the same assumption to be entertained in regard to husbands. "If it is administratively convenient to provide a conclusive presumption for men, it is inconsistent to require a demonstration of dependency in fact for women," Judge Johnson said. "The administrative convenience, supposed or real, in providing men with a conclusive presumption of dependency is simply irrelevant to this case. The question is whether it is administratively convenient to require women to demonstrate dependency in fact. From the majority's reasoning, the answer must be clearly in the negative because it is easier just to grant the presumption. Thus, on the strength of the majority's logic, there can be no rational basis."

Judge Johnson also found a basis in *Reed* for invalidating the statutory classification in *Frontiero*. *Reed*'s "basic message . . . is that administrative convenience is not a shibboleth, the mere recitation of which dictates constitutionality," he said. "Rather, whatever [the] governmental benefit that can be supposed should be balanced with the impact upon the subject class and the arbitrariness of the classification." If the challenged statutes were subjected to such an analysis, Johnson concluded, they would be found to violate the due process clause of the Fifth Amendment.

Having lost in the three-judge court, counsel for the Frontieros filed a notice of appeal to the Supreme Court on April 26, 1972. The Court noted probable jurisdiction on October 12, indicating that it was willing to hear the case on the merits. At the same time, *Frontiero* attracted support from the American Civil Liberties Union, whose Women's Rights Project decided to file an *amicus curiae* brief urging reversal of the three-judge court's decision.

Defending the lower court decision and the challenged statutory classification, counsel for the government argued that the distinction was a reasonable one for Congress to have made. Congress could reasonably assume that most wives of armed forces men were dependent upon their husbands for support, and, given the large number of males in the services, "Congress could properly determine that it would be an unnecessary burden on the dependency benefits program to require that each application for benefits be examined and investigated. It was therefore justified in concluding that the statutory objectives would best be served by granting benefits to all married male personnel, notwithstanding that a small proportion of servicemen whose wives are not dependent would receive a windfall in the form of unneeded benefits." It was similarly reasonable, the government argued, for Congress to assume that most husbands of female service members were not dependent on their wives for support, and that the much smaller number of claims for dependent benefits by females could be examined individually without undue administrative burden.

The statutory classification, government counsel thus argued, was a reasonable one, as distinguished from the unreasonable classification in *Reed*. "Here, in contrast, the classification chosen by Congress to achieve administrative economies is based upon reasonable presumptions of dependency, which are in accord with the realities of American life. The statute therefore does not infringe the Fifth Amendment rights of female members of the armed forces, and *Reed* does not require that it be declared unconstitutional."

The government also argued that the sexual classification involved should not be regarded as an inherently suspect classification, as one based on race or national origin would be. First, this classification dealt only with economic benefits, and "the Court has held that when, as here, the government operates in the area of economics and social welfare, legislative classifications must be sustained if they have a reasonable basis, even though they be 'imperfect' or may in practice result in some inequality." Secondly, the government contended, a sexual classification was not analogous to those based on race or national origin, which were condemned because they typically were aimed at discriminating against disadvantaged minorities. Women, however, were a majority in the nation and not suffering from inability to assert political influence. Unlike racial or national origin classifications, sexual classifications did not express a legislative judgment of inferiority but rather reflected sociological and physiological differences. A holding that sexual classifications were presumptively invalid was inappropriate, the government argued, since the sexual "characteristic frequently bears a reasonable relation to a legitimate governmental purpose."

Finally, the government argued that it would be inappropriate for the Court to invalidate the statutes in question because political processes could be depended upon to remedy any inequalities that might exist. Congress was already considering legislation extending dependent benefits to female members of the armed forces on the same terms as those available to males, and the Department of Defense had recommended such a change in congressional policy. Additionally, the government noted, the Equal Rights Amendment had been proposed by Congress, and if sexual classifications were to be constitutionally condemned, "the appropriate method to accomplish it is by constitutional amendment or legislation and not by abrupt judicial departure from long-applied constitutional principles."

On behalf of the Frontieros, Joseph Levin and Morris Dees argued that the challenged statutes were invalid whether the traditional test or the "suspect classification" test was applied to them. The statute, they argued, "seizes upon a group, women, who have historically suffered employment discrimination and diminished opportunities for employment, and uses that inferior economic status as a justification for heaping on further discrimination—reduced housing and medical benefits which men in the same circumstance automatically receive."

Although counsel argued that the sexual classification should be held suspect in the same manner as a racial classification, they also argued that it could not be validly justified on the grounds of administrative efficiency or convenience even under traditional equal protection principles. The government's "interest in ease of administration," they contended, "cannot by any test justify the further visitation of inequalities upon women which the present dependency definitions enact. Such discrimination runs counter to our basic concepts of fairness and equality inherent in due process." The traditional equal protection test had been applied by the Court in *Reed,* they noted, to invalidate Idaho's discriminatory probate statute, and "the dependency rules challenged here are almost indistinguishable from the mandatory preference rule struck down in *Reed*—under the guise of procedural convenience, they foster substantive inequality."

Joining counsel for the Frontieros in asking that the statutes be invalidated the American Civil Liberties Union *amicus curiae* brief argued that sexual classifications fell in the inherently suspect category and thus were presumptively invalid. The ACLU reviewed the history of the status of women in American society and concluded that it closely paralleled that of blacks. "Although the legislature may distinguish between individuals on the basis of their need or ability, it is presumptively impermissible to distinguish on the basis of an unalterable identifying trait over which the individual has no control and for which he or she should not be disadvantaged by the law," the ACLU argued.

> Legislative discrimination grounded on sex, for purposes
> unrelated to any biological difference between the sexes,
> ranks with legislative discrimination based on race, another
> congenital, unalterable trait of birth, and merits no greater
> judicial deference. The time is now ripe for this Court to re-
> pudiate the premise that, with minimal justification, the legis-
> lature may draw "a sharp line between the sexes," just as this
> Court has repudiated once settled law that differential treat-
> ment of the races is constitutionally permissible.

Frontiero v. Richardson thus presented the Court with the
opportunity to move a step beyond *Reed v. Reed* and to hold that
sexual classifications were inherently suspect and presumptively
invalid under the principles of equality guaranteed by the Constitution. The case was argued orally on January 17, 1973, and the
Court's decision was announced on May 14. In an opinion by
Justice Brennan, joined by Justices Douglas, White, and Marshall,
sexual classifications were held to fall within the inherently suspect category. A majority of the Court, however, did not accept
this reasoning, since Justice Stewart concurred in a brief opinion
on the basis of *Reed v. Reed*, and Justice Powell, joined by Chief
Justice Burger and Justice Blackmun also concurred but rejected
the idea that sexual classifications were inherently suspect. Justice
Rehnquist alone dissented.

FRONTIERO V. RICHARDSON
411 U.S. 677, decided May 14, 1973

Mr. Justice Brennan announced the judgment of the Court and an
opinion in which Mr. Justice Douglas, Mr. Justice White, and Mr. Justice
Marshall join.

The question before us concerns the right of a female member of the
uniformed services to claim her spouse as a "dependent" for the purposes of
obtaining increased quarters allowances and medical and dental benefits
under 37 USC Sections 401, 403 . . . and 10 USC Sections 1072, 1076 . . . ,
on an equal footing with male members. Under these statutes, a serviceman

may claim his wife as a "dependent" without regard to whether she is in fact dependent upon him for any part of her support. . . . A servicewoman, on the other hand, may not claim her husband as a "dependent" under these programs unless he is in fact dependent upon her for over one-half of his support. . . . Thus, the question for decision is whether this difference in treatment constitutes an unconstitutional discrimination against service-women in violation of the Due Process Clause of the Fifth Amendment. A three-judge District Court for the Middle District of Alabama, one judge dissenting, rejected this contention and sustained the constitutionality of the provisions of the statutes making this distinction. . . . We noted probable jurisdiction. . . . We reverse. . . .

In an effort to attract career personnel through re-enlistment, Congress established . . . a scheme for the provision of fringe benefits to members of the uniformed services on a competitive basis with business and industry. Thus . . . a member of the uniformed services with dependents is entitled to an increased "basic allowance for quarters" and . . . a member's dependents are provided comprehensive medical and dental care.

Appellant Sharron Frontiero, a lieutenant in the United States Air Force, sought increased quarters allowances, and housing and medical bene-fits for her husband, appellant Joseph Frontiero, on the ground that he was her "dependent." Although such benefits would automatically have been granted with respect to the wife of a male member of the uniformed services, appellant's application was denied because she failed to demonstrate that her husband was dependent on her for more than one-half of his support. Appellants then commenced this suit, contending that, by making this dis-tinction, the statutes unreasonably discriminate on the basis of sex in viola-tion of the Due Process Clause of the Fifth Amendment. In essence, appel-lants asserted that the discriminatory aspect of the statutes is twofold: first, as a procedural matter, a female member is required to demonstrate her spouse's dependency, while no such burden is imposed upon male members; and, second, as a substantive matter, a male member who does not provide more than one-half of his wife's support receives benefits, while a similarly situated female member is denied such benefits. Appellants therefore sought a permanent injunction against the continued enforcement of these statutes and an order directing the appellees to provide Lieutenant Frontiero with the same housing and medical benefits that a similarly situated male member would receive.

Although the legislative history of these statutes sheds virtually no light on the purposes underlying the differential treatment accorded male and female members, a majority of the three-judge District Court surmised that Congress might reasonably have concluded that, since the husband in our society is generally the "breadwinner" in the family—and the wife typically the "dependent" partner—"it would be more economical to require married female members claiming husbands to prove actual dependency than to extend the presumption of dependency to such members" . . . . Indeed, given the fact that approximately 99% of all members of the uniformed services are male, the District Court speculated that such differential treatment might conceivably lead to a "considerable saving of administrative expense and manpower" . . . .

At the outset, appellants contend that classifications based upon sex, like classifications based upon race, alienage, and national origin, are inherently suspect and must therefore be subjected to close judicial scrutiny. We agree and, indeed, find at least implicit support for such an approach in our unanimous decision only last Term in Reed v. Reed . . . .

In Reed, the Court considered the constitutionality of an Idaho statute providing that, when two individuals are otherwise equally entitled to appointment as administrator of an estate, the male applicant must be preferred to the female. Appellant, the mother of the deceased, and appellee, the father, filed competing petitions for appointment as administrator of their son's estate. Since the parties, as parents of the deceased, were members of the same entitlement class, the statutory preference was invoked and the father's petition was therefore granted. Appellant claimed that this statute, by giving a mandatory preference to males over females without regard to their individual qualifications, violated the Equal Protection Clause of the Fourteenth Amendment.

The Court noted that the Idaho statute "provides that different treatment be accorded to the applicants on the basis of their sex; it thus establishes a classification subject to scrutiny under the Equal Protection Clause" . . . . Under "traditional" equal protection analysis, a legislative classification must be sustained unless it is "patently arbitrary" and bears no rational relationship to a legitimate governmental interest. . . .

In an effort to meet this standard, appellee contended that the statutory scheme was a reasonable measure designed to reduce the workload on probate courts by eliminating one class of contests. Moreover, appellee argued that the mandatory preference for male applicants was in itself reasonable since "men [are] as a rule more conversant with business affairs than . . . women." Indeed, appellee maintained that "it is a matter of common knowledge, that women still are not engaged in politics, the professions, business or industry to the extent that men are." And the Idaho Supreme Court, in upholding the constitutionality of this statute, suggested that the Idaho

Legislature might reasonably have "concluded that in general men are better qualified to act as an administrator than are women."

Despite these contentions, however, the Court held the statutory preference for male applicants unconstitutional. In reaching this result, the Court implicitly rejected appellee's apparently rational explanation of the statutory scheme, and concluded that, by ignoring the individual qualifications of particular applicants, the challenged statute provided "dissimilar treatment for men and women who are . . . similarly situated" . . . . The Court therefore held that, even though the State's interest in achieving administrative efficiency "is not without some legitimacy," "[to] give a mandatory preference to members of either sex over members of the other, merely to accomplish the elimination of hearings on the merits, is to make the very kind of arbitrary legislative choice forbidden by the [Constitution] . . . ." This departure from "traditional" rational-basis analysis with respect to sex-based classifications is clearly justified.

There can be no doubt that our Nation has had a long and unfortunate history of sex discrimination. Traditionally, such discrimination was rationalized by an attitude of "romantic paternalism" which, in practical effect, put women, not on a pedestal, but in a cage. . . .

. . . [O]ur statute books gradually became laden with gross, stereotyped distinctions between the sexes and, indeed, throughout much of the 19th century the position of women in our society was, in many respects, comparable to that of blacks under the pre–Civil War slave codes. . . .

It is true, of course, that the position of women in America has improved markedly in recent decades. Nevertheless, it can hardly be doubted that, in part because of the high visibility of the sex characteristic, women still face pervasive, although at times more subtle, discrimination in our educational institutions, in the job market and, perhaps most conspicuously, in the political arena. . . .

Moreover, since sex, like race and national origin, is an immutable characteristic determined solely by the accident of birth, the imposition of special disabilities upon the members of a particular sex because of their sex would seem to violate "the basic concept of our system that legal burdens should bear some relationship to individual responsibility. . . ." And what differentiates sex from such nonsuspect statuses as intelligence or physical disability, and aligns it with the recognized suspect criteria, is that the sex characteristic frequently bears no relation to ability to perform or contribute to society. As a result, statutory distinctions between the sexes often have the effect of invidiously relegating the entire class of females to inferior legal status without regard to the actual capabilities of its individual members.

We might also note that, over the past decade, Congress has itself manifested an increasing sensitivity to sex-based classifications. In Title VII of the Civil Rights Act of 1964, for example, Congress expressly declared that no employer, labor union, or other organization subject to the provisions of the Act shall discriminate against any individual on the basis of "race, color, religion, *sex,* or national origin." Similarly, the Equal Pay Act of 1963 provides that no employer covered by the Act "shall discriminate . . . between employees on the basis of *sex.*" And Sec. 1 of the Equal Rights Amendment, passed by Congress on March 22, 1972, and submitted to the legislatures of the States for ratification, declares that "[equality] of rights under the law shall not be denied or abridged by the United States or by any State on account of sex." Thus Congress itself has concluded that classifications based upon sex are inherently invidious, and this conclusion of a coequal branch of Government is not without significance to the question presently under consideration. . . .

With these considerations in mind, we can only conclude that classifications based upon sex, like classifications based upon race, alienage, or national origin, are inherently suspect, and must therefore be subjected to strict judicial scrutiny. Applying the analysis mandated by that stricter standard of review, it is clear that the statutory scheme now before us is constitutionally invalid. . . .

The sole basis of the classification established in the challenged statutes is the sex of the individuals involved. . . . [A] female member of the uniformed services seeking to obtain housing and medical benefits for her spouse must prove his dependency in fact, whereas no such burden is imposed upon male members. In addition, the statutes operate so as to deny benefits to a female member, such as appellant Sharron Frontiero, who provides less than one-half of her spouse's support, while at the same time granting such benefits to a male member who likewise provides less than one-half of his spouse's support. Thus, to this extent at least, it may fairly be said that these statutes command "dissimilar treatment for men and women who are . . . similarly situated" . . . .

Moreover, the Government concedes that the differential treatment accorded men and women under these statutes serves no purpose other than mere "administrative convenience." In essence, the Government maintains that, as an empirical matter, wives in our society frequently are dependent upon their husbands, while husbands rarely are dependent upon their wives. Thus, the Government argues that Congress might reasonably have concluded that it would be both cheaper and easier simply conclusively to presume that wives of male members are financially dependent upon their husbands, while burdening female members with the task of establishing dependency in fact.

The Government offers no concrete evidence, however, tending to support its view that such differential treatment in fact saves the Government any money. In order to satisfy the demands of strict judicial scrutiny, the Government must demonstrate, for example, that it is actually cheaper to grant increased benefits with respect to *all* male members, than it is to determine which male members are in fact entitled to such benefits and to grant increased benefits only to those members whose wives actually meet the dependency requirement. Here, however, there is substantial evidence that, if put to the test, many of the wives of male members would fail to qualify for benefits. And in light of the fact that the dependency determination with respect to the husbands of female members is presently made solely on the basis of affidavits, rather than through the more costly hearing process, the Government's explanation of the statutory scheme is, to say the least, questionable.

In any case, our prior decisions make clear that, although efficacious administration of governmental programs is not without some importance, "the Constitution recognizes higher values than speed and efficiency" . . . . And when we enter the realm of "strict judicial scrutiny," there can be no doubt that "administrative convenience" is not a shibboleth, the mere recitation of which dictates constitutionality. . . . On the contrary, any statutory scheme which draws a sharp line between the sexes, *solely* for the purpose of achieving administrative convenience, necessarily commands "dissimilar treatment for men and women who are . . . similarly situated," and therefore involves the "very kind of arbitrary legislative choice forbidden by the [Constitution] . . . . " We therefore conclude that, by according differential treatment to male and female members of the uniformed services for the sole purpose of achieving administrative convenience, the challenged statutes violate the Due Process Clause of the Fifth Amendment insofar as they require a female member to prove the dependency of her husband.

Reversed.

Mr. Justice Stewart concurs in the judgment, agreeing that the statutes before us work an invidious discrimination in violation of the Constitution. Reed v. Reed . . . .

Mr. Justice Rehnquist dissents for the reasons stated by Judge Rives in his opinion for the District Court. . . .

Mr. Justice Powell, with whom the Chief Justice and Mr. Justice Blackmun join, concurring in the judgment.

I agree that the challenged statutes constitute an unconstitutional discrimination against service-women in violation of the Due Process Clause of the Fifth Amendment, but I cannot join the opinion of Mr. Justice Brennan, which would hold that all classifications based upon sex, "like classifications based upon race, alienage, and national origin," are "inherently suspect and must therefore be subjected to close judicial scrutiny" . . . . It is unnecessary for the Court in this case to characterize sex as a suspect classification, with all of the far-reaching implications of such a holding. Reed v. Reed . . . , which abundantly supports our decision today, did not add sex to the narrowly limited group of classifications which are inherently suspect. In my view, we can and should decide this case on the authority of Reed and reserve for the future any expansion of its rationale.

There is another, and I find compelling, reason for deferring a general categorizing of sex classifications as invoking the strictist test of judicial scrutiny. The Equal Rights Amendment, which if adopted will resolve the substance of this precise question, has been approved by the Congress and submitted for ratification by the States. If this Amendment is duly adopted, it will represent the will of the people accomplished in the manner prescribed by the Constitution. By acting prematurely and unnecessarily, as I view it, the Court has assumed a decisional responsibility at the very time when state legislatures, functioning within the traditional democratic process, are debating the proposed Amendment. It seems to me that this reaching out to pre-empt by judicial action a major political decision which is currently in process of resolution does not reflect appropriate respect for duly prescribed legislative processes.

There are times when this Court, under our system, cannot avoid a constitutional decision on issues which normally should be resolved by the elected representatives of the people. But democratic institutions are weakened, and confidence in the restraint of the Court is impaired, when we appear unnecessarily to decide sensitive issues of broad social and political importance at the very time they are under consideration within the prescribed constitutional processes.

While a majority of the Court had once again refused to hold that sexual classifications were inherently suspect, all the justices except Justice Rehnquist did agree in *Frontiero* that the sexual discrimination embodied in the statutes under challenge violated the due process clause of the Fifth Amendment. Sharron and Joseph Frontiero had therefore finally won their long battle with the Air Force, but, by the time the Court decided the case,

Sharron had left military service. When her four-year enlistment expired in October 1972, she resigned from the Air Force, and the couple moved to Gloucester, Massachusetts. The Frontieros did, however, receive all the back pay and allowances that had been denied to Sharron under the discriminatory benefits policy that they had challenged. When informed of the Supreme Court's decision, Mrs. Frontiero understandably commented, "I think it's about time. That's great."

From the standpoint of equalitarian policy, *Frontiero* was a disappointment to the ACLU and other groups that sought to persuade the Court to hold that sexual classifications fell within the inherently suspect category. And in subsequent cases, the Court has continued to resist such a step. In *Kahn v. Shevin,* decided in 1974, the Court upheld a Florida statute that granted widows a five-hundred-dollar tax exemption but denied such an exemption to widowers. The Court rejected the argument that such a policy was discriminatory against males in violation of the equal protection clause.

Writing for the Court, Justice Douglas held that such disparate treatment of widows and widowers was justified by the fact that widows were likely to be economically disadvantaged on the deaths of their husbands, while widowers did not usually suffer such economic problems. "We deal here," Douglas said, "with a state tax law reasonably designed to further the state policy of cushioning the financial impact of spousal loss upon the sex for whom that loss imposes a disproportionately heavy burden." Applying traditional equal protection policy, Douglas held that the states "have large leeway in making classifications and drawing lines which in their judgment produce reasonable systems of taxation." Justices Brennan, Marshall, and White dissented, arguing that, under *Frontiero* and *Reed,* the Florida statute was invalid.

In *Geduldig v. Aiello,* another 1974 decision, the Court sustained a California employment disability insurance system that excluded employment disabilities arising from normal pregnancies from compensation under the program. Since only women workers could become pregnant, it was argued, the California program discriminated against females by excluding disability resulting from pregnancy while compensating male workers for disabilities that were peculiarly male in nature.

Again refusing to apply the suspect classification test, the Court applied traditional equal protection standards and held that particularly "with respect to social welfare programs, so long as the line drawn by the State is rationally supportable, the courts will not interpose their judgment as to the appropriate stopping point." The state's interest in maintaining the solvency of the disability compensation program as well as its interest in keeping employee contributions to the program at a low level were rational grounds, the Court said, for excluding pregnancies from the category of compensable disabilities.

In dissent, Justice Brennan, joined by Justices Douglas and Marshall, charged that the Court seemed "willing to abandon that higher standard of review" it had used to judge the validity of sexual classifications in *Reed* and *Frontiero* "without satisfactorily explaining what differentiates the gender-based classification employed in this case from those found unconstitutional in Reed and Frontiero. The Court's decision threatens to return men and women to a time when 'traditional' equal protection analysis sustained legislative classifications that treated differently members of a particular sex solely because of their sex."

Needless to say, the equal protection principles applicable in cases of alleged sexual discrimination are presently in a state of flux in the Court's decisions. Although the Court did take some significant steps in *Reed* and *Frontiero,* it has refused to hold that sex is an inherently suspect classification similar to race and national origin. It is therefore clear that the Fourteenth Amendment equal protection clause and the Fifth Amendment due process clause permit sexual classifications that probably would be prohibited by the proposed Equal Rights Amendment, and the next major step in the field of sexual equality hinges on what happens to ratification of the ERA in the state legislatures.

INDEX TO CASES

GENERAL INDEX

219